Baltic food & drink

The calorie-rich Baltic diet provides the perfect insulation against long north European winters, but may not do your waistline any favours. It is a diet very much determined by local landscape and agriculture, with rye fields lending flavour to the distinctively rich Baltic bread, seas and rivers yielding culinary treats from salted herring to smoked eel, and meadow-grazing dairy herds providing the raw materials for delicious sour cream and cheese. Pork is by far the most popular of the locally reared meats. Although global trends have ensured that there is more variety on Baltic menus than ever before, these staple foodstuffs still form the mainstay of the eating-out experience.

D1197994

Pork

If there is one thing that appears on absolutely every Baltic restaurant menu, it is the pork chop (*karbonaad* in Estonia, *karbonāde* in Latvia, *karbonadas* in Lithuania). At its most basic, this is a simple slice of (often fatty) meat thrown into a pan for a brief sizzle, although the classic Baltic chop – cooked in tasty beer-batter and accompanied by a tangy mound of sauerkraut – can be a real culinary treat.

Fish

As you might expect for a region with a long coastline and a wealth of freshwater lakes, fish plays an important part in the Baltic diet. Traditionally, fishermen would home-cure a large part of their catch by smoking it in smoking sheds (which often doubled as the family sauna). **Smoked fish** is still a delicacy of the coastal regions, offered as a starter in restaurants or as a snack in street cafés. Usually you will be given the whole fish, complete with head, skin and bones, served on a plate but with no cutlery – picking out the flesh with your fingers is all part of the ritual. All kinds of salt- and freshwater fish are seen as suitable for smoking, although it is the **eel** which is considered the real delicacy. Peeling the succulent white meat from the rubbery skin is a laborious, but ultimately rewarding experience.

Freshwater fish from the Baltic lakes and rivers – especially **trout**, **pike** and **pike perch** – feature regularly on restaurant menus throughout the region. Some of the most characterful of the fish recipes are to be found in the shoreline settlements of Lake Peipsi in Estonia, where the local catch is stewed or baked with lashings of locally grown onions.

Another Baltic standby is salted or marinated **herring**: universally available as a starter, it is also served as a snack to accompany vodka or other spirit shots.

Borscht

Opinions differ as to the precise origin of borscht, the beetroot-based **soup** that has for centuries been a popular staple among peasant communities across northeastern Europe. The form of borscht consumed with most relish in the Baltic States is the cold, summer variety, which goes under the name of *šaltibarščiai* in Lithuania and *augsta zupa* in Latvia. Comprising shredded beetroot, yoghurt, garlic, gherkin and a garnish of chopped herbs and sour cream, it's alarmingly pink in colour and looks more like a fancy pudding than a savoury dish. If you're looking for a refreshing summer lunch with a local twist, however, you can't do much better.

Potatoes

Nowhere is the Baltic love affair with the potato more profound than in Lithuania, where this outwardly unassuming vegetable plays a starring role in the national cuisine. Widest known – and most immediately recognizable – of the potato-based dishes is **cepelinai** (literally "zeppelins"), in which finely grated potato mush is formed into cylinders, stuffed with minced meat and then boiled to produce starchy, glutinous blobs that aren't to everyone's taste. **Potato pancakes** (*bulviniai blynai*), made by dropping big dollops of shredded potato into hot oil, are an important part of the culinary repertoire and can be quite delicious when served with mushroom sauce, smoked salmon, or – most traditionally of all – bacon bits swimming in sour cream. There are many regional variations on the potato pancake theme, *Žemaičių blynai* (stuffed with meat and moulded into a heart shape) being among the most satisfying.

Black rye bread

Considered as something of an occasional treat in other European countries, **black rye bread** (*leib* in Estonia, *rupjmaize* in Latvia, *duona* in Lithuania) is an everyday staple in the Baltic States, and accompanies every meal from breakfast onwards. Made from a mixture of rye and wheat flour (the proportion differs from bakery to bakery), and often flavoured with caraway seeds or other natural goodies (Lithuanian *ajerų duona* is baked on a bed of bulrushes), Baltic bread is extraordinarily rich in nutrients and has the added advantage of staying fresh and springy for days.

Rīga Balsam

Few Baltic spirits are as immediately recognizable as **Rīga Balsam** (*Rīgas balzams*), the sticky black syrup sold in traditional, black-labelled clay bottles. Brewed in the city since the eighteenth century, the 45-percent-proof firewater tastes rather like cough medicine and is made from an appropriately healthy-sounding list of ingredients – which include a reputed 24 different herbs, along with forest berries, ginger and birch buds. Downing the stuff neat can be something of an ordeal, although combined with hot blackcurrant juice or coffee, it becomes the perfect winter warmer. The same company distils Ķimelis, a nectar-sweet liqueur made from caraway seeds which has many Latvian adherents – although outsiders may find it something of an acquired taste.

△ Trakai Island Castle

local saying has it. Down the street at no. 22 is the **Karaim Ethnographic Exhibition** (Karaimu etnografinė paroda; Wed–Sun 10am–6pm; 4Lt), a modern pavillion with sepia photographs of nineteenth-century Karaim families (see box opposite), the men in their dark caftans and black-and-white felt hats, the women in embroidered velvet jackets and ornate clogs with two-inch heels. Filigree jugs and coffee cups add further to the oriental flavour, aided somewhat incongruously by some medieval Persian swords and a suit of samurai armour. Further on, at no. 30, is the nineteenth-century **Kenessa** (Kenesa), or Karaim prayer house, a simple ochre cube with a greening roof.

The Island Castle

A hundred metres or so beyond the Kenessa, Karaimų descends to the shores of Lake Galvė, where stalls selling amber jewellery and hawkers renting out rowing boats and pedalos vie for your attention. Forming a wondrous backdrop to the waterfront scene is the **Island Castle** (Šalos pilis), about 500m offshore, a satisfyingly romantic cluster of red-brick watchtowers and squat round turrets topped with spindly weathercocks, grouped around a central, sky-scraping keep. The whole place was a ruin intil 1962, when the Lithuanian government decided to rebuild the castle as it must have looked in Vytautas the Great's time. It was a display of national pride to which Moscow chose to turn a blind eye, although Nikita Khruschev was said to be infuriated by the project.

Two wooden footbridges lead across the water to the castle, now home to a **museum** (Tues–Sun: May–Sept 10am–7pm; Oct–April 10am–5pm; ⓦwww.trakaimuziejus.lt; 10Lt), which interweaves the castle's history with local ethnography. The most important exhibits are displayed in the warren of halls within the central **keep**, separated from the rest of the castle by an inner moat, and holding within its sturdy frame a surprisingly delicate, galleried courtyard. Inside are scale models of the castle at different stages of its development, medieval weaponry and the colourful garments traditionally worn by the local Karaim. There's also a crowd of mannequins dressed in the traditional dress of the local Lithuanian population – white smocks and straw hats for the men, full skirts with black aprons embroidered with flower designs for the women. Exhibits in the outer buildings evoke medieval castle life: there are wild-boar skins, drinking horns and a jumble of furniture, including a bizarre table-and-chair set fashioned from stag antlers in the "Hunters' Room". The museum winds up with an eminently missable history of pipe-smoking through the ages, where you'll chance upon Meerschaum pipes carved into whimsical shapes such as reclining female nudes and horses' heads.

In summer, a **lake steamer** (10Lt return) runs from the castle to the northern end of Lake Galvė (also accessible by road), where the Tyszkiewicz family built the summer residence of **Užutrakis Palace**, and called in French landscape gardener Edouard André (who also worked for the family in Palanga) to lay out a wooded park. The palace is not open to the public, but the leafy park is a pleasant place for a wander and a good spot for savouring the views back towards Trakai.

Eating, drinking and entertainment

Trakai's main claim to culinary fame is the Karaim-introduced *kibinas*, a crescent-shaped pastry filled with grey meat that unleashes a deadly drip of hot fat after a few bites. *Kibinai* can be bought from snack stalls and cafés throughout the town; there is also a respectable handful of sit-down restaurants offering familiar Lithuanian and north-European fare.

In August, Lithuania's National Philharmonic and National Opera travel out to Trakai to take part in the **Trakai Festival**, a series of outdoor performances in the courtyards of both the Island and Peninsula castles. The tourist offices in Vilnius and Trakai can fill you in on the schedule and sell tickets – advance booking is essential.

Cafés and restaurants

Akmeninė Užeiga Bražuolės village ℡8-528/25186, ⊛www.akmenineuzeiga.lt. Lakeside, thatched-roof hotel-restaurant 5km north of town, offering international cuisine, Russian and Georgian specialities and an outdoor lakeside grill in summer. Mains hover around the 30–40Lt range. Daily 11am–10pm.

Apvalaus stalo klubas Karaimų 53A ℡8-528/55595, ⊛www.asklubas.lt. Smart lakeside pavilion offering views of Trakai castle and quality international cuisine. Choose between steaks, breast of duck, or excellent freshwater fish, and try and leave room for the desserts. With mains in the region of 45Lt it is pricier than most, but still affordable. Daily 11am–10pm.

Kybynlar Karaimų 29 ℡8-528/55179, ⊛www.kybynlar.lt. A lakeside restaurant with a Karaim-influenced, oriental theme (which extends to the costumed staff), this is probably the best place to sample *kibinai* – which here come in several flavours, cheese- or vegetable-filled versions included. The menu is also strong on Near Eastern fare such as stuffed vine leaves, spicy meatballs and skewer-grilled kebabs. Daily 11am–10pm.

Senoji kibininė Karaimų. One of the older *kibinai* outlets, occupying a wooden hut decorated with domestic knick-knacks at the northern end of town, about 1km south of the castle. The chewy-grey-meat-filled *kibinai* on offer here are a bit of an acquired taste, but there's plenty in the way of inexpensive mainstream Lithuanian fare – marinated-herring salads, potato pancakes and *koldūnai* included. Daily 10am–10pm.

Šokolado sostinė corner of Vytauto and Birutės. Anyone with a dangerous chocolate addiction should give this place a wide berth, as it specializes in anything made from the sweet brown stuff. Expect delicious, handmade truffles, all manner of cookies and cakes, good coffee and speciality teas. Daily 11am–6pm.

Kernavė

Just outside the village of **KERNAVĖ**, 30km northwest of Vilnius, a cluster of four flat-topped hills overlooking the River Neris once made up the military and administrative centre of the pre-Christian Lithuanian state. Originally crowned with wooden stockade forts, the hills almost certainly served as the main power base of Mindaugas, the thirteenth-century strongman who welded the Lithuanian tribes into a unified and expansionist state. The site was abandoned at the end of the fourteenth century after repeated sackings by the Teutonic Knights – the last of which, in 1390, probably included volunteer crusader Henry Bolingbroke, the future King Henry IV of England. Now protected as an **archeological reserve** (archeologinis rezervatas), the hills can be scaled by means of wooden stairways for sweeping views of the surrounding terrain.

The site's combination of historical pedigree and natural beauty has ensured its popularity with present-day neo-pagans, who congregate here for summer solstice bonfires on the night of June 23/24. Another good time to visit is the first or second weekend in July, when the **Kernavė Festival of Experimental Archeology** (Eksperimentinės archeologijos festivalis; information on ☎8-382/47371, ⓦwww .kernave.org) provides enthusiasts with the chance to dress up as medieval Lithuanian warriors and peasants and give demonstrations of pottery and metalwork.

Kernavė is a well-signed, twelve-kilometre journey west of the main Vilnius–Panevėžys highway. There are four to six daily **buses** to Kernavė from Vilnius, but many of these leave uncomfortably early in the morning; catching the 1.30pm bus from Vilnius and returning at 6pm (5pm on Saturdays and Sundays) is currently your best option.

The Museum of the Centre of Europe

According to a study made by the French National Geographical Institute in 1989, the official centre of Europe is located at 25 degrees 19' longitude, 54 degrees 54' latitude – in other words 25km north of Vilnius just beside the main road to Utena. The exact spot is marked by a sundial about 400m west of the road, accessible via a (signed) track. A handful of passers-by stop off here to take a look, though there's little to detain you.

However, the institute's findings do serve as a handy raison d'être for the grandly titled **Museum of the Centre of Europe** (Europos parkas; ⓦwww.europosparkas .lt; 9am–dusk; 12Lt), a significantly more worthwhile destination, located – somewhat confusingly – 17km to the southeast (it's 19km out of Vilnius: leave town via Kalvarių gatvė and it's well signed from there). Set amidst forested hills, the museum is basically an open-air **sculpture park**, established on the initiative of local artist Gintaras Karosas in 1991, and featuring an ever-growing display of over 65 works by sculptors from all over the world. There's something to please everyone in a collection that ranges from the impenetrably abstract to the facile: falling into the latter category is Karosas's *Infotree* right by the entrance, where a maze constructed from over three thousand old television sets comments on the role of the media as the bearers of state propaganda – a statue of Lenin is buried inside. The main body of sculptures is 1km further on, conveniently grouped around a café-restaurant (where you can pick up an English-language plan of the park to aid your wanderings; 1Lt). Karosas's set-piece *Monument of the Centre of Europe*, a small pyramid with the names (and distances in kilometres) of various world capitals arranged around it, is probably less captivating than the title would suggest. Highlights elsewhere include Magdalena Abakanowicz's *Space of Unknown Growth*, a family of giant concrete eggs lurking in a small dell; Dennis Oppenheim's *Drinking Structure with Exposed Kidney Pool*, a strange and rather unnerving cross between a caravan and an elephant; and Aleš Vesely's rather jolly *Sculpture idea – structure*, a metal, temple-like chamber on a spring-mounted floor, which starts to slowly bounce up and down when you enter.

Travel details

Buses

Vilnius to: Anykščiai (3 daily; weekends only; 2hr); Birštonas (5 daily; 2hr 30min); Biržai (4 daily; 3hr 40min–4hr 20min); Druskininkai (6 daily; 2hr 5min–3hr 30min); Kaunas (every 15–30min; 1hr 30min–1hr 55min); Klaipėda (7 daily; 4hr); Nida (1 daily; 6hr); Palanga (7 daily; 4hr 15min); Panevėžys (10 daily; 1hr 50min–3hr); Šiauliai (8 daily; 3hr 15min); Šilutė (4 daily; 5hr 30min); Trakai (Mon–Fri 20 daily, Sat & Sun 15 daily; 40–50min).

Trains

Vilnius to: Ignalina (6 daily; 2hr); Kaunas (Mon–Fri 11 daily; Sat & Sun 8 daily; 1hr 40min–2hr); Klaipėda (2 daily; 5hr); Marcinkonys (Mon–Fri 5 daily; Sat & Sun 3 daily; 2hr); Paneriai (Mon–Fri

24 daily; Sat & Sun 17 daily; 10min); Šeštokai (2 daily; 3hr 30min); Šiauliai (1 daily; 3hr 50min); Trakai (Mon–Fri 7 daily, Sat & Sun 4 daily; 40min).

International trains

Vilnius to: Daugavpils (3 weekly; 3hr); Kaliningrad (2 daily; 6hr 30min); Lvov (2 weekly; 16hr 10min); Minsk (2 daily; 4hr 10min); Moscow (2 daily; 16hr); St Petersburg (3 weekly; 12hr); Warsaw (1 daily; 7hr).

International buses

Vilnius to: Amsterdam (1 weekly; 26hr); Berlin (1 daily; 18hr); Brussels (1 weekly; 30hr); Gdańsk (1 daily; 11hr); Kaliningrad (2 daily; 8hr); Kraków (2 weekly; 12hr); Minsk (3 daily; 4–6hr); Olsztyn (4 weekly; 8hr 30min); Rīga (5 daily; 5hr); Tallinn (2 daily; 10hr 15min); Warsaw (3 daily; 9hr).

Flights

Vilnius to: Amsterdam (2 daily; 2hr 35min); Berlin (1 daily; 1hr 45min); Brussels (1 daily; 2hr 30min); Copenhagen (1 daily; 1hr 40min); Dublin (1 daily; 3hr 30min); Frankfurt (2 daily; 2hr 15min); Helsinki (2 daily; 1hr 25min); Kiev (1 daily; 1hr 40min); London (2 daily; 3hr); Moscow (2 daily; 1hr 55min); Paris (3 weekly; 3hr 20min); Prague (2 daily; 2hr 20min); Rīga (1 daily; 55min); Stockholm (1 daily; 1hr 10min); Tallinn (2 daily; 1hr 35min); Warsaw (1 daily; 1hr 10min).

3.2

Eastern and central Lithuania

A vast, rolling expanse of grazing land and cereal crops broken up by deep swathes of forest, eastern and central Lithuania are the heartland of what is still a predominantly agricultural country. There's a modest scattering of fair-sized industrial cities, each filled with the energies one would expect from a fast-changing, post-communist country, but even these lie only kilometres away from bucolic market towns and isolated villages – the kind of communities that

EASTERN & CENTRAL LITHUANIA

LATVIA

Rīga   Rīga   Rīga

St Petersburg

Livāni
Preiļi
Joniškis
Biržai
Pašvalys
Mēmele
Hill of
Crosses
Rokiškis
Šiauliai
Panevėžys
Kupiškis
Daugavpils
Radviliškis
Šeduva
Dusetos
Zarasai
Tytuvėnai
Nevėžis
Niūronys
Visaginas
Raseiniai
Anykščiai
AUKŠTAITIJA
NATIONAL
PARK
AUKŠTAITIJA
Kėdainiai
Ukmergė
Molėtai
Paluše
Ignalina
Jurbarkas
Nemunas
Širvintos
Švenčionys
Raudondvaris
Jonava
Neris
Šakiai
Kaunas
Rumšiškės
Elektrėnai
Kazlų Rūda
Vilkaviškis
Prienai
Biřstonas
Trakai
VILNIUS
Marijampolė
Alytus
Markys
Smarhon'
Kalvarija
Lazdijai
DZŪKIJA
NATIONAL
PARK
Šalčininkai
Merkinė
Varėna
BELARUS
POLAND
Suwałki
Sejny
Marcinkonys
Druskininkai
Grūtas Park
Sculpture Park
Lida

ŽEMAITIJA

Kaliningrad

KALININGRAD
(RUSSIA)

SUVALKIJA

DZŪKIJA

Vitebsk

Minsk

Minsk

N

0   50 km

Warsaw   Grodno   Grodno

Lithuanian-born Polish novelist Tadeusz Konwicki described as "the desert islands of Central Europe".

Eastern and central Lithuania are traditionally made up of three distinct ethnographic areas: Aukštaitija in the northern and central parts of the country, Dzūkija in the south and east and Suvalkija in the southwest. **Aukštaitija** (which literally means "Uplands", although it's not particularly higher than any other part of the country) is such a big, amorphous region that it no longer serves as a common badge of identity to the people who live there – they're more likely to see themselves as inhabitants of a particular city or district. There's more in the way of local patriotism in **Dzūkija**, a densely forested region famous for its wild mushrooms, wood-carving traditions and folk music – especially the unaccompanied narrative songs performed by women. The hard-working farming folk of **Suvalkija** (named after the regional centre of Suwałki, which is now just over the border in Poland) are said to speak the purest form of Lithuanian in the country – their dialect was chosen to form the basis of the official literary language by nineteenth-century reformers.

The region sees far fewer tourists than either Vilnius or the Baltic coast, but there's a great deal to discover. With an absorbing Old Town and an impressive clutch of museums, Lithuania's second city of **Kaunas** is as rewarding as any of the big urban centres of the Baltics, and also offers easy access to the Baroque monastery at **Pažaislis** and the unmissable open-air ethnographic museum at **Rumšiškės**. The region's remaining cities are largely modern, concrete affairs: **Panevėžys** is a useful transport hub for northern Lithuania, but offers far less in the way of attractions than **Šiauliai**, a youthful, energetic place that's also the main jumping-off point for the pilgrim-tramped route to the mysterious **Hill of Crosses**. There's much more in the way of atmosphere in the small towns of central Lithuania, with both **Biržai** and **Kėdainiai** boasting a wealth of historic monuments bequeathed by the aristocratic Radvila clan, and sleepy **Anykščiai** offering lazy woodland walks and a brace of quirky museums. For a taste of wild, unspoilt nature, the **Aukštaitija National Park** covers the most accessible chunk of northwestern Lithuania's extensive lakeland region, while the **Dzūkija National Park** presents a superb opportunity to sample the enticing woodland environments of the south – the laid-back spa town of **Druskininkai** is the best base from which to explore it.

Getting around the region **by car** is relatively swift if you're travelling via the two main highways, which serve the Vilnius–Kaunas–Klaipėda and Vilnius–Panevėžys–Rīga routes respectively. Main roads elsewhere are mostly single-lane affairs and can be slow-going, although given the unspoilt beauty of the countryside this is no great hardship. Vilnius, Kaunas and Panevėžys are the main nodal points of an extensive **bus** network that covers all the places mentioned in this chapter – again, bear in mind that services on country roads can take an age to get anywhere. If Vilnius is your starting point then a number of places can be accessed **by train**, with routes fanning out towards Kaunas, the Aukštaitija National Park, the Dzūkija National Park and Šiauliai.

Aukštaitija National Park

Northeast of Vilnius extends a rippling, green landscape scattered with a glittering archipelago of lakes, occupying the troughs and hollows gouged out of the Baltic plain by glaciers during the last Ice Age. Among the most attractive and easily visited of the lakeland regions is the **Aukštaitija National Park**, 100km north of Vilnius, where the River Žeimena and its tributaries feed over one hundred lakes of various shapes and sizes. It's an understandably popular area with canoeists, who use the network of lakes and rivers as an aquatic highway traversing one of Lithuania's most unspoilt regions. It's prime walking territory, too, with waterside trails leading up into the low, rounded hills that cluster around the lake shores. Some seventy percent of the park is made up of forest – predominantly pine, spruce and birch. The densest woodland is concentrated in the sparsely populated northern parts of the park, and it's here that you're most likely to come across roe deer, red deer and wild boar, and more rarely elk, marten and beaver.

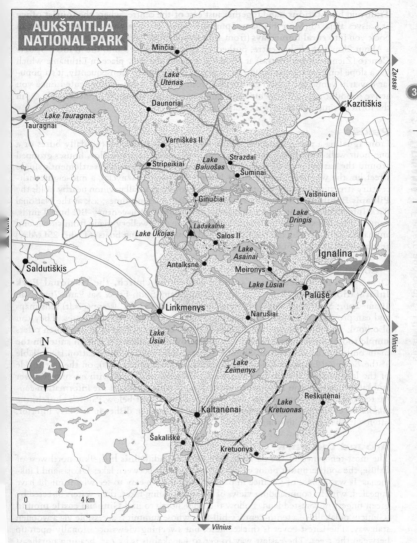

AUKŠTAITIJA
NATIONAL PARK

Minčia

Lake
Utenas

Daunoriai

Kazitiškis

Lake Tauragnas
Tauragnai

Varniškės II

Stripeikiai

Lake
Baluošas

Strazdai

Šuminai

Vaišniūnai

Ginučiai

Lake
Dringis

Ladakalnis

Lake Ūkojas

Salos II

Lake
Asainai

Ignalina

Antalksnė

Meironys

Saldutiškis

Lake Lūsiai

Palūšė

Linkmenys

Narušiai

Lake
Ūsiai

Lake
Žeimenys

N

Reškutėnai

Kaltanėnai

Lake
Kretuonas

Šakališkė

Kretuonys

0   4 km

Vilnius

Entry tickets (2Lt) to the park are available from the **information centre** in the park's main settlement, **Palūšė** (see overleaf). Both the information centre in Palūšė and the tourist office in nearby **Ignalina** can provide details of the handful of small hotels and rural homestays in and around Palūšė, as well as the park's rough-and-ready campsites, most of which are just lakeside patches of grass with no running water or toilet facilities.

Ignalina

The park's main jumping-off point is **IGNALINA**, a small town of pastel-hued wooden houses that lies just outside the park, on the Vilnius–Visaginas road and rail routes.

Train and bus stations stand together just east of the centre, where the tourist office at Laisvės alėja 70 (Mon–Fri 9am–5pm; ☎8-386/52597, ⓦwww.lsa.lt/ignalina) can book you into rural homestays (from 40Lt upwards) all over the park.

About 2km east of the centre, pushed up against a wooded hill, the **Winter Sports Centre** (Žiemo sporto centras) at Sporto 3 is about the only place in Lithuania which has a slope long enough (at 300m) to be worth skiing down. Consequently, it's a popular day-trip venue for winter-sports fans from Vilnius – skis can be rented once you arrive for 30Lt a day. The centre also offers **accommodation** (☎8-386/54193; ●) in the form of simple doubles with shared facilities.

Palūšė

From Ignalina a minor road runs 5km west towards **PALŪŠĖ** (10 daily buses or a one-hour walk from Ignalina train station), a village of dainty, yellow houses grouped around the eastern end of Lake Lūšiai. Slightly uphill from the settlement's single street lies the wooden **Church of St Joseph** (Šv Jozefo bažnyčia), a mid-eighteenth-century structure with a squat, two-storey bell tower. A small pavilion nearby holds the **Pilkapis Exhibition** (Pilkapio ekspozicija; erratic opening times; ask at the National Park Information Centre – see below), consisting of fifth-century-BC burial finds, namely a female skeleton accompanied by a trove of jewellery made from stones and animal bones. Down by the lakefront, a shed rents out rowing boats (6Lt/hr; 25Lt/day) and canoes (12Lt/hr; 35Lt/day) during the summer.

Practicalities

Occupying the former priest's house beside the church, the **National Park Information Centre** (June–Aug Mon–Thurs 9am–5pm, Fri & Sat 9am–7pm, Sun 10am–2pm; Sept–May Mon–Fri 9am–5pm; ☎8-386/52891, ⓔanp@is.lt) sells maps and can provide information on renting out canoes and advice on routes. They can also book you into the *Tourism Centre* (Turismo centras; ●) next door, which offers simple rooms with shared facilities in cabins over the summer, and en suites in the main building all year round. Slightly more salubrious accommodation is available at the *Ecological Education Centre* (Ekologinio švietimo centras; ●) on the north side of the lake just off the road to Meironys, where rooms come with en-suite shower and kitchenette. If you have your own transport, you could ask the information centre to book you a room in Ginučiai mill (see below). Just below Palūšė's church, the *Aukštaičių Užeiga* **restaurant** offers traditional Lithuanian dishes in a folksy interior, often with live music in summer.

Around the park

The most renowned of the park's beauty spots is **Ladakalnis hill**, 9km northwest of Palūšė, the southernmost point of a ridge that extends between lakes Ūkojas and Linkmenas. It was a place of sacrifice in pagan times, and it's easy to see why it might have appealed, with its commanding views of six surrounding lakes, their waters bisected by green fingers of forested land. Follow the ridge north to find **Ginučiai castle mound** (Ginučių piliakalnis), a tenth-century hill-fort whose summit is accessible via a wooden stairway. The forest cover is thicker here, but sweeping views occasionally open up between the trees. The easiest way to get to Ladakalnis is by car, heading northeast from Palūšė along the Tauragnai road and turning north onto a dirt road. Alternatively, you can walk from Palūšė (3–4hr), following a trail along the northern shores of Lake Lūšiai which takes you through a pair of wonderfully preserved villages full of timber houses, **Salos-I** and **Salos-II**.

Five kilometres north of Ladakalnis, **GINUČIAI** is a picturesque village of pea-green houses squeezed between lakes Alnajos and Sravinaitis. The nineteenth-century water mill in the centre of the village is now a national park-operated guesthouse (booked through the information centre in Palūšė; ●), offering tasteful, wooden-floored rooms with shared facilities – there's no breakfast but you do get use of a kitchen. The former millpond is a popular bathing spot in summer, and you can rent boats at the bridge where the two lakes meet. Ginučiai also boasts the one **campsite** in the park which comes with a water supply and hole-in-the-ground toilets.

Ten kilometres east of Ginučiai, on the shores of Lake Dringis, **VAIŠNIŪNAI** is another lovely village of timber houses and granaries, watched over by a huge roadside Rupintojėlis figure sculpted by a local craftsman. Heading west from Ginučiai along dirt roads will bring you after 5km to **STRIPEIKAI**, where the **Ancient Beekeeping Museum** (Senovinės bitininkystės muziejus; May to mid-Oct daily 10am–7pm; 3Lt), displays an oddly riveting collection of traditional beehives, carved out of tree trunks into various shapes, and spread across a grassy meadow like timber tombstones.

Anykščiai and around

One hundred and ten kilometres northwest of Vilnius, **ANYKŠČIAI** (pronounced "A-*neeksh*-chey") is one of the most attractive towns in the Lithuanian northeast, nestling in a rolling patchwork of forest and green pasture either side of the River Šventoji. The beauty of the region occupies a treasured place in the Lithuanian psyche, thanks largely to local-born priest Antanas Baranauskas (1835–1902) and his poem *Forest of Anykščiai (Anykščių Šilelis)* – a lyrical evocation of nature, regarded as one of the nation's most sacred texts. The town has an absorbing museum devoted to Baranauskas and makes a good base-camp for woodland walks, while horse-lovers will be intrigued by nearby **Niūronys** – where there's a museum devoted to the creatures. With four to five **buses** a day from Vilnius, Anykščiai is an easy day-trip from the capital – if you miss one of these services, head for Ukmergė and change there.

The Town

Perched on a hill just above the town's bus station, the **Baranauskas and Vienuolis-Žukauskas Memorial Museum** at Vienuolio 4 (Baranausko ir Vienuolio-Žukausko memorialinis muziejus; daily 8am–5pm; 3Lt) pays homage to both the author of the *Forest of Anykščiai* and the self-appointed keeper of the Baranauskas flame, Antanas Žukauskas (1882–1957), who wrote short stories under the pen-name of Vienuolis ("the monk"). The museum was originally the site of the Baranauskas family farmstead, and Vienuolis bought it in 1922 with the express intention of turning its one surviving building – a log-built granary – into a national shrine. Now enclosed in a concrete-and-glass shell to protect it from the elements, the granary contains a chair and table belonging to Baranauskas and a few facsimile manuscripts, but little to convey the scale of his achievements – as well as being a prolific author, he was one of nineteenth-century Lithuania's leading ecclesiastics, rising to become Bishop of Seinai (now Sejny in Poland) in 1897. You can also look around the house Vienuolis built for himself next door to the granary; its mid-twentieth-century interior of floral wallpaper and ticking grandfather clocks has been lovingly preserved.

Across the river from the museum, Anykščiai's unassuming town centre is dominated by the neo-Gothic **Church of St Matthew** (Šv Mato bažnyčia), whose twin towers – at 79m each – are the tallest in the country. The impressively cavernous interior features some lovely nineteenth-century, floral-motif wall coverings and brightly coloured stained glass by contemporary artist Anortė Mackelaitė.

To reach what remains of the **forest** Baranauskas waxed so lyrically about, head southwest from the church along Vilniaus gatvė and keep on going past the town cemetery. The road soon turns into an asphalted path surrounded on both sides by dense woodland rich in pine, birch, oak and elm. Following the trail for 5km leads eventually to the **Puntukas boulder** (Puntuko akmuo), a six-metre-high lump of rock deposited by a retreating glacier some 12,000 years ago and nowadays a much-loved landmark – no self-respecting local newly-weds would dream of having their photograph taken anywhere else. One side of the boulder is decorated with an Assyrian-style bas-relief of pointy-helmeted pilots Darius and Girėnas, who plummeted to their deaths while attempting to fly from New York to Kaunas in 1933 (see box, p.365).

Anykščiai has one other attraction: the **narrow-gauge railway** (siaurukas; ⓦwww .siaurukas.eu) that runs northwest to Panevėžys (see opposite) and east to Lake Rubikiai (Rubikių ežeras). Regular passenger services were discontinued in 2001 but the line has succesfully reinvented itself as a tourist attraction, operating Saturday and Sunday excursions to Rubikiai (currently departing Anykščiai at 11am and returning at 2.30pm) from mid-May to mid-October. Tickets (12Lt return) can be bought from the Anykščiai tourist office (see below) or from the conductor on the train itself. Anykščiai's **train station**, ten minutes' walk north of the Baranauskas museum along Gegužės, is a handsome wooden building that hasn't changed much since the inter-war years, and there's a small museum of narrow-gauge rolling stock in a former engine shed.

Practicalities

Anykščiai's **tourist office**, just below the Baranauskas museum at Gegužės 1 (daily 9am–5pm; ☎8-381/59177, ⓦwww.antour.lt), can book you into a clutch of rural homestays (❶–❷) in the region, including several around Lake Rubikiai, 10km east of town – few of these are anywhere near public transport routes so you'll need a car. The best **hotel** is the *Mindaugo Karūna*, just east of the centre at Liudiškių 18 (☎8-381/58520, ⓦwww.mindaugokaruna.lt; ❹), a sports and conference centre with cosy en suites, and indoor and outdoor swimming pools on the premises. A cheaper option is the *Puntukas*, in the centre at Baranausko 8 (☎8-381/51345; ❷), offering frumpy rooms with shared facilities and a handful of more expensive en suites with new furniture and TV. The cosiest of the **cafés** is *Erdvė*, on the main square, offering a full menu of meat and fish dishes and bench seating in the yard. *Bangelė*, occupying a weir-side building above the River Šventoji, is a good place for a drink.

Niūronys

Six kilometres north of Anykščiai, just off the Rokiškis road, the village of **NIŪRONYS** is the site of the rather delightful **Museum of the Horse** (Arklio muziejus; daily 10am–6pm; 3Lt), occupying an ensemble of five traditional, timber-built buildings arranged farmstead-style beside the village's main crossroads. Lithuania's relationship with the beast is explored through a series of displays, including photographs of working horses through the ages, a re-created village smithy and a barn full of horse-drawn ploughs, rakes and traps. The museum is far from being a tribute to a disappearing culture: in fact the use of horses on Lithuanian farms has increased over the last decade and a half, the break-up of Soviet-era collective farms having led to fewer working tractors in circulation. Between spring and autumn, you'll see plenty of characteristically stocky, Lithuanian farm horses grazing in the fields outside, and there's a paddock where kids can ride ponies. Horse-and-carriage excursions (horse-and-sledge in winter) are a great way to take in the local countryside, but should be booked in advance (☎8-381/51722; if you can't get through to an English-speaker, Anykščiai tourist office might be able to help).

Three **buses** a day run to the village from Anykščiai, and walking back to town through the gently undulating landscape of forest and pastureland (1hr 20min) is no

Bėk, bėk, žirgelį

Only a horse-mad nation like the Lithuanians could come up with a festival entitled Bėk, bėk, žirgelį ("Run, ye little horse!"), a celebration of all things equine which takes place in the field below the Museum of the Horse on the first or second weekend in June – the tourist office in Anykščiai will have full details. Farmers from all over the region descend on the village with their horses and traps, and large crowds assemble to watch a day-long programme of races involving everything from donkeys to thoroughbreds. There's also plenty in the way of craft stalls, beer tents and grilled food. Extra buses from Anykščiai are laid on for the occasion.

great hardship. The *Pasagelė* café next to the museum doles out scrumptious potato pancakes, as well as soup of the day and more substantial pork dishes.

Panevėžys

The fifth-largest city in Lithuania, **PANEVĖŽYS** is an unenticing, grey sprawl which owes its place on tourist itineraries to its position on the Vilnius–Rīga highway rather than any particular attractions. It's a very useful transport hub if you're shuttling around by bus between north Lithuanian towns like Anykščiai, Biržai and Šiauliai – and with fast connections to and from both Kaunas and Vilnius, you'll rarely end up having to stay here overnight.

If you do have time to kill, head uphill from the bus station to the main square, then follow the west-bound Vasario 16-os gatvė to find the **Panevėžys Regional Museum** at no. 23 (Panevėžio kraštotyros muziejus; Tues–Sat 10am–5pm; 1.50Lt), a small, but entertaining collection comprising exhibits as diverse as mammoth tusks and milk churns. Its main focus is rural life in the nineteenth century, illustrated through a reconstructed, peasant living room. Upstairs, glass cases are crammed with butterflies and bugs, while a bunker-like basement holds exhibitions of contemporary art. The nearby **Photography Gallery**, Vasario 16-os 31 (Fotografijos Galerija; Tues–Sat 10am–5pm; 2Lt), has a regular programme of quality exhibitions; somewhat less predictable are the shows sporadically held at the **Panevėžys Art Gallery**, a block south of here at Respublikos 3.

The helpful **tourist office** is on the main square at Laisvės 11 (Mon–Fri 9am–5pm; ☎8-45/508081, ✉pantic@takas.lt). If you do end up **staying** the night, try the fairly comfortable *Romantic*, in a lakeside park north of the centre at Kranto 24 (☎8-45/584860, ⊛www.hotel.romantic.lt; ❹), or *Panevėžys* at Laisvės 26 (☎8-45/501601, ⊛www.hotelpanevezys.lt; ❸), an uninspiring, if habitable, concrete box in the centre. The best place for a drink or snack is *Galerija XX*, Laisvės 7, a lively café decked out with old clocks and sepia photographs of pre-World War I Panevėžys.

Biržai

Two hundred kilometres north of Vilnius and 20km east of the main Vilnius–Rīga highway lies the border town of **BIRŽAI**. It was put on the map by the Radvila family, who owned the town from the fifteenth to the nineteenth centuries, turning it into a flourishing trade centre and key military stronghold in the process. Nowadays, Biržai is a pretty uneventful place, but it's worth visiting for its **fortress**, lapped by the waters of Lake Širvėna.

The Town

Attractively set in a leafy park (called the "Biržai Castle Cultural Reserve") at the northern end of the town's main artery, Vytauto gatvė, Biržai's **fortress** is actually a twentieth-century reconstruction of the much-modified original dating from 1586, built by Kristupas Radvila, "the Thunderer" (1547–1603). Surrounded by grassy ramparts and reached via a dainty drawbridge, it's a creamy, elegantly arcaded, Renaissance-style building, looking more like a stately home than a castle. The Radvilas, who had plenty of estates elsewhere in Lithuania, abandoned the fortress when it was blown up by the Swedes in 1704. What remained of it was put to the torch seven decades later as part of a lavish theatrical entertainment put on by the hooligan-aristocrat Karol Stanisław Radvila.

The fortress now houses the **Biržai District Museum** (Biržų krašto muziejus; Wed–Sun 9am–5pm; 2Lt), which starts off with a rather daunting collection of rows of ancient swords and axe heads. Things pick up with a scale model of the fortress as it looked in the time of "the Thunderer", overlooked by striking portraits of Augustus II "the Strong" of Poland-Lithuania and Peter the Great of Russia – the pair met here in 1701 to agree on a common front against the invading Swedes. Upstairs, wooden sculptures of Catholic saints throng a room dedicated to folk art.

A short stroll southeast through the park will bring you to the gleaming-white **Church of St John the Baptist**, its twin nineteenth-century towers piled wedding-cake style in three tiers. Immediately to the east lies a broad, flagstoned square dominated by a monument to Lithuanian Bolshevik poet, Julius Janonis (1896–1917). Squatting on top of an enormous concrete pole, he looks more like a pillar-dwelling saint of old than a rabble-rousing bard.

From the square, head east along Basanavičiaus, cross the Apašča River and turn left up Malūno gatvė to reach the most picturesque part of reed-shrouded **Lake Širvėna**. A rickety footbridge leads over the heads of inquisitive swans to the lake's northern shore, where a wooded park surrounds the stately **Astravas Palace** (Astravo dvaras) – a summer retreat built by the Tyszkiewicz family after the Radvilas sold them the town of Biržai in 1812. You can't visit the interior, but it's a lovely sight nonetheless, its mock-Renaissance lookout tower giving it the appearance of a grandiose village fire station.

Practicalities

Biržai is served by a handful of direct **buses** from Vilnius and by regular services from Panevėžys and Pašvalys. Biržai's bus station is at the northern end of Vytauto gatvė, near the castle park. Once you've done the rounds of the sights there's not much reason to stay, but if you do decide to stop over, the **tourist office** at Janonio 2 (Mon–Fri 9am–5pm; ☎8-450/33496, ⓦwww.birzai.lt) has details of a few rural homestays (①) in outlying villages; otherwise the *Tyla* **hotel**, 2km north of the centre at Tylos 2 (☎8-450/31191, ⓦwww.tyla.lt; ④), is the only sure-fire source of accommodation in town. There are a couple of serviceable **cafés** on the main strip and a handful of gloomy beer bars serving up the local tipple, Biržų alus (Biržai beer).

Kaunas and around

With a population of 420,000, **KAUNAS** is the third-biggest city in the Baltic States, a bustling, metropolitan place and a major commercial and industrial centre. It served as the temporary capital of Lithuania for twenty years following World War I, and contains museums and galleries of national importance, yet still seems overwhelmingly provincial and self-absorbed in relation to Vilnius.

Although not as extensive as that of the capital, Kaunas's medieval **Old Town** still boasts an enjoyable ensemble of red-brick buildings and ice-cream-coloured churches, gathered around a handsome main square. Extending east of here along the shop- and café-lined Laisvės alėja, the **New Town** is characterized by the modernist and Art Deco buildings hastily thrown up during the inter-war period to make Kaunas look worthy of its capital-city status. Strewn along the way are some highly individual museums, offering everything from fine art to folk sculpture and carnival masks. Easily accessible out-of-town attractions include the Baroque monastery of **Pažaislis** and the superb open-air Museum of Lithuanian Life at **Rumšiškės**. Traces of the Jewish community that once thrived in Kaunas are thin on the ground; many were executed by the Nazis at **Ninth Fort**, located northwest of the city and preserved as a grimly moving memorial.

Only 100km west of Vilnius and easily reached by **bus or rail**, Kaunas can be treated as a day-trip from the capital – although you'll need a few days to get the most out of it and explore some of the outlying attractions as well. Its good transport links also make it an ideal base from which to roam the whole of central Lithuania.

Some history

Kaunas started out as one of Lithuania's key border strongholds, defending the south of the realm from frequent incursions from the Teutonic Knights. After the Battle of Žalgiris in 1410, the Teutonic danger receded, leaving Kaunas free to grow rich from commerce – its position on the Nemunas River providing access to a network of trade routes. Several centuries of prosperity followed, marred only briefly by the sacking of the town by the Russians in 1655. Kaunas also became an important ecclesiastical centre, the city's Catholic seminary producing many of the nation's spiritual leaders.

A major turning point in Kaunas's development was the Tsarist Empire's decision to make it the lynchpin of their western defences in the 1880s. The Russians thoroughly redeveloped the place, constructing a new city centre around a long straight boulevard (now Laisvės alėja; see p.362) and a ring of nine forts. Kaunas flourished, although its forts were in such a state of disrepair by 1914 that commander-in-chief Grand Duke Nikolai suggested that the city's name be changed from Kovno (Russian for "Kaunas") to Govno (Russian for "shit"). The fortifications were in any case never put to the test: scared witless by the German offensive of summer 1915, Kaunas's commander General Grigoriev ran away to Vilnius rather than lead the city's defence, for which he was sentenced to eight years' hard labour.

After World War I, Vilnius was occupied by the Poles, and Kaunas had to step into the breach. Declared the "provisional" capital, Kaunas seemed an unlikely seat of power, not least because it lacked the set-piece administrative buildings that a national capital needed. Visiting in the early 1920s, British traveller Owen Rutter found Kaunas to be "not worthy of the name city and, quite frankly, it is filthy. Moreover, its hotels are the worst in the Baltic States." By the 1930s, however, Kaunas had been transformed, with a rash of construction turning the city into a showroom for modern architecture – the Resurrection Church, Vytautas the Great War Museum and main Post Office being the principal surviving monuments from this go-ahead era.

In the wake of World War II, Kaunas lost its political role, but gained an important place in the national psyche. Taking in fewer Russian immigrants than other big centres, Kaunas remained a Lithuanian-speaking city, proudly aware of its status as a repository of national values. It was here that art student Romas Kalanta burnt himself to death in 1972 to protest against Soviet power, sparking days of rioting. During the pro-independence upsurge of the late 1980s, Kaunas was the kind of place where Russian-speaking visitors would be met with blank stares or given wrong directions by locals who claimed to know no other language than their own.

Initially slow to reap the benefits of post-independence economic change, Kaunas is now beginning to transform itself into a modern European city. Quirky souvenir shops in the Old Town and chic, glass-fronted cafés along Laisvės alėja lend the place a welcoming and animated air. One thing that hasn't changed is the city's deep-seated feeling of inferiority vis-à-vis near-neighbour Vilnius – comments about the culture and sophistication of the capital are usually met here with silence and a grinding of teeth.

Arrival and information

The **bus and train stations** are within 400m of each other on Vytauto prospektas on the eastern edges of the city centre. It takes the best part of forty minutes to walk to the Old Town, so you might want to hop on trolleybus #1, #5 or #7 and get off at Vilniaus gatvė. Kaunas's **airport** is 12km northeast of the centre – minibus #120 runs into town.

The **tourist information centre**, ten minutes' walk from the bus and train stations at Laisvės alėja 36 (Kauno regiono turizmo informacijos centras; April–Sept Mon–Fri 9am–7pm, Sat 9am–3pm; Oct–March Mon–Fri 9am–6pm; ☏8-37/323 436, ⓦwww .kaunastic.lt), handles information about the whole region, including Birštonas (see p.378), and can help with accommodation bookings. You can also pick up a copy of *Kaunas in Your Pocket* here (ⓦwww.inyourpocket.com; 5Lt), a reliable source of accommodation, restaurant and bar listings which is updated yearly – also available from bookstores, newspaper kiosks and some hotel foyers.

Accommodation

Kaunas is well endowed with pricey, business-standard **hotels**, and although budget and mid-range choices are thinner on the ground, they're not impossible to find. Many of the more expensive hotels offer weekend discounts – it always pays to ask. The cheapest beds in town are to be found in **private rooms** with downtown landladies (from 80Lt single, 140Lt double); Litinterp, Gedimino 28-7 (☏8-37/228 718, ⓦwww .litinterp.lt), can set you up in one of these.

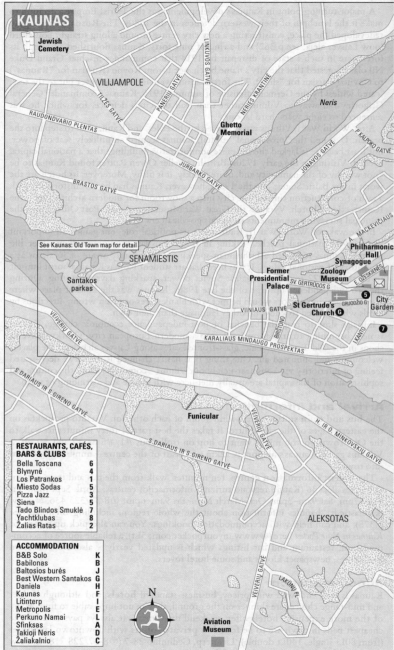

▲ Ninth Fort & Klaipėda

KAUNAS

Jewish
Cemetery

VILIJAMPOLE

Neris

Ghetto
Memorial

RAUDONDVARIO PLENTAS

TILŽĖS GATVĖ

PANERIŲ GATVĖ

LINKUVOS GATVĖ

NERIES KRANTINĖ

JURBARKO GATVĖ

BRASTOS GATVĖ

JONAVOS GATVĖ

P. KALPOKO GATVĖ

A. MACKEVIČIAUS

See Kaunas: Old Town map for detail

SENAMIESTIS

Santakos
parkas

Former
Presidential
Palace

Zoology
Museum

Philharmonic
Hall
Synagogue

E. OŽEŠKIENĖS

SV. GERTRŪDOS G

St Gertrude's
Church ⑥

GRUODŽIO G.

BRISTONO

VIINIAUS GATVĖ

GRUODŽIO G.

⑤

KANTO

City
Garden

⑦

VEIVERIŲ GATVĖ

KARALIAUS MINDAUGO PROSPEKTAS

S. DARIAUS IR S. GIRENO GATVĖ

Funicular

VEIVERIŲ GATVĖ

H. IR O. MINKOVSKIŲ GATVĖ

S. DARIAUS IR S. GIRENO GATVĖ

ALEKSOTAS

**RESTAURANTS, CAFÉS,
BARS & CLUBS**

Bella Toscana	6
Blynynė	4
Los Patrankos	1
Miesto Sodas	5
Pizza Jazz	3
Siena	5
Tado Blindos Smuklė	7
Yachtklubas	8
Žalias Ratas	2

ACCOMMODATION

B&B Solo	K
Babilonas	B
Baltosios burės	J
Best Western Santakos	G
Daniela	H
Kaunas	F
Litinterp	I
Metropolis	E
Perkuno Namai	L
Sfinksas	A
Takioji Neris	D
Žaliakalnio	C

VEIVERIŲ GATVĖ

LAKŪNŲ PL.

Aviation
Museum

N

▼ Botanical Gardens

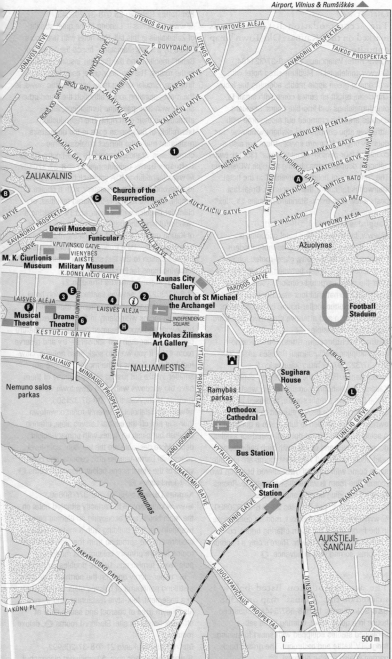

UTENOS GATVÉ

TVIRTOVÉS ALÉJA

JONAVOS GATVÉ

P. DOVYDAIČIO G.

UTENOS GATVÉ

SAVANORIŲ PROSPEKTAS

TAIKOS PROSPEKTAS

ANYKŠČIŲ GATVÉ

DARBININKŲ GATVÉ

KAPSŲ GATVÉ

BIRŽŲ GATVÉ

RADVILÉNŲ PLENTAS

ROKŠŲKIO GATVÉ

ŽANAVYKŲ GATVÉ

KALNIEČIŲ GATVÉ

ŽEMAIČIŲ GATVÉ

P. KALPOKO GATVÉ

❶

AUŠROS GATVÉ

V. KUDIRKOS GATVÉ

M. JANKAUS GATVÉ

J. BASANAVIČIAUS

ŽALIAKALNIS

K. PETRAUSKO GATVÉ

J. MATEIKOS GATVÉ

Ⓐ

AUKŠTAIČIŲ

MINTIES RATO

Ⓑ

GATVÉ

SAVANORIŲ PROSPEKTAS

AUŠROS GATVÉ

AUKŠTAIČIŲ GATVÉ

GÉLIŲ RATO

**Church of the
Resurrection**

Ⓒ

ŽEMAIČIŲ GATVÉ

P. VAIČAIČIO

VYDŪNO ALÉJA

Devil Museum

V.PUTVINSKIO GATVÉ

Funicular

Ažuolynas

GATVÉ

**M. K. Čiurlionis
Museum**

VIENYBÉS
AIKŠTÉ

Military Museum

K. DONELAIČIO GATVÉ

PARODOS GATVÉ

**Kaunas City
Gallery**

Ⓓ

❷

LAISVÉS ALÉJA

Ⓔ

❸

RAKANDŲ

ⓘ

**Church of St Michael
the Archangel**

Ⓕ

❹

LAISVÉS ALÉJA

**Football
Staduim**

**Musical
Theatre**

**Drama
Theatre**

❻

INDEPENDENCE
SQUARE

KĘSTUČIO GATVÉ

Ⓗ

PERKŪNO ALÉJA

KARALIAUS

MICKEVIČIAUS

**Mykolas Žilinskas
Art Gallery**

MINDAUGO PROSPEKTAS

❶

NAUJAMIESTIS

VYTAUTO PROSPEKTAS

*Nemuno salos
parkas*

**Sugihara
House**

*Ramybés
parkas*

VAIŽGANTO GATVÉ

Ⓛ

**Orthodox
Cathedral**

Nemunas

KARO LIGONINÉS

VYTAUTO PROSPEKTAS

KAUNAKIEMIO GATVÉ

Bus Station

TUNELIO GATVÉ

**Train
Station**

PRANCŪZŲ GATVÉ

J. BAKANAUSKO GATVÉ

**AUKŠTIEJI-
ŠANČIAI**

M. K. ČIURLIONIO GATVÉ

A. JUOZAPAVIČIAUS PROSPEKTAS

LIVINSKIO GATVÉ

LAKŪNŲ PL.

0   500 m

Old Town

The accommodation listed below is marked on the "Kaunas: Old Town" map opposite.

Apple Hotel Valančiaus 19 ☎8-37/321404, ⓦwww.applehotel.lt. Medium-sized hotel with welcoming green apple motifs adorning the lobby. The clean, bright en suites come with small TV, pine furnishings and lino-like floors. Standard doubles are a bit cramped but most come with attractive attic ceilings and skylight windows; "lux" doubles offer a bit more space. There are also a couple of four-person "family blocks" (300Lt): two adjacent double rooms sharing a single WC/shower. The "museum of holiday souvenirs" in the hotel stairwell is far cooler than it sounds. Breakfast costs a few litas extra. Standard doubles ③, "lux" doubles ④

Daugirdas Daugirdo 4 ☎8-37/301561, ⓦwww.daugirdas.lt. This hotel occupies a sixteenth-century house and its more modern neighbour – with the lofty, glass-roofed lobby area occupying the gap between the two. Rooms offer the deep-carpeted comforts you'll find in any good international four-star. Bonuses include the barrel-vaulted, cellar-bound breakfast room, central location and attentive staff. Two rooms are wheelchair-accessible. ⑦

Kaunas Archdiocesan Guesthouse (Kauno arkivyskupijos svečių namai) Rotušės aikštė 21 ☎8-37/322597, ⓦhttp://kaunas.lcn.lt /sveciunamai. Part of the seventeenth-century Kaunas archbishopric complex at the western end of the Old Town's main square, and used by the Soviet army before being returned to its original owners – who decided to turn it into a guesthouse. A selection of functional but well-cared-for singles, doubles, triples and quads, with high ceilings, parquet floors and small TVs. Most rooms are en suite; some come with a WC/shower shared between two rooms. One room is wheelchair-accessible. Rooms ②–④ depending on size and facilities.

Kunigaikščio menė Daukšos 28 ☎8-37/320800, ⓦwww.hotelmene.lt. A smart, modern guesthouse in the heart of the Old Town offering bright, comfortable rooms with shower. There's only a handful of rooms, so ring well in advance. ⑤

New Town

The accommodation listed below is marked on the "Kaunas" map on p.358.

B&B Solo Dysnos 10 ☎8-687/54443. Suburban house in a quiet street, offering three self-contained studios equipped with smart furnishings, fridge, TV, kettle and bathroom. The grassy back garden is also at your disposal. ④

Babilonas Raseinių 25 ☎8-37/202545, ⓦwww.babilonas.lt. Lurking in the quiet streets of Žaliakalnis is this tall, thin hotel with five floors linked by a spiral staircase – hence the "Tower-of-Babel" moniker and the Babylon-inspired paintings in the rooms. The top-floor suite, complete with fireplace, circular dining table and fastastic views, is the most appealing room, although the standard en suites, with their pale pine furnishings, are attractive in their own right. The reproduction bas-reliefs of Babylonian gods in the downstairs restaurant make the perfect breakfast-time companions. Standard rooms ⑤, top-floor suite ⑦

Baltosios Burės Gimbutienės 35 ☎8-37/370467, ⓦwww.jachtklubas.lt. A yacht-club-owned motel just beyond Pažaislis monastery, with a choice of simple, box-like rooms with shared facilities, or chintzier doubles with shower and TV. Boasting a wonderful pine-shrouded position on the shores of Kauno marios, it's a bit of a hike without your own transport – take trolleybus #5 from opposite the bus station to the last stop, then walk for 2km following signs for Pažaislis. ①–③

Best Western Santakos Gruodžio 21 ☎8-37/302702, ⓦwww.santaka.lt. Swish hotel in a converted warehouse, offering atmospheric, spacious rooms with plenty in the way of exposed brickwork and wood-beamed ceilings. Most feature bathtubs rather than just showers – try and reserve room #104 if you want to soak in an antique, claw-foot bathtub. Rooms in the modern annexe are smaller in size but just as classy – many of them have big windows with good downtown views. ⑦

Daniela Mickevičiaus 28 ☎8-37/321505, ⓦwww.danielahotel.lt. Seventy-room downtown four-star just off the central Laisvės alėja, offering smallish but plush en suites with primary-colour decor. More desirable are the top-floor, split-level suites with barrel-vaulted attic ceilings, and good views of the street scene below. Standard rooms ⑥, split-level suites ⑦

Kaunas Laisvės alėja 79 ☎8-37/750850, ⓦwww.kaunashotel.lt. Perfectly situated hotel on the main boulevard, occupying an elegant early-twentieth-century building with a metallic-cube modern annexe sprouting from the rear. Standard rooms feature primary colours and modern, pale-wood furnishings. Deluxe doubles are roomier – the upper-storey ones on the northern side offer a striking panorama of Laisvės alėja. Breakfast is in a basement, folk-style restaurant, and there's also a gym (free of charge) and sauna (free at off-peak times) on site. Standard rooms ⑥, deluxe rooms ⑦

Metropolis Daukanto 21 ☎8-37/205992, ⓦwww.takiojineris.com. A somewhat gloomy but

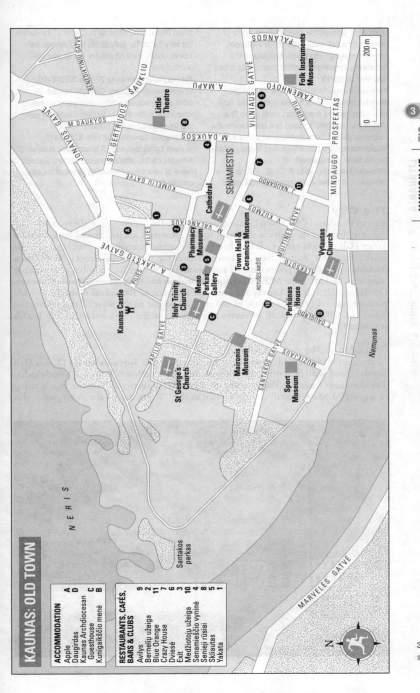

KAUNAS: OLD TOWN

ACCOMMODATION

Apple	A
Daugirdas	D
Kaunas Archdiocesan Guesthouse	C
Kunigaikščio menė	B

RESTAURANTS, CAFÉS, BARS & CLUBS

Avilys	9
Berneliu užeiga	2
Blue Orange	11
Crazy House	7
Dviesė	6
Exit	3
Medžiotoju užeiga	10
Senamiesčio vyninė	4
Senieji rūsiai	8
Skliautas	5
Yakata	1

0   200 m

N E R I S

Santakos parkas

St George's Church

Kaunas Castle

Holy Trinity Church

Maironis Museum

Sport Museum

PAPILIO GATVĖ

PILIES

A. JAKŠTO GATVĖ

PILIES

M. VALANČIAUS

KUMELIŲ GATVĖ

JONAVOS GATVĖ

SV. GERTRUDOS

M. DAUKŠOS

M. DAUKYOS

ŠAUKLIŲ

BENEDIKTINIŲ GATVĖ

Little Theatre

Cathedral

Pharmacy Museum

Meno Parkas Gallery

Town Hall & Ceramics Museum

ROTUŠĖS AIKŠTĖ

Perkūnas House

Vytautas Church

Folk Instruments Museum

SENAMIESTIS

V. KUZMOS

MUITINĖS GATVĖ

ALEKSOTO

I. DAUGĖRDO

J. NAUGARDO

MUZIEJAUS GATVĖ

SANTAKOS GATVĖ

VILNIAUS GATVĖ

L. ZAMENHOFO

A. MAPU

KĘPULŲ GATVĖ

MINDAUGO PROSPEKTAS

PALANGOS

Nemunas

MARVELĖS GATVĖ

N

S

361

charmingly olde-worlde establishment, some of whose rooms still come with 1950s wallpaper, brown furnishings and proper bathtubs in the bathrooms. Ongoing renovation means that prices may well go up. ❸

Perkūno Namai Perkūno 61 ☎8-37/320230, Ⓦwww.perkuno-namai.lt. One of the better business-class options if you don't mind being 2km east of the Old Town. Located in a quiet residential neighbourhood, it features roomy en suites with Scandinavian-style furnishings, and friendly, attention-to-detail management. ❼

Sfinksas Aukštaičių 55 ☎8-37/301982, Ⓦwww.sfinksas.lt. A twelve-room hotel in a residential street fifteen minutes' walk northeast of the centre, but very handy for leafy strolls in Ąžuolynas park. The en suites are a bit chintzy, but supremely comfortable. ❻

Takioji Neris Donelaičio 27 ☎8-37/306100, Ⓦwww.takiojineris.com. Centrally located multi-storey business hotel undergoing extensive renovation at the time of writing. Check the website for room types and prices.

Žaliakalnio Savanorių 66 ☎8-37/321412, Ⓦwww.takiojineris.com. A tower-block hotel uphill from the centre, offering snazzy, modern doubles, many of which have sweeping views of the city centre. ❻

The City

Kaunas's medieval **Old Town** (Senamiestis) sits near the confluence of the rivers Nemunas and Neris; at its centre is the main square, **Rotušės aikštė**, graced by a splendid Town Hall. Within easy reach lie a handful of impressive medieval churches and some quirky museums. East of the Old Town extends the nineteenth-century **New Town** (Naujamiestis), cut by pedestrianized **Laisvės alėja**. Off here lie a number of rewarding museums, including the **M.K. Čiurlionis Museum** and the eccentric **Devil Museum**. On the outskirts, leafy **Ąžuolynas park** and the tranquil **Botanical Gardens** provide pleasant retreats from the bustle of the city, while just to the west of the centre, the suburb of **Vilijampolė** still preserves a few traces of the city's once-thriving Jewish community.

Rotušės aikštė and around

At the centre of the Old Town is the broad expanse of **Rotušės aikštė** (Town Hall Square), lined with fifteenth- and sixteenth-century merchants' houses in pastel shades. The dominant feature is the magnificent **Town Hall**, its tiered Baroque facade rising to a graceful 53-metre-tall tower. Known as the "White Swan" for its elegance, this

△ Rotušės aikštė, Kaunas

building dates back to the sixteenth century and during its history has been used as an Orthodox church, a theatre and a university department, though these days it houses a "Palace of Weddings" – the city's most popular registry office where nuptials are celebrated on Saturdays throughout the year. The Town Hall's vaulted cellar provides an atmospheric home for a **Ceramics Museum** (Tues–Sun 11am–5pm; 3Lt), displaying work by some of the best of contemporary Lithuania's applied artists.

Over on the northern side of the square, the **Lithuanian Pharmacy Museum** (Tues–Sat 10am–6pm; 3Lt) begins with a boring history of medicine but picks up with a reconstructed nineteenth-century pharmacy, full of decorative storage cabinets and exotically shaped glass vials. A few doors along at no. 26, the **Meno parkas** art gallery (Mon–Fri 10am–6pm, Sat 10am–4pm; free) is one of Kaunas's best venues for high-profile contemporary art exhibitions.

Looming towards you at the western end of the square is the Baroque **Holy Trinity Church**, its towers topped with cast-iron crosses adorned with sun motifs. Behind it lies a dignified group of creamy-coloured buildings belonging to Kaunas seminary, traditionally the most important seat of Catholic learning in the country, and a key centre of intellectual resistance to Tsarism in the years before World War I. A smooth, granite statue at the southwestern corner of the square honours one of the seminary's most famous rectors, **Jonas Mačiulis-Maironis** (1862–1932), an enthusiastic patron of Lithuanian culture who also wrote lyric poetry suffused with love for the motherland – his *Voices of Spring* (1895) is the most widely read volume of verse in Lithuania. Behind the statue, the eighteenth-century town house where Maironis lived during his rectorship is now the **Maironis Museum of Lithuanian Literature** (Maironio lietuvių literatūros muziejus; Tues–Sat 9am–5pm; closed on last Friday of each month; 3Lt). The ground-floor display of materials chronicling the development of Lithuanian literature is frustratingly labelled in the local language only – and the sight of exhibits like Šatrijos Ragana's cello is unlikely to mean much to people who have never read her novellas. Upstairs, however, Maironis's perfectly preserved living quarters boast some of the most eye-catching interiors in the whole of the country, with a fabulous display of Art Deco and folk-inspired wall coverings.

A few steps south, at Muziejaus 7, the **Lithuanian Sport Museum** (Lietuvos sporto muziejus; Wed–Sun: summer 10am–6pm; winter 9am–5pm; 2Lt) presents a very different perspective on the nation's cultural history, with photographs of champion basketball teams and gold-medal Olympians – with discus throwers Romas Ubartas (Barcelona 1992) and Virgilius Alekna (Sydney 2000 and Athens 2004) – occupying centre stage. Padding out the collection are all kinds of souvenirs picked up by Lithuanian sporting teams at various international competitions: a hideous doll in the form of a marmot turns out to have been the official mascot of the 1992 Winter Student Games in Poland.

Hogging the northeastern corner of the square, Kaunas's austere, red-brick **Cathedral** (Katedra Basilika) dates back to the reign of Vytautas the Great, although it has been much rebuilt since. After the plain exterior, the vivacious interior, full of brightly coloured frescoes and plaster cherubs looking down from pillars, comes as something of a surprise. There are nine altars in total, with the large, statue-adorned, Baroque high altar (1775) by Tomasz Podhayski stealing the limelight.

Pre-dating the cathedral by several centuries is **Kaunas Castle** (Kauno pilis), the scant remains of which lie just northwest of the square. Little more than a restored tower and a couple of sections of wall are left, the rest having been washed away by the Neris, but in its day the fortification was a major obstacle to the Teutonic Knights. The fifteenth-century **St George's Church** (Šv Jurgio bažnyčia), next door, is an impressive Gothic pile in crumbling red brick, where restoration has so far done little to arrest fifty years of decay. West of here, foot- and cycle-paths converge on the spit of land where the river Neris flows into the Nemunas.

There's better-preserved Gothic finery south of the main square. The **Perkūnas House** (Perkūno namas) at Aleksoto 6 is an elaborately gabled, red-brick structure, thought to have been built as a merchants' meeting hall or possibly a Jesuit chapel, standing on the reputed site of a temple to Perkūnas, the pagan god of thunder (a statue of the god was found on the site in the nineteenth century). From here Aleksoto descends to the banks of the Nemunas and the glowering **Vytautas Church** (Vytauto bažnyčia), built by Vytautas the Great in around 1399 to give thanks for his deliverance from the armies of the Tatars. During its long existence it has suffered various indignities, including use as a munitions magazine and potato store, and, like many other Lithuanian churches, it also had a stint as an Orthodox place of worship.

Three blocks east of the church at Zamenhofo 12B, the **Lithuanian Folk Instruments Museum** (Wed–Sun 10am–5pm; 4Lt) contains a fascinating array of archaic-looking instruments, including *kanklės* (traditional Baltic zithers) of all sizes, and sonorous wooden horns wrapped in birch bark.

Laisvės alėja and around

Running east from the Old Town through Kaunas's **Naujamiestis** (New Town) is **Laisvės alėja** (Freedom Avenue), a broad, pedestrianized shopping street. The whole street was, bizarrely, a no-smoking zone from 1990 until 2000, when the city council finally gave up trying to enforce it. At the western end of Laisvės, near the junction with Vilniaus, an elegant, ochre mansion in a well-tended park served as the **Presidential Palace** (Prezidentūra; Tues–Sun 11am–5pm; ⊛ www.istorineprezidentura.lt; free) during Kaunas's period as the provisional capital, and now houses a history museum honouring its four inter-war occupants – Antanas Smetona, Jonas Stamgaitis, Aleksandras Stulginskis and Antanas Merkys. It was Smetona who enjoyed the longest stint in the presidential hot seat, and Smetona-related memorabilia unsurprisingly take up most space in the elegant sequence of staterooms. However, the most revered relic in the collection – unsurprisingly for this basketball-mad country – is the ceremonial casket awarded to European champions Lithuania when they won the trophy for the second time in 1939.

Opposite the palace, a passageway leads off Laisvės into a yard containing **St Gertrude's Church** (Šv Gertrudos bažnyčia; Mon–Sat 10am–7pm, Sun 7.30am–noon), a fourteenth-century, red-brick structure so dwarfed by the surrounding apartment blocks that it looks more like a clay-house lantern souvenir than a church. Inside there's an especially ornate Baroque pulpit topped by a gesticulating statue of St John Nepomuk, and a much-venerated crucifix on the high altar – you'll see the devout crawling round it on their knees.

Back on Laisvės, the **Tadas Ivanauskas Zoology Museum** (Kauno Tado Ivanausko zoologijos muziejus; 5Lt) at no. 106 is a three-floor, something-for-everybody collection of stuffed and pickled creatures. It's all great fun and pretty self-explanatory, although the armadillo-to-zebra display of mammals on the ground floor is probably worth saving until last.

Moving east, the junction with L. Sapiegos is enlivened by a bronze **statue of Vytautas the Great**, the fifteenth-century Grand Duke who extended Lithuania's borders as far as the Black Sea. Immediately opposite is the **City Garden** (Miesto sodas), where, on May 14, 1972, the 19-year-old art student Romas Kalanta immolated himself in protest against Soviet rule. The act sparked several days of anti-Soviet rioting, and an estimated five hundred people were arrested. Kalanta's act is commemorated by local sculptor Robertas Antinis's memorial sculpture *Field of Sacrifice*, a rust-coloured assemblage of horizontal shards. The southern end of the park is marked by the **Musical Theatre**, the country's prime venue for operetta and the site – in May 1929 – of an attempt on the life of Prime Minister Augustinas Voldemaras. The assassin missed, killing the PM's grand-nephew instead.

Making a brief detour north from the City Garden up Sapiegos brings you to the **Kaunas Philharmonic Hall** at no. 9, where the Lithuanian Seima (Parliament) held its deliberations from 1919 until 1926, when President Smetona's imposition of authoritarian rule rendered it surplus to requirements. Just round the corner at Ožeškienės 17, the nineteenth-century **Choral Synagogue** (Choralinė sinagoga; Sat 10am–noon & 6–6.30pm, Sun–Fri 6–6.30pm) is the sole Jewish place of worship left in a city that used to boast them by the handful. The sky-blue, balustraded interior contains an intricately carved Aron ha Kodesh, or high altar, which somehow survived the Nazi occupation. In the yard behind the synagogue is another striking monument by Robertas Antinis, this time honouring the child victims of the Holocaust with a slab of metal studded with tiny stars.

Vienybės aikštė and the Military Museum

Kaunas celebrates its role in sustaining Lithuanian national identity on **Unity Square** (Vienybės aikštė), at the junction of S. Daukanto and K. Donelaičio, a block north of Laisvės. Here a **monument** depicting Liberty as a female figure faces an eternal flame flanked by traditional wooden crosses, with busts of prominent Lithuanians from the nineteenth century between the two. Overlooking all this is the **Military Museum of Vytautas the Great** (Vytauto Didžiojo karo muziejus; summer Wed–Sun 10am–6pm; winter Wed–Sun 9am–5pm; closed last Thurs of every month; 4Lt), a grey, angular symbol of inter-war modernity which was intended to put Kaunas on the architectural map when it was completed in 1937. Swords, pikes and scale models of stockade forts conjure up the martial vigour of the medieval Lithuanian state, while the independence struggles of 1918–20 are remembered in an impressive display of uniforms and weaponry. The museum also functions as a shrine to the Lithuanian pilots Darius and Girėnas (see box below), whose death in a plane crash during a transatlantic flight provided the inter-war Lithuanian state with its defining moment of heroism and sacrifice. One room displays poignant pictures of the pair being feted at farewell dinners before their departure from New York, while the ripped and blood-spattered shirts they were

---

Darius and Girėnas

Most European nations had aviator heroes in the inter-war years, and in Darius and Girėnas, Lithuania was not to be left out. Born in western Lithuania and taken to live in the US at an early age, Steponas "Stephen" Darius (1896–1933) and Stasys "Stanley" Girėnas (1893–1933) both fought with US forces in World War I, learning to fly towards the war's end. Darius was the more flamboyant of the two, winning a Purple Heart for bravery in 1918, and turning up in Lithuania to take part in the seizure of Klaipėda in 1923 (see p.442). A sports nut who excelled at just about every activity that involved kicking, throwing or hitting a ball, Darius was also influential in turning basketball into inter-war Lithuania's most popular team game.

Darius had long dreamed of flying non-stop from New York to Kaunas and enlisted Girėnas as his co-pilot. Money raised by the Lithuanian community in North America helped fund the purchase of a secondhand plane, which they named the *Lituanica*. They took off on July 15, 1933, only to crash two days later in an East Prussian forest, tantalizingly short of their target. The cause of the accident remains unknown. The vast crowds who had assembled at Kaunas airport to greet their arrival were shattered by the news, and a deep sense of national loss spread across the country. As the first famous dead Lithuanians of the modern media age, Darius and Girėnas were quickly enshrined as national martyrs. Their embalmed bodies were on permanent display until 1944, when they were banished to a storeroom by a Soviet regime that disapproved of patriotic cults. In 1964 they were finally laid to rest at Aukštieji Šančiai cemetery in the southeast of the city, but public remembrance of their exploits was broadly discouraged.

Post-independence, Lithuania has been quick to restore Darius and Girėnas to the national pantheon: the pair feature prominently on the 10Lt banknote, and have been honoured with a monument next to the Kaunas sports stadium that bears their name. A scale model of the *Lituanica* hangs from the ceiling of the departure lounge of Vilnius airport, although it's not clear whether this is intended to inspire travellers or scare them witless.

wearing when they crashed are kept in a case nearby. Preserved in an enormous glass box upstairs, the wreckage of their bright-orange plane, the *Lituanica*, looks more like a contemporary art installation than a tragic relic.

The M.K. Čiurlionis Art Museum

Part of the same building as the Military Museum, the **M.K. Čiurlionis Art Museum** (M.K. Čiurlionio dailės muziejus; summer Tues–Sun noon–6pm; winter Tues–Sun 11am–5pm; closed last Tues of every month; 4Lt), houses an exhaustive collection of

Mikalojus Konstantinis Čiurlionis (1875–1911)

Born in the southeastern town of Varėna and raised in the nearby spa resort of Druskininkai from the age of 3, Lithuania's most famous painter and composer was introduced to music by his father, who was the organist at Liškiava church (see p.390). The talented youth soon caught the attention of Count Michał Ogiński, who installed Čiurlionis in his private music school in Plungė, and went on to finance further study abroad. Čiurlionis graduated from the Warsaw Conservatoire in 1899, and was set to continue his studies in Leipzig when Ogiński died and the money dried up. Equipped with a sound grasp of musical theory however, Čiurlionis set about composing lengthy symphonic pieces, the best known of which are the tone poems *In the Forest* (*Miške*; 1900) and *The Sea* (*Jūra*; 1907). At the same time Čiurlionis was pursuing his career as an artist, enrolling in the newly opened Warsaw School of Fine Arts in 1904.

Čiurlionis believed that both music and art could be used to tap the raw emotive power of the human spirit. This dovetailed rather nicely with his belief in the Lithuanians themselves as a uniquely spiritual nation, who were closer to their Indo-European origins than many of their neighbours and therefore represented a bridge between European religions and Eastern mysticism. He believed that Lithuanian spirituality was expressed in its folk art, and – even though he didn't always use folk imagery in his own paintings – he strongly advocated a return to folk traditions in order to develop a true Lithuanian culture.

Like many urbanized Lithuanians of his generation however, Čiurlionis grew up speaking Polish, and only mastered Lithuanian after 1907 on the promptings of his fiancée, the essayist and critic Sofia Kymantaitė. In 1907 the couple helped to organize the first Lithuanian Art Exhibition in Vilnius, hoping to raise public perception of the arts in general and Čiurlionis's own paintings in particular. The response was disappointingly lukewarm. Unable to make a living from painting or composing in Vilnius, Čiurlionis headed for St Petersburg in 1909 in the hope of breaking into the flourishing art scene there. His work made a big impression on critics and fellow painters, but none of the local dealers offered him an exhibition. Back in Vilnius, lack of both money and an appreciative audience drove Čiurlionis into apathy, depression and, ultimately, serious mental illness. Thus weakened, he was unable to withstand the onslaught of pneumonia, and died at a sanatorium outside Warsaw on April 10, 1911.

Čiurlionis died in obscurity because he was a Lithuanian artist working at a time when there was no Lithuanian art establishment capable of promoting his works. Within a decade of his demise, however, Lithuania was an independent state desperately in need of cultural icons, and Čiurlionis fitted the bill perfectly. An art museum bearing his name was established in 1925, and proceeded to buy all Čiurlionis's paintings from his widow. The symphonic poems, hardly ever peformed during their composer's lifetime, became regular fixtures in the repertoire of the Lithuanian Philharmonic.

In the early years of the Soviet occupation, Čiurlionis's taste for mysticism was considered decadent and reactionary, and it wasn't until the late 1960s that the local communist party began to curry intellectual favour by readmitting Čiurlionis to the national pantheon. Nowadays, Čiurlionis's soulful, contemplative art is considered to be one of the most eloquent expressions of the Lithuanian national character.

pictures by Lithuania's greatest artist. During his short career (he died of pneumonia at the age of 36 in 1911), Čiurlionis created a unique body of work, producing enigmatic paintings influenced by the French Symbolists, many of them suffused with religious imagery. A composer as well as a painter, Čiurlionis believed that the feelings aroused by symphonic music could also be expressed in two-dimensional art – the dreamy, pulsating and often hypnotic results of his labours are on show by the cartload here. He produced small-format watercolours and pastels for the most part, rendering them in hazy greens, yellows and blues, and giving them contemplative titles like *Sorrow*, *Truth* or *Thought*. Castles, mountains and rivers feature prominently in his works, but they're often lost in wavy washes of colour – leading some to claim him as a precursor of abstract art.

If you've had enough Čiurlionis, there's a solid collection of Lithuanian art from the inter-war years, when Kaunas was the site of the country's only art school. Particularly striking are the Expressionist landscapes of bendy trees and collapsing skies produced by Antanas Samuolis (1899–1942), and the Gauguin-esque portraits of Viktoras Vizgirda (1904–93). There's also a good deal of Lithuanian folk art, notably the wooden statuettes of saints that traditionally decorate wayside shrines.

The Devil Museum

Kaunas has a second unique art collection nearby in the shape of the **A. Žmuidzinavičius Art Museum**, at Putvinskio 64 (A. Žmuidzinavičiaus kūrinių ir rinkinių muziejus; June–Sept Tues–Sun noon–6pm; winter Tues–Sun 11am–5pm; closed last Tues of every month; 4Lt). Better known as the **Devil Museum** (Velnių muziejus), this houses a vast collection of figures put together by the artist Antanas Žmuidzinavičius (1876–1966), who devoted his life to the collection of all kinds of folk art, specializing in the demonic masks worn by Lithuanian revellers at Shrovetide – when the spirit of winter is driven away by donning Hallowe'en-like disguises. There's an extensive display of the masks here, sporting fearsome horns, yellow teeth and lolling red tongues. Ranged elsewhere are all manner of devil-related objects donated to the museum by artists both domestic and foreign, including some rather desirable Latvian crockery decorated with cavorting, impish forms. Although there's a lot of disappointing junk, too (think pitch-fork-wielding garden gnomes), some exhibits will stick in the memory – look out for Kazys Derškevičius's sinister representation of Hitler and Stalin as devils dancing on a Lithuania composed of skulls. The museum also has an impressive collection of more mainstream wooden folk sculpture, with several representations of the Rupintojėlis, or Sorrowful Christ, a popular subject in Lithuanian folk art, in which Christ is traditionally depicted seated with his head in his hands. Other sculptures include a squadron of dragon-spearing St Georges, and numerous depictions of St Isidore – shown scattering seed from a flaxen bag, the sower-saint is a typical example of Lithuanian religious syncretism, mixing Catholic iconography with pagan fertility symbols of the pre-Christian era.

Church of St Michael the Archangel

Marking the eastern end of Laisvės alėja, the silver-domed **Church of St Michael the Archangel** (Igulos bažnyčia) stands imperiously over Nepriklausomybes aikštė ("Independence Square"). Originally an Orthodox church built for the Tsarist garrison in the 1890s, this neo-Byzantine structure has preserved its military associations despite several changes of regime and denomination, serving as the (Protestant) German army church in World War I, and becoming the (Catholic) Lithuanian army church immediately afterwards. Its bare interior is a reflection of the fact that it was an art gallery for most of the Soviet period. A rather garish modern altar painting of the Archangel adds a dash of colour to the place, and a side altar to the right harbours a superb example of a Rupintojėlis, or "Sorrowful Christ", sculpture. A curtained doorway in the church lobby leads down to the so-called **Museum for the Blind**: initiated by Kaunas University students in 2005, the museum aims to raise awareness about the problems of the unsighted by encouraging sighted people to spend time in a light-free environment in which they must survive by using touch alone. The museum doesn't keep regular opening hours: the nearby Kaunas tourist office (see p.357) will check the situation on your behalf.

The Mykolas Žilinskas Art Gallery

Occupying a contemporary building in the northeast corner of Nepryklausomybės aikštė, the **Mykolas Žilinskas Art Gallery** (Mykolo Žilinsko dailės galerija; June–Sept Tues–Sun noon–6pm; Oct–May 11am–5pm; closed last Tues of every month; 6Lt) showcases the globe-spanning collection of fine and applied art amassed by the Kaunas-born Žilinskas, who prospered in German business circles after 1945, and gifted his treasures to his home city in order to form this museum. Dominating a room of Egyptian amulets, Roman glassware and Ming vases is a show-stopping eighteenth-century set of over fifty ceramic figures representing the apotheosis of Catherine the Great – as well as the Empress herself, there are Greek gods, and figures in Turkish and Tatar garb representing the grateful subject nations of the Russian Empire. Less ostentatious, but still too good to eat your dinner off, are Art Deco plates from the 1920s and propagandist porcelain from Soviet Russia decorated with Cubist workers waving hammers and sickles. Among the paintings are several roomfuls of Flemish and Italian masters: Žilinskas's favourite painting was the turbulent maritime scene of *On the Coast of the Strong Sea* by Leonardo Coccarante (1680–1750), although visitors will also be drawn by Lithuania's only Rubens, a sombrely effective *Crucifixion*. Right outside the gallery, Petras Mozūras's towering statue of an unabashedly naked man is something of a local talking point.

The Kaunas City Gallery

A short distance northeast of Nepriklausomybės aikštė, the **Kaunas City Gallery** (Kaono paveikslų galerja; Tues–Sun 11am–5pm; 4Lt) houses another artistic donation by a rich local-born Lithuanian, Algimantas Miškinas – his collection takes in minor works by most twentieth-century Lithuanian artists, but lacks any real highlights. The gallery possesses a number of rather more interesting pieces relating to the Fluxus movement of the 1960s, a loose grouping of avant-garde artists inspired by Lithuanian-born New Yorker George Maciunas. Situated in the entrance hall, Ay-O's *Black Hole dedicated to George Maciunas* is an interactive piece you really need to experience for yourself; the Fluxus Room upstairs contains more graphics by the same artist, plus plenty of other materials relating to the movement.

Žaliakalnis

Ten minutes' walk northeast of Nepriklausomybės, on the northern side of Putvinskio, lies the lower station of a 1930s **funicular railway** (funikulierius; daily 7am–7pm; 0.50Lt), which is operated by a pair of beautifully maintained, almost museum-piece vehicles, each presided over by a red-uniformed conductor. The funicular climbs up to **Žaliakalnis** (Green Hill), a leafy residential area favoured by the Kaunas middle classes during the inter-war years. Near the upper terminal is the **Church of the Resurrection** (Prisikėlimo bažnyčia), a masterpiece of 1930s architecture whose soaring tower is topped by a slender cross. Having served as a radio factory during the communist period, the church has undergone thorough restoration in the years since Soviet occupation, its bright-white paint job adding a touch of futuristic glamour to the Kaunas skyline. A lift (Mon–Fri noon–6pm, Sat & Sun 11am–6pm; 5Lt) ascends the first thirty metres of the seventy-metre-high belfry to an expansive **viewing terrace** on the church's roof, affording panoramic views in every direction.

East of the centre: the Sugihara House and Ąžuolynas

Just east of the bus and train stations paths lead up to another prosperous area of quiet, residential streets – the kind of place where foreign diplomats set up home during the period when Kaunas was the provisional capital. One of these was Chiune Sugihara (see box opposite), the unassuming consul who has been dubbed "Japan's Schindler" for his action in supplying thousands of Jewish refugees with Japanese visas – allowing them to escape a city threatened by Nazi invasion. The **Sugihara House** (May–Sept Mon–Fri 10am–5pm, Sat & Sun 11am–4pm; Oct–April Mon–Fri noon–4pm; donation requested), occupying the consul's former home at Vaizganto 30, displays fascinating photographic evidence of Sugihara's activities – one picture shows him still issuing visas from the window of a train compartment moments before his final departure from the city.

From the Sugihara House it's a short walk northeast to the **Darius and Girėnas Sports Stadium**, which, as the best equipped in the country, is where the Lithuanian football team play most of their matches. Immediately behind it lies **Ąžuolynas** ("oakwood"), a wonderfully leafy square-kilometre of park filled with ash, elm, lime and oak.

South of the centre: the Botanical Gardens

A further swathe of residential suburbs runs along the hillside on the south bank of the River Nemunas. The one destination of real interest here is the **Botanical Gardens** (Botanikos sodas; daily: June–Aug 9am–6.30pm; Sept–May 8.30am–5.30pm; 4Lt), a relaxing stretch of rose gardens, flowerbeds and shrubberies that lies at the end of minibus route #49 (from Birštono in the Old Town). Highlights include a lily-choked serpentine and a central Orangery (Oranžerija; daily June–Aug 11am–6.30pm, Sept–May 10am–5pm) containing banana palms, Bengal fig trees and a goldfish-stocked pond.

Chiune Sugihara (1900–86)

A career diplomat and Russian specialist in the Japanese foreign ministry, Chiune Sugihara was posted to Kaunas as Japanese consul in March 1939 in order to report on Soviet intentions in the region. When Soviet forces occupied Lithuania in July 1940, most foreign diplomats were ordered to leave without delay, but Sugihara and the Dutch consul, Jan Zwartendijk, where allowed to stay for one more month.

At the time, thousands of Jewish refugees from Nazi-occupied western Poland were arriving in Kaunas, only to discover that the Soviet authorities refused to give them transit visas unless they first obtained valid visas for their next destination. As the only representative of a country bordering the Soviet Union left in the city, Sugihara was besieged with requests for help. However, he couldn't give the refugees normal Japanese entry visas because of objections from his ministry in Tokyo, so he opted instead to hand out Japanese transit visas – under the pretence that the refugees were ultimately bound for Dutch colonies in the east. Local Soviet officials turned a blind eye to Sugihara's scheme, but approval from Tokyo was slow in coming – so Sugihara simply went ahead on his own initiative, writing out the relevant documents by hand, thereby providing an estimated 6000 people with passage out of the country. When he finally left Kaunas on September 1, he presented his consular stamp to a refugee so that more visas could be issued on his behalf. Sugihara went on to serve in the Japanese embassy in Prague, but was sacked by the foreign ministry in 1945 – a belated punishment for his refusal to do things by the book in Kaunas.

Sugihara built a career as a businessman after the war and remained ignorant of the fate of those he had helped escape, until a survivor sought him out in 1969. Enthused by the renewal of old contacts, Sugihara visited Israel the same year. However, he remained largely unrecognized until 1984, when the Yad Vashem Institute declared him one of the "Righteous Among the Nations" – the title given to gentiles who took personal risks to save Jewish lives. Hillel Levine's biography of Sugihara, published in 1996 (see "Books", p.461), was the first attempt to tell the whole story – although it outraged Sugihara's family with its warts-and-all treatment of a subject who had visited brothels as a young diplomat and been married to a White Russian emigré before settling down with his second (still living) spouse.

Before World War II, Kaunas, like Vilnius, had a large **Jewish population**. Nearly all were killed during the war and little remains of their presence. The main area of Jewish settlement was **Vilijampolė** (known for much of its history by the Russian name of Slobodka), a suburb just across the Neris from the Old Town, and it was here that the Nazis created a closed ghetto in July 1941. An attractive grid of timber houses, today's Vilijampolė contains little in the way of memorials to the people who once lived and died here. A granite obelisk at the junction of Linkuvos and Kriščiukaičio bears an inscription in Lithuanian and Hebrew stating simply that "on this spot stood the gates of the Kaunas ghetto 1941–44". From here you'll have to zigzag your way north through residential streets to find a small (and easily missed) plaque at Goštautų 4 that marks the former location of the ghetto hospital, burned down by the Nazis on October 4, 1941, with staff and patients still inside. Finally, there's an overgrown, barely accessible **Jewish cemetery** (Senosios žydų kapinės) clinging to a hillside in the northwest of the suburb, just off Kalnų.

The Ninth Fort

Many of Kaunas's Jews ended their lives at the **Ninth Fort** (Devintasis fortas) on the northwestern fringes of the city, one of several forts built around Kaunas by the Russians in the lead-up to World War II, and known by their numbers ever since. The Ninth Fort was used by the Lithuanians as a camp for political prisoners during the inter-war years, was subsequently used by the Soviet NKVD in 1940, and then transformed into a holding prison and killing ground by the Nazis from June 1941 onwards. It's thought that as many as 50,000 people lost their lives here over the next four years

Jewish Kaunas

Jews first came to Kaunas in the early fifteenth century at the invitation of Grand Duke Vytautas the Great, and were settled in Vilijampolė in order to keep them separate from the Lithuanian population of the city centre. The Jews soon established a trading settlement in the centre, although outbreaks of anti-Semitism resulted in their periodic expulsion (notably in 1495, 1753 and 1761), adding to the importance of Vilijampolė as their natural refuge. The Jews had re-established themselves in the centre of Kaunas by the late nineteenth century, and by the time of World War I they made up the majority of the population in the Old Town. On the eve of World War II, there were approximately 35,000 Jews in Kaunas (of which 6000 lived in Vilijampolė), about forty percent of the city's total.

Although there was little social integration betwen the Jewish and Lithuanian populations of pre-war Kaunas, outbreaks of explicit anti-Semitism were rare. However, the arrival of the German troops on June 23, 1941 unleashed an unexpectedly ferocious wave of popular violence. On June 25, Lithuanian gangs ran riot in Vilijampolė, killing an estimated 1000 civilians and decapitating chief rabbi Zalman Ossovsky. Two days later in central Kaunas, a group of over fifty Jews was driven onto the forecourt of the Lietūkis garage and clubbed to death by the locals, with German soldiers looking on. Gruesome footage of the incident has subsequently been used in several Holocaust-related documentaries.

On July 10, all the city's Jews were herded into the newly established ghetto in Vilijampolė. Many were relieved by the move, thinking that this would protect them from the violence of Lithuanian hooligans. However, regular "actions", in which arbitrarily chosen groups of Jews were rounded up and shot by the Germans, became commonplace as the autumn of 1941 wore on. The enthusiasm of the local Lithuanian population for anti-Semitic excesses continued to astound even the Germans. Colonel Jäger of Einsatzgruppe A, the organization charged with organizing mass killings throughout northeastern Europe, notoriously reported that Kaunas, "where

– at least 30,000 of them were Jews from Kaunas or the surrounding region: the others came from locations as diverse as Munich and Marseilles.

Surrounded by banked-up earthworks, the fort forms the centrepiece of an extensive park criss-crossed by paths and planted with trees. A flagstoned avenue leads to a huge Soviet-era memorial, a jagged concrete outcrop pitted with the shapes of human faces and fists. Like all such monuments of the period, it's dedicated to the "victims of Fascism" and fails to mention the Jews by name – Soviet ideology always denied the true nature of the Holocaust in an attempt to portray Marxism-Leninism as the sole target of Nazi hatred. Nearby are smaller, post-1991 memorials, honouring particular communities of Jews who ended up here, and a sign indicating one of the trenches where many of them were shot.

An innocuous-looking doorway in a red-brick wall leads through to the **Ninth Fort Museum** (Wed–Sun 10am–4pm; 6Lt), which occupies a series of dark grey chambers that served as soldiers' dormitories during the tsarist period, and prisoners' cells after that. Wide-ranging displays cover the fort's role as a tsarist Russian garrison and its subsequent use as a Lithuanian political prison, before moving on to cover the Jewish experience in World War II. Among the poignant reminders of those incarcerated here is a section of glass-covered wall covered in graffiti by those about to be murdered – "we are 500 Frenchmen," wrote Abraham Wechsler of Limoges.

An additional department of the museum, the so-called **"New Museum"** (same times, same ticket) occupies the concrete wedge-shaped building on the northeastern side of the Ninth Fort complex, and covers the Soviet occupation, deportations of 1941 and 1949, and the survival struggles of Lithuanian exiles in Siberia.

trained Lithuanian volunteers are available in sufficient numbers, is comparatively speaking a shooting paradise."

Right from the start it was clear that those members of the community required by the Germans for work duty stood a good chance of surviving (for the time being), while the others were likely to be murdered. This placed Jewish leaders – who controlled the distribution of work permits – in the unenviable position of deciding who lived and who died. Some argued that a refusal to issue any work permits at all would be the only morally correct action to take, until the new chief rabbi Abraham Dov Shapiro decreed that an attempt to save some Jewish lives was better than no attempt at all. On October 28, the Jews of Vilijampolė were assembled by their community leaders so that several thousand of them could be selected for work duties by the SS. Of the 20,000-plus that were surplus to requirements, approximately 10,000 of them were taken away and shot within weeks – most were murdered in the notorious Ninth Fort (see above) just outside the city.

Despite frequent actions and arbitrary shootings, Vilijampolė's surviving Jews attempted to preserve a semblance of normal life in the years that followed. The able-bodied continued to work in factories inside and outside the ghetto, squares were ploughed up and used to grow vegetables, and a 35-piece ghetto orchestra gave regular concerts. In April 1944, the Germans decided to clear the ghetto of its remaining 8000 inhabitants. The women were sent to Stutthof, the men to Dachau, where 75 percent of them perished. By the time the Red Army arrived in August there were no Jews left in Kaunas – save for the fortunate handful who had found hiding places in the city or had escaped to join partisans in the surrounding forests.

After the war, most survivors moved to Vilnius or emigrated entirely, and the local Jewish population currently stands at just over 1000. The wonderfully restored synagogue on Ožeškienės gatvė (see p.364) functions as their social and spiritual centre.

The Ninth Fort is 4km out of central Kaunas, right beside the main highway to Klaipėda. **To get there**, catch any westbound inter-city service from the main bus station and get off when you see the memorial looming up on your left.

Pažaislis monastery

Some 7km east of the city centre, the Baroque **Pažaislis monastery** (Pažaislio vienuolynas) is worth visiting for its location as much as its fine architecture, situated as it is in a belt of forest beside the shores of the so-called Kaunas Sea, or Kauno marios, an artificial lake created to feed a hydroelectric power station in the late 1950s. Surrounded by sandy shores shaded by pines, it's a popular recreation spot in summer and an invigorating place for a stroll whatever the season. **Getting there** is easy – take trolleybus #5 from opposite the bus station to the end of the line and carry on walking in the same direction, bearing left and under the railway tracks after about five minutes.

The monastery was built for the Camaldolese Order in 1667 by one of the Grand Duchy of Lithuania's leading aristocrats, Krzysztof Zygmunt Pac. Looted by Napoleon's troops in 1812 and closed down by the Tsarist authorities in 1832, it was subsequently used as an Orthodox church until its resettlement by Lithuanian-American nuns in the 1920s. The Soviets used it as a psychiatric hospital, and it wasn't until 1992 that the nuns returned. Presiding magisterially over a grassy courtyard, the monastery church is one of the most striking examples of the Baroque style in the country, with a twin-towered facade thrusting forward from a huge octagonal drum topped by a bulbous cupola. The interior (officially open Tues–Sun 11am–5pm, but often closed without explanation) is vibrantly decorated with frescoes, with Giuseppe Rossi's *Coronation of the Virgin* filling the central dome, and Michelangelo Palloni's scenes from the lives of Christ and St Benedict covering the walls. The church's period as an Orthodox foundation is recalled by the tombstone of Aleksii Fedorovich Lvov (1798–1870), outside the main door and to the right – he penned the music to the Tsarist Empire's national anthem, *God Save the Tsar*. The monastery grounds are used for **concerts** in summer, when the Lithuanian Philharmonic Orchestra frequently plays here.

Eating and drinking

You can eat and imbibe very well and very reasonably in Kaunas, and you shouldn't have to stray far from the central strip formed by Laisvės alėja, Vilniaus gatvė and Rotušės aikštė in order to find a convivial place to settle. As usual in Lithuania, there's not always a clear boundary separating cafés, restaurants and bars, with establishments often catering for a coffee-swilling crowd during the daytime, serious diners in the evening and even more serious drinkers as the night draws on.

Old Town

Avilys Vilniaus 34. Upmarket pub in a tastefully renovated brick cellar that brews its own beer – including the light, lager-like Avylis, and the stronger, honey-flavoured and strangely addictive Medaus. There's a long list of beer cocktails (beer plus spirit shots in the same glass) for those who favour the fast track to oblivion. The food menu features plenty of hearty meat dishes, augmented by desserts such as handmade chocolate truffles and fresh, locally made ice cream. Sun–Thurs noon–midnight, Fri & Sat noon–2am.

Bernelių Užeiga Valančiaus 9. Lively restaurant in an attractive suite of rustic rooms, including an atmospheric, wood-beamed attic hung with dried herbs. The traditional Lithuanian menu doesn't just restrict itself to the obvious (*cepelinai*, plus anything else made from potatoes), but also extends to deliciously flavoured stews and roasts rarely found outside the older recipe books. The drinks menu lists indigenous knock-you-for-six spirits like *samanė* alongside margaritas, piña coladas and other global concoctions. And very reasonable prices too. Sun–Thurs 11am–midnight, Fri & Sat 11am–1am.

Crazy House Vilniaus 16. Lives up to its name with a barrel-vaulted cellar filled with visual and practical jokes – we'll leave you to decide whether they're funny or not. Straightforward meat-and-potatoes menu, and a full range of spirits and cocktails. Sun–Thurs 11am–midnight, Fri & Sat 11am–2am.

Dviesė Vilniaus 8. Cheap and filling savoury pies and doughnut-like *spurgos*, in a bland, ground-floor café space and a more interesting cellar, with exposed medieval masonry and wrought-iron fish. Daily 10am–11pm.

Medžiotojų užeiga Rotušės aikštė 10. Upscale but not overpriced restaurant with a gamey theme that's reflected in the hunting trophies dotted around the walls. Chose between simple wooden tables in one half, or a more formal dining room in the other. Meat-gluttons will be satisfied with whatever they order here, although venison and wild boar are the specialities. The desserts, too, are deeply satisfying. Daily 11am–midnight.

Senamiesčio vyninė Daukšos 23. Warm colours and the odd bit of exposed brickwork make this a civilized place to feast on mainstream Lithuanian fare, bolstered by a good range of freshwater fish and an above-average choice of wines, with mains around 20–25Lt. There's usually a daily two-course lunch offer chalked up on a board outside. Mon–Fri 10am–11pm, Sat & Sun noon–11pm.

Senieji rusiai Vilniaus 34. Candlelit, red-brick cellar with swords hanging theatrically from the walls. The international menu includes excellent grilled steaks and pan-fried and baked fish. With main courses hovering around the 30Lt mark, prices are very reasonable. Sun–Thurs 11am–midnight, Fri & Sat 11am–2am.

Yakata Valančiaus 14. This small seven-table sushi restaurant is the perfect antidote to the meat-heavy stodge on offer elsewhere. Noodle soups and a serviceable teriyaki chicken help to round out the menu. Daily 11am–midnight.

New Town and beyond

Bella Toscana Daukanto 12. One of the best places for coffee, hot chocolate and cakes in the New Town. Also offers a breakfast menu of scrambled eggs and pancakes. Mon–Fri 7am–10pm, Sat & Sun 10am–10pm.

Blynynė Laisvės 56. An order-at-the-counter café serving all manner of sweet and savoury pancakes, alongside a simple repertoire of potato-based dishes – a good place to tuck into a slice of *bulvių plokštainis*. Daily 9am–7pm.

Miesto Sodas Laisvės alėja. Bright, roomy café-restaurant on the main strip with everything from T-bone steaks to salads. The big, street-side windows make this the perfect place for a people-watching lunch. Cocktails and jazzy piano-tinkling in the evenings. Sun–Wed 11am–11pm, Thurs–Sat 11am–midnight.

Pizza Jazz Laisvės alėja 68. Dependable source of thin-crust pies, as well as lasagne and other pasta dishes, in a bright and breezy atmosphere. Daily 11am–11pm.

Tado Blindos Smuklė Kęstučio 93. Mid-priced Lithuanian-themed place located in a basement with rustic accoutrements adorning the walls. The folk decor isn't convincing, but the cooking more than compensates: *koldūnai*, *cepelinai* and potato pancakes, plus salads and fish if you're after something a little less calorific. Daily 11am–midnight.

Yachtklubas Gimbutienės 35. Roomy restaurant on the shores of the Kaunas reservoir, a short distance beyond Pažaislis monastery. The varied but never-too-pricey menu covers familiar pork and chicken territory, with fish dishes adding a bit of interest. Good views of the yacht moorings and access to lakeside walks make this a mellow lunchtime venue. Sun–Thurs 10am–10pm, Fri & Sat 10am–midnight.

Žalias Ratas Laisvės 36B. A building that looks like a country cottage, tucked incongruously in a yard behind the tourist office. Homely, trad cooking, wooden benches, staff clad in traditional plaid and a big white stove in the middle of the room. A good place to try *cepelinai* (served until 3pm). Moderately priced. Daily 11am–midnight.

Entertainment and festivals

There's a lot of serious culture on offer in Kaunas, although visitors are often caught out by the seriously early performance times – 5 or 6pm being the norm. The city's musical flagship is the **Kaunas Philharmonic** (Kauno Filharmonija), Sapiegos 5 (T8-37/200478; box office daily 2–6pm), site of regular performances by the Kaunas Chamber Orchestra and the Kaunas State Choir (probably the top choral group in the country), as well as Friday-evening visits from the Vilnius-based Lithuanian National-al Symphony Orchestra. The **Musical Theatre** (Muzikinis teatras), Laisvės alėja 91 (T8-37/200933; box office Tues–Sat 10am–1pm & 3–6pm, Sun 10am–3pm) is the venue for light opera and musicals.

Lithuanian-language **drama** – including major touring productions from Vilnius – can be seen at the Drama Theatre (Dramos teatras), Laisvės 71 (T8-37/224064, Wwww.dramosteatras.lt; box office Tues–Sat 11am–2pm & 3–6.30pm, Sun 1hr before performance). Kaunas Little Theatre (Kauno Mažasis teatras), Daukšos 34 (T8-37/206546; box office Wed–Fri 3–7pm, Sat 11am–6pm, Sun 1hr before performance), is the place to see contemporary drama in a smallish, intimate space. The Kaunas State Puppet Theatre (Kauno valstybinis lelių teatras) at Laisvės 87A (T8-37/220061,

(®www.kaunoleles.lt) puts on performances for kiddies, usually starting at noon, although there are occasionally adult-oriented shows in the evening.

Cinemas showing mainstream international films include Planeta, Vytauto 6; Romuva, Laisvės 54; and Senasis Trestas, Mickevičiaus 8A.

Clubs and bars

Many of the hipper establishments along Laisvės feature live music and dancing at weekends – otherwise late drinkers move on to the clubs, for which there's a small entrance charge.

Exit Maironio 19, ®www.exit.lt. Minimally decorated, youth-oriented bastion of dance culture in the Old Town, attracting big-name house and techno DJs from the Baltics and beyond. Fri & Sat only, 10pm–4/5am.

Orange ("B.O." for short) Muitinės 9. Home-from-home drinking den drawing a wide cross-section of arty nonconformists and mainstream boozers eager to enjoy the laid-back vibe and vaguely alternative sounds on the CD player. An upstairs party room hosts DJ nights and gigs at weekends, and cheap pizzas are available too. Mon–Thurs 9.30am–2am, Fri 9.30am–3am, Sat 3pm–3am, Sun 3pm–1am.

Los Patrankos Savanorių 124. Enjoyably cavernous place which has more in the way of lighting effects, dry ice and podium dancers than the other places in town. A long trudge uphill from the centre – taxis might come in useful. Tues–Sat 8pm–4am or later.

Siena Laisvės alėja 93. Basement club beneath the *Miesto Sodas* restaurant, serving up a selection of mainstream sounds to a relaxed, fun-seeking crowd. Thurs–Sat 9pm–4am.

Skliautas Rotušės aikštė 26. A cosy, barrel-vaulted chamber in an alleyway just off the Old Town's main square, decked out in sepia photos of pre-war Kaunas. A good place for a cheap, filling lunch, although it is as a relaxing evening watering hole that *Skliautas* comes into its own. Daily 10am–midnight.

Festivals and events

The most prestigious of the year's culture-fests is the **Pažaislis Music Festival** (®www.pazaislis.lt) in July and August, when concerts featuring top classical performers from Lithuania and abroad are held in churches throughout the city centre and in the grounds of Pažaislis monastery – concerts held here are definitely worth attending if you have the chance. Information and tickets are available from Kaunas Philharmonic (see p.373).

The tourist office can provide details of other annual events: the **Kaunas Jazz Festival** (®www.kaunasjazz.lt) brings together the best Lithuanian musicians and several international guests during the last week of April, while the **Kaunas Modern Dance Festival** attracts a broad spectrum of innovative groups from the Baltic region in early October. The **Days of Kaunas** (®www.kaunodienos.lt), a city festival held over a weekend in mid-to-late May, culminates with a massive open-air pop concert in the Old Town's main square.

Shopping

Most of Kaunas's high-street stores are to be found along Laisvės alėja; the new, mall-style shopping centres such as Akropolis, Mindaugo prospektas, are the best places to look for international brand names. Galleries selling locally made ceramics, jewellery and artworks congregate along the Old Town streets of Vilniaus, Valančiaus and their neighbours.

Crafts and souvenirs

Kauno dizaino salonas Valančiaus 5. Wacky ceramics, avant-garde glassware and a big range of earrings, brooches and pendants. Mon–Fri 10am–6pm, Sat 10am–4pm.

Kauno langas Valančiaus 5 ®www.klangas.lt. Artist-made jewellery, plus paintings and sculpture. Mon–Fri 10am–6.30pm, Sat 10am–4pm.

Kauno mažoji galerija Daukšos 20. Quirky ceramics, handmade cards and amber earrings, necklaces and bracelets. Mon–Fri 10am–7pm, Sat 11am–4pm.

Linas Medis Vilniaus 32. Wooden kitchenware and toys (including mobiles to hang in kiddies' bedrooms), and linen bedspreads. Mon–Fri 10am–6.30pm, Sat 10am–5pm.

Tekstilininkų ir dailininkų galerija Valančiaus 15. Offbeat, unique bags, hats and other accessories made by local craftspeople. Mon–Fri 11am–6pm, Sat 11am–4pm.

Antiques and collectables

Antikvariatas Kumelių 17 Classy furniture, clocks, silverware and paintings. Mon–Sat 11am–5pm.
Antiquarius Šv Gertrūdos 56 ⓦ www.vabolis.com. Porcelain, agricultural implements, furniture and other oddments. Mon–Fri 11am–6pm.

Books

Knygų Laisvės alėja 29. Small selection of English-language paperbacks, international art books, locally produced tourist titles and maps. Mon–Fri 9am–7pm, Sat 10am–5pm.
Pegasas Vilniaus 43. Maps, guidebooks and a sprinkling of English-language novels. Mon–Fri 10am–7pm, Sat 10am–6pm.

Listings

Airlines Air Lithuania, Kęstučio 69 ⓣ 8-37/229706, ⓦ www.airlithuania.lt. Flights from Kaunas to Oslo, Mälmo and Hamburg.
Car rental Budget, Savanorių 443A ⓣ 8-37/490440, ⓦ www.budget.lt; Litinterp, Gedimino 28-7 ⓣ 8-37/228718, ⓦ www.litinterp.lt.
Internet Interneto kavinė, Vilniaus 26 (Mon–Sat 9am–10pm, Sun 10am–9pm).
Left luggage In the train station (daily 7am–7pm with a break for lunch).
Pharmacy Corner of Vytauto and Čiurlionio (open 24hr).
Post Office Laisvės alėja 102 (Mon–Fri 7am–7pm, Sat 7am–5pm).

Taxis Einesa ⓣ 8-37/331011 or Milvasa ⓣ 1400.
Travel agents Baltic Clipper, Laisvės 61–1 (ⓣ 8-37/320300), sells international plane tickets; Müsų Odisėja, M.K. Čiurlionio 15 (ⓣ 8-37/408410, ⓦ www.tourinfo.lt) organizes coach trips and hotel reservations throughout Lithuania; Studentų kelionės, Kęstučio 57–4 (ⓣ 8-37/220552, ⓦ www.studentukeliones.lt) deals in youth and student discount travel. Kautra, Laisvės 36 (ⓣ 8-37/209836, ⓦ www.kautra.lt) and at the bus station (ⓣ 8-37/322222) sells long-distance and international bus tickets.

Outside Kaunas: Rumšiškės

Twenty kilometres east of Kaunas, just off the main Vilnius-bound highway, **RUMŠIŠKĖS** is an unremarkable modern village built to accomodate locals whose homes were submerged by the creation of the Kaunas Sea (see p.372). However, the rolling green countryside just outside provides a perfect setting for the open-air **Museum of Lithuanian Life** (Lietuvos liaudies buities muziejus; Easter–Oct Wed–Sun 10am–6pm; 6Lt), where approximately 150 original buildings – mostly from the nineteenth century – from all over Lithuania have been gathered together. Covering 175 hectares, it's a big site, and you'll need a couple of hours to do it justice – an English-language map (5Lt from the ticket office) will help you find your way around.

Adventure sports

Kaunas is a good starting point for an adventurous day out, with a handful of adrenalin-sport opportunities located a short drive from the city.

Ekspedicija ⓣ 8-615 73393, ⓦ www.ekspedicija.lt. Climbing wall in a pine-shrouded location 30km west of town on the Vilkija road. They can also organize one-day canoe trips from the Kauno marijos reservoir downstream to the city itself (from 20Lt/person depending on size of group).

Lokės pėda Lokėnelių kaimas, 5km north of Jonava on the Kaunas–Ukmergė road ⓣ 8-699 21144, ⓦ www.lokespeda.lt. Adventure park featuring eight harness-assisted tree-top walks, each offering a range of balance-challenging obstacles and zip-wire slides (40Lt/3hr). Also safaris on four-wheeled motorcycles through local woods and riverside meadows (ⓦ www.motosafaris.lt; 250Lt/90min). Both tree-walks and safaris are oversubscribed in summer, and you're advised to book in advance by Internet to reserve a slot. May–Sept daily 10am–7pm; Oct–April open at weekends but check website for precise times.

The buildings are arranged in four groups, each representing Lithuania's principal ethnographic areas, with – roughly at any rate – Aukštaitija to the north, Žemaitija to the south, Suvalkija to the west and Dzūkija somewhere in the middle. Each group of buildings is separated from the next by a couple of hundred metres of farmland or forest, making the whole ensemble perfect for a countryside stroll. Many of the farmhouse interiors reveal how self-sufficient rustic households had to be, with furniture and farm tools crafted by the man of the house during the long winters, and bedspreads – very often the only sign of colour in the wood-floored, wood-panelled rooms – woven or embroidered by the womenfolk. Despite the obvious harshness of nineteenth-century farming life, its re-creation here comes across as invitingly idyllic, with long Žemaitijan farmhouses groaning under vast overhanging thatched roofs, and horses grazing in the fields nearby. At the northern end of the museum, an octagonal wooden church, resembling a sail-less windmill, marks the approaches to an Aukštaitijan grid-plan village, its neat cottage gardens, porched houses and picket fences looking like an ideal piece of rural suburbia. Occupying a hill brow at the centre of the museum is the main street of a typical late-nineteenth-century town, its parallel rows of wooden buildings full of craft workshops where you can watch woodcarvers, ceramicists and weavers at work – they'll have some of their handicrafts for sale here, too. You can pick up snacks and soft drinks at the town's *arbatinė*, or "tea room".

The museum is closed throughout the winter except on the Sunday preceding **Shrove Tuesday** (Užgavėnės), when folklore enthusiasts dress up in mummers' costumes and burn an effigy known as the *morė* to mark the death of winter.

Practicalities

Rumšiškės is served by Kaunas–Vilnius **buses** (but not express minibuses), which pick up and drop off at the bus shelter on the main highway; from here it's a straightforward 25-minute walk south to the museum entrance. On the way you'll pass a small **tourist office** at S. Nėries 4–6 (June–Aug Mon–Fri 9am–5pm; T 8-346/47247, E turinfo@takas.lt), which can organize **bed-and-breakfast accommodation** (2) in Rumšiškės and surrounding villages.

Kėdainiai and around

An easy day-trip from Kaunas, or a pleasant stop-off en route to Panevėžys or Šiauliai, **KĖDAINIAI** is a 35,000-strong, semi-industrialized provincial centre. With its well-preserved churches of every denomination, a brace of surviving synagogues and an elegantly proportioned main square, Kėdainiai exudes the sense of cultural tolerance and taste for fine architecture that characterized the courtly culture of early seventeenth-century Lithuania. It was then that this minor market town on the River Nevėžis became the property of the Calvinist branch of the Radvila family, who sought to utilize its money-earning potential as a stop-off on the Vilnius–Baltic Sea trade routes, while simultaneously turning it into an important focus of Protestant culture. It was hero of campaigns against the Swedes, Kristupas Radvila (son of Kristupas "the Thunderer" of Biržai; see p.355), who set the ball rolling, endowing Calvinist churches and encouraging merchants of various faiths to settle in the town, while his German-educated son Jonušas (who took first a Catholic, then an Orthodox wife in order to preserve his alliances with non-Protestant sections of the aristocracy) set up a printing press in the hope of weaning intellectuals away from Vilnius. Protestant emigrants from Scotland were particularly numerous, building prosperous town houses which still surround Kėdainiai's main square. However, this economic and cultural flowering was short-lived – Kėdainiai was repeatedly sacked during the Swedish-Russian wars of the 1650s, and didn't really recover until the late nineteenth century, by which time its importance as a processing point for the local cucumber harvest had made it the pickled gherkin capital of the Baltics – a status it still enjoys. Kėdainiai is served by hourly **buses** from Kaunas and Panevėžys, and a handful from Vilnius and Šiauliai.

Arrival, information and accommodation

Kėdainiai's train station is at the northern end of town, but as this is only served by two Vilnius–Šiauliai services a day, you're more likely to arrive at the bus station, 2km to the southwest, on the town's main through road, **Basanavičiaus gatvė**.

Head up Basanavičiaus and turn left into Didžioji to find the **tourist office** at Didžioji 1 (Mon–Fri 9am–5pm; ☎8-347/60363, ⓦwww.visitkedainiai.lt), which has plenty in the way of free English-language brochures and can book you into a small number of rural **B&Bs** in the region. Best of the **hotels** is ⅉ *Grėjaus Namas*, Didžioji 36 (☎8-347/51500 & 67153, ⓦwww.grejausnamas.lt; ❹–❺), a seventeenth-century structure built for Scottish settler Jacob Grey. Comfortable en suites with pastel-green colour schemes are decorated with photographs of Scottish castles, while the deluxe room has the added advantage of sofa, bathtub and minibar. Top-floor rooms have skylight windows. *Aroma Rex*, Didžioji 52 (☎8-347/55555, ⓦwww.aroma.lt; ❸), is a homely substitute, with five cosy, ensuite rooms with TV – although if you're allergic to the colour brown, you may have problems with the decor.

The Town

Kėdainiai's easily explored historic heart stretches either side of Didžioji gatvė, a largely pedestrianized shopping street that runs through a neat chequerboard of well-preserved buildings. The street culminates in Didžioji rinka, or Great Square, where the quaint town houses built by Kėdainiai's seventeenth-century Calvinist community – most of them Scottish immigrants – can still be admired.

The Kėdainiu District Museum and around

Occupying a former Carmelite convent at Didžioji 19, the **Kėdainiai District Museum** (Tues–Sat 9am–5pm; 2Lt) offers an involving display of artifacts recalling the town's past glories. Alongside portraits of sundry Radvilas and a case containing Kristupas Radvila's ceremonial sash, there's a model of Kėdainiai's main market square as it looked in its seventeenth-century heyday, made out of colourful clay houses that look like gaudily iced cakes. In the next room there's a pre-World War I photograph of the same square – so packed with horses and carts that it looks as if every peasant from central Lithuania came to trade here. Elsewhere there's a display of beautifully carved wooden crosses and a room full of nineteenth-century furniture made from antlers that has to be seen to be believed. Photographs crowding the walls of former convent cells include a snap of Nobel prize-winning author **Czesław Miłosz**, who was born to a Polish-speaking minor gentry family in Šeteniai, 15km northeast of town, on June 30, 1911 – he lived there for ten years before heading for High School in Vilnius. Winding lazily past his childhood home is the Nevėžis River, which, disguised by the name of Issa, was to crop up in his autobiographical fiction some fifty years later (see "Books", p.459). Behind the museum, and accessible via a narrow alleyway, the eighteenth-century **St Joseph's Church** (Šv. Juozapo bažnyčia) is a delightful wooden church with Baroque belfry, built by the Carmelites to wrest spiritual power away from the local Calvinists.

The Reformed Church

A couple of blocks east of the museum at Senoji 1, the seventeenth-century **Reformed Church** (Reformatų bažnyčia; June–Sept: 11am–4pm; rest of year: ask at the museum if it can be opened up for you; 2Lt) is the town's trademark edifice, a high-sided oblong with a pair of ice-cream-cone towers either side of the main portal. Begun under Kristupas Radvila and finished under Jonušas, it's a wonderful exercise in ascetic religious architecture, its light, lofty and only minimally decorated interior clearly designed to induce feelings of spiritual contemplation. The communists were so impressed by its spaciousness they turned the building into a basketball court. Now used for occasional services attended by a dwindling congregation of local Protestants, the church is mainly visited for the Radvila family vault, which lies beneath the main altar. The grandest of the sarcophagi are a richly ornamented Baroque affair containing the remains of Jonušas Radvila and the next-door casket of his grandfather Kristupas "the Thunderer", embossed with suitably fearsome lions' heads. The smaller coffins, each mounted on balled feet as if intended to be periodically rearranged by a macabre interior designer, belong to Jonušas's four siblings, all of whom died in infancy.

Didžioji Rinka and Senoji Rinka

Immediately east of the church lies the **Didžioji Rinka**, or Great Square, a broad, open space bordered by a handsome collection of old-ish buildings. Most eye-catching are the merchants' houses at the square's northern end, their brightly painted, curvy gables resembling jellies at a children's party. In the middle of the square stands a **monument to Jonušas Radvila**, famous in Lithuania (and infamous in Poland) for attempting to rupture the Polish-Lithuanian Commonwealth in 1655 by allying the Grand Duchy of Lithuania with Sweden instead. Lonušas died in battle later the same year, and his projected political realignment remained a pipe dream.

Moving north from the Didžioji Rinka along Senoji gatvė brings you out onto another large square, **Senoji Rinka**, or Old square, once monopolized by the town's Jewish stall holders. Encouraged to settle in the area by the Radvilas in the seventeenth century, Kėdainiai's Jewish community played a prominent role in the town's social and economic life until August 28, 1941, when the Nazis shot an estimated 2076 victims in one day. Two synagogues survive, standing end-to-end at the far side of the square. The larger of the two (colloquially known as the summer synagogue because it wasn't equipped with central heating) is now an arts school, while its smaller neighbour (the "winter synagogue", naturally) serves as the **Kėdainiai Multicultural Centre** (Daugiakultūris centras; Tues–Sat 10am–5pm; 2Lt), hosting seasonal exhibitions by contemporary artists and photographers. Whatever's on show, it's definitely worth having a peek at the spirit-soothing, light-blue interior, its ceiling held up by a quartet of spindly columns. The upstairs gallery, punctuated by twelve small windows symbolizing the twelve tribes of Israel, was where female members of the congregation were allowed to follow services.

The Kėdainiai minaret

Returning to Basanavičiaus and heading north towards the train station brings you after twenty minutes' walk to a unkempt town park, sprawling along both banks of the Dotnuvėlė, a tributary of the Nevėžis. Spearing skywards in the northwestern corner of the park is the rather incongruous-looking **Kėdainiai minaret**, a folly built by General Totleben, who lived in a manor house that stood nearby until its destruction in World War II. A veteran of the Russo-Turkish War of 1877–78, when he commanded Tsarist armies in Bulgaria, Totleben considered it Russia's destiny to save the Near East from Ottoman misrule – and built this minaret in celebration of his big idea.

Eating and drinking

Best place **to eat** in the town centre is the restaurant of the *Grėjaus namas* hotel (see p.377), a barrel-vaulted, Baroque space offering solid international cuisine and courtyard seating in summer. Further afield, *Po šiaudiniu stogu* at Jazminų 1 is a log cabin located in a suburban area of family houses and gardens some twenty minutes' walk west of the centre: all of Lithuania's potato-based favourites are here (including *Kėdainiai blynai*: potato pancakes stuffed with mincemeat), alongside pork chops, grill-steaks and pan-fried carp and other fish. A couple of cafés on the main street serve alcoholic drinks until 10 or 11pm, after which you should head for the *Vikonda* **nightclub** 200m north of the old town at Basanavičiaus 22 (⦿ www.vikondosklubas .lt), which hosts DJ-led party nights and pop-rock gigs at weekends, and more sedate drinking opportunities most other nights.

Birštonas

Some 44km south of Kaunas, just off the main road to Druskininkai (see p.384), the spa town of **BIRŠTONAS** has been a popular getaway ever since the days of Vytautas the

Great, when the Grand Duke and his entourage adopted the local castle as their favourite hunting lodge. The local mineral springs became fashionable in the 1920s, when Lithuania's leading spa town of Druskininkai was occupied by Poland, and Birštonas was called upon to deputize. While spa tourism and the provision of rest cures remain Birštonas's raison d'être, the place retains a village-like feel and a rural pace of life. The settlement straggles along the banks of the River Nemunas, whose slow-moving meanderings have hereabouts produced a series of huge loops known as the Nemunas Bends. With the region's dense forest and wildlife under the protection of the Nemunas Bends Regional Park (Nemuno kilpų regioninio parkas), Birštonas presents plenty of opportunities to explore the local riverside paths on foot or by bicycle.

Birštonas is easily reached by half-hourly **bus** from Kaunas. Coming from the Vilnius direction, the route via Trakai and Aukštiadvaris (served by five daily Vilnius–Prienai buses) ploughs through some of Lithuania's prettiest countryside, characterized by pretty lakeside villages set amidst low, rolling hills.

The Town

Birštonas's focal point is the **Nemunas River**, which passes 2km west of town before looping back on itself and sweeping past Birštonas to the east. It's on the eastern side of town, beside the river, that you'll find the town centre, with a sprinkling of spa buildings and a red-brick neo-Gothic parish church. Beside the church, the **Birštonas Sacral Museum** (Birštono sakralinis muziejus; Wed–Sun 10am–5pm; donation requested) honours local archbishop Teofilius Matulionis (1873–1962), who struggled to preserve religious freedoms during the Soviet occupation. It was in this house that Matulionis secretly consecrated Vincentas Sladkevičius (1920–2000) as bishop of Kaišiadorys, despite the opposition of the Soviet powers. Prevented from taking up his post until the early 1970s, Sladkevičius was subsequently made a cardinal by Pope John Paul II in 1988. Animated wooden statuettes of saints, previously displayed in wayside shrines, round off a charming display. Just up the street, at Vytauto 9, the **Birštonas Museum** (Birštono muziejus; Wed–Sun 10am–5pm; free) has a rather modest collection of local agricultural implements and old spa-resort postcards. A couple of blocks west, the photographs on display in the **Nemunas Bends Regional Park Visitors' Centre** (Nemuno kilpų regioninio parko lankytojų centras; Mon–Fri 9am–5pm; free) provide a colourful introduction to the flora and fauna of the surrounding forests.

Into the park

The easiest way to access the Nemunas Bends Regional Park is to walk or cycle northwest along the riverbank from the centre of town and into the **Zverinčius Forest** (Žvėrinčiaus miškas), which extends for some 7km into a pocket of land almost encircled by the meandering river. Criss-crossed by trails (pick up a map from the tourist office), the forest is thick with soaring pines, although the ancient and knobbly conifer known as the Vytautas Oak, 4km out of Birštonas and a popular target for strollers, is thought

---

Taking the cure in Birštonas

Birštonas has several sanatoria, of which the centrally located Tulpės (℡8-319/65525, ⓦwww.tulpe.lt) is the best equipped. The Tulpės' modern indoor pool (Mon–Fri 8.30am–8.30pm, Sat & Sun 9am–8pm; 25Lt for 90min) is fed by mineral water and also boasts water slides, kiddies' paddling areas, saunas and sweeping views towards the Nemunas River. As far as individual treatments are concerned, Tulpės offers mineral baths, herbal baths and aromatherapy, as well as mud treatments in which towelling bags of heated mud are applied to aching bones and muscles. All treatments (15–20Lt) can be booked at the main reception desk, although you may have to undergo a brief blood-pressure test before undergoing some procedures.

to be one of the oldest trees in Lithuania. River islands lying off the northern end of the forest are an important nesting ground for little terns from May to August.

West of Birštonas, the road to Prienai runs beside the upstream loop of the Nemunas, passing after 2km one of the region's best-known beauty spots: the **Škėvonys Escarpment** (Škėvonių atodanga). Stretching north from the *Seklytėlė* café-restaurant (see below), this 500-metre-long sandstone cliff rises some 35m above the river, and provides an excellent view of the looping Nemunas below.

Practicalities

Birštonas' bus station is on the main street, Jaunimo gatvė, a short distance from the **tourist office** at Jaunimo 3 (T8-319/65740, Wwww.birstonas.lt), where you can book accommodation and rent bikes. There's a handful of good hotels in town, beginning with the central *Audenis* at Lelijų 3 (T319 61300, Wwww.audenis.lt; ④), a nine-room affair offering roomy en suites with unfussy decor and quiet colours, and some great attic rooms with skylight windows. *Sofijos Rezidencija*, near the tourist office at Jaunimo 6 (T8-319/45200, Wwww.sofijosrezidencija.lt; ⑤), features gloriously over-the-top design touches, including copies of Renaissance paintings, loud and luscious fabrics and canopied beds. Set among pines on the riverside path just northwest of the centre, *Sonata*, Algirdo 34 (T8-319/65825, Wwww.sonatahotel.lt; ⑤), offers en-suite rooms in warm colours, and plenty in the way of relaxing woodland scenery. All three hotels have good **restaurants**, although the most scenic eating and drinking option is *Seklytėlė*, Prienų 10, a rustic-style café-restaurant 2km west of town on the Škėvonys Escarpment (see above), with a sweeping panorama of the Nemunas from its terrace.

The Birštonas **Jazz Festival**, held on the last weekend of March on even-numbered years, is Lithuania's oldest such festival – initiated during the culturally stagnant Brezhnev era in 1980, it immediately attained cult status as a celebration of artistic freedom. The weekend always begins and ends with Dixieland jazz although there's a great deal more sandwiched in between. Information and tickets are available from the tourist office.

Dzūkija National Park

With its deep swathes of sandy-soiled pine forest punctuated by the occasional one-street village, the **Dzūkija National Park** (Dzūkijos nacionalinis parkas; Wwww .atostogos.lt/dzukijanp) is about as far away from urban Lithuania as you can get. This 56,000-hectare stretch of rolling terrain on the east bank of the River Nemunas has never been a major agricultural area, most of the population making a living from forestry, beekeeping or gathering the berries, nuts and mushrooms for which the Dzūkijan woodland is famous. The local villages, sparsely inhabited by an ageing population, have preserved traditional features that elsewhere in the country can only be seen in ethnographic museums: timber houses adorned with intricate, filigree-effect window frames and gardens sporting boldly carved wooden crosses topped with shrines or sun symbols. The forest itself is teeming with animal life: eagles, buzzards and woodpeckers inhabit the canopy, while elk, deer and wild boar root around among the lichens and ferns below.

Canoe trips

One of the best ways to enjoy Dzūkija's woodland scenery is to **canoe** down the Nemunas tributaries, Merkys and Ūla, athough permits (available from the visitors' centre in Marcinkonys for a nominal fee) are required for the Ūla. You can only travel along national park-authorized itineraries, which are as follows: the half-day trip down the Merkys from Puvočiai to Merkinė, the one-day trip down the Ūla from Zervynos to Žiūrai, and the two-day trip down the Ūla from Zervynos to Puvočiai. Canoe rental (40Lt/day) and their transport to (and from) the river can be organized by the visitors' centre in Marcinkonys or the youth hostel in Zervynos.

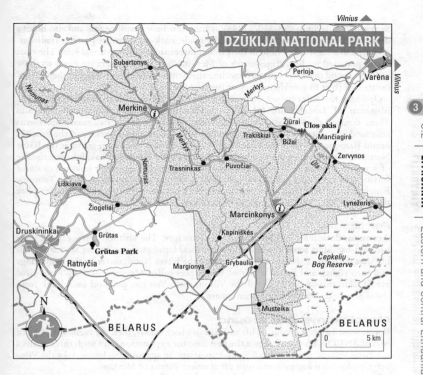

There are two main routes into the region: the main Vilnius–Druskininkai road runs along the park's northern boundaries, passing through **Merkinė** en route, while the Vilnius–**Marcinkonys** rail line cuts through the more densely forested southern section of the park. There are national park visitors' centres at both Merkinė and Marcinkonys – the latter is marginally better as a base for woodland walks and is also within striking distance of the **Čepkelių bog reserve**, a protected area of marshland on the park's southern border.

A few village homestays and tent-pitching sites aside, the park doesn't offer a great deal in the way of **accommodation**, and most visitors end up staying just outside the park in Druskininkai (see p.385).

Approaching the park along the main Vilnius–Druskininkai highway, you'll notice a series of exquisitely carved roadside **shrine-poles** topped with all manner of faces and figures, which start just after Varėna, 82km out from the capital, and continue until well past Merkinė. They're based on themes contained in the Symbolist paintings and symphonic compositions of Mikalojus Konstantinis Čiurlionis (see box, p.366), who was born in Varėna and grew up in Druskininkai. The poles, sculpted by contemporary folk artists, were erected in 1976 to commemorate the centenary of his birth.

Merkinė and around

Twenty-five kilometres beyond Varėna, Vilnius–Druskininkai buses pick up and drop off at a dusty road junction at the eastern end of **MERKINĖ** – hardly the best of introductions to what turns out to be a neat country town of one-storey wooden dwellings and cottage gardens. There's a handful of incongruous concrete buildings on the main square, one of which houses the **National Park Vistors' Centre**, Vilniaus 3 (Mon–Fri

8am–noon & 1–5pm; ☎8-310/57245); it has a few basic maps for sale and also holds a display of handicrafts – notably the locally made, dark-earthenware pottery, traditionally fired in a log-fuelled hole in the ground rather than a conventional kiln. The craft is still practised in the villages north of Merkinė, and most potters are eager to show visitors around their workshops providing that you arrange things through the visitors' centre first (best to give them a day or two's notice).

Opposite the information centre, a former Orthodox church now serves as the **Museum of Local Lore** (Merkinės kraštotyros muziejus; June–Sept Wed–Sun 11am–6pm; 2Lt), with wooden looms, spinning wheels and agricultural implements crammed into a junk-shop interior. Heading downhill along J. Bakšio, past the lipstick-bright Baroque facade of the Church of the Assumption, you soon arrive at the River Nemunas. Overlooking the north bank, a grassy **castle mound** (piliakalnis) was the site of a wooden stockade fort in the fourteenth century, an important link in a chain of fortifications protecting southern Lithuania from frequent incursions by the Teutonic Knights. Climbable via a wooden stairway, it's a great spot from which to contemplate the curve of the river and the grey-green forests beyond.

Practicalities

Accommodation around Merkinė is pretty meagre. The visitors' centre can organize bed-and-breakfast accommodation in a few local farmhouses, and there are tent-pitching sites without facilities on the far bank of the River Nemunas (cross the road bridge and turn right), and beside a pair of small lakes called Mergelės akelės ("little girls' eyes"), 2km east of town just off the Vilnius road. You can get **food and drink** from the supermarket on Merkinė's main square.

Marcinkonys and around

If you want to get a flavour of life in Dzūkija's backwoods, then the mellow village of **MARCINKONYS** is on balance the best base for exploration, and with three trains a day from Vilnius, it makes an easy day-trip. If you're approaching by car, take the Vilnius–Druskininkai highway and turn off at either Varėna or Merkinė.

Marcinkonys is a narrow, two-kilometre-long village, built around a single street, Miškininkų gatvė, heading off north from the train station. After 100m or so it passes the **Ethnographic Museum** (Etnografinės muziejus; June–Sept Tues–Sat 9am–5pm; Oct–May Mon–Fri 11am–4pm; 2Lt), a wonderfully restored old farmhouse, packed with domestic utensils, hand-woven textiles and the kind of practical pine furniture that would command a high price in today's interior design stores. A barn on the opposite side of the farmyard displays craft items made by present-day Dzūkijans, including a cluster of traditional wooden distaffs carved with wheel-like sun motifs.

Another 800m up the main street, the **National Park Visitors' Centre** at Miškininkų 61 (Mon–Fri 9am–5pm; ☎8-310/44466) has a few Lithuanian-language leaflets and basic maps for sale, and can point you in the direction of worthwhile local walks. Continuing north along the main street brings you after another 1km to one of the most appealing wooden **parish churches** in the country, a twin-towered, canary-yellow building, overlooking a pine-shaded graveyard. About 400m east of the church lies **Gaidzų kopa**, one of the most impressive of the local dunes.

The easiest walk in the area – which can be done in full or in part – is the **Zackagiris Nature Path** (Zackagirio gamtinis takas), a thirteen-kilometre-long circuit that starts at the visitors' centre and loops through the forest on either side of the village. For a short fifty-minute walk, head west along the trail to enjoy a quiet waterside trek along the Grūda River, where several hives carved by beekeepers from living tree trunks can be seen. The eastern part of the circuit passes through thick pine forest growing on an undulating bed of sand dunes.

The visitors' centre can book you into a handful of rural homestays (❶–❷), although they're mostly well outside the village and you'll need your own transport to get around. **Accommodation** in Marcinkonys itself is provided by the *Eglė* just behind the visitors' centre, offering prim en suites with TV and breakfast

(℡8-310/44469; ③). There's a tent-pitching site, with no facilities, beside Lake Kastionis (Kastinio ežeras), 1km northeast of the train station. *Kavinė po liepa* **café**, midway between the visitors' centre and the ethnographic museum, sells simple snacks and locally brewed Perloja beer.

Čepkelių bog

Five kilometres southeast of Marcinkonys, the area's trademark sandy-floored pine forest suddenly gives way to the soggy terrain and stunted plants of **Čepkelių bog** (Čepkelių raistas). Although lying just outside the boundaries of the Dzūkija National Park, the bog is a state-protected area into which you are strictly forbidden to wander. However, you can get as far as the reserve's northwestern corner, where paths bordering the bog afford good views of the Čepkelių landscape along the way. Bristling with heath plants, lichens and coniferous shrubs, it's a memorably stark spectacle. Keep still and you may catch sight of capercaillie strutting their way through the Čepkelių heather.

To get to the marshes, pick up the lane behind Marcinkonys train station and follow it southwest (ignoring a sign to the left reading "Čepkelių" after 800m – this simply leads to the reserve's administration office), a lovely walk through blissfully quiet forest. After 4km you arrive at a picnic spot and a signboard that directs you to the edge of the bog.

The Ūla Valley

Running along the northeastern boundaries of the park, the **Ūla** is one of the park's most beautiful rivers, winding its way between sandy, tree-covered banks before emptying into the Merkys (which in turn joins the Nemunas at Merkinė). The most picturesque of the half-forgotten villages along its banks is **ZERVYNOS**, 10km northeast of Marcinkonys and only one stop away on the train. As well as a wonderful collection of traditional timber buildings and a number of nearby forest trails, the village can boast a friendly **youth hostel** (mid-May to mid-Sept; ℡8-620/52720, ✉svirnelis@hotmail.com; 12Lt), offering dorm beds in a rustic, facility-free cabin. Meals are available for a few extra litais and staff can arrange canoeing on the Ūla River.

Six kilometres northwest of Zervynos and 2km beyond the river's-edge village of Mančiagirė, a wooden stairway leads down from the main Merkinė-bound road to a lovely wood-shrouded stretch of riverbank. A signed path leads off from here to the tiny lake known as **Ūlos akis** ("Eye of the Ūla"), where hot springwater agitates the dark sand on the lake floor to create a bubbling-cauldron effect.

A further 3km down the road from Ūlos akis lies the invitingly sleepy village of **ŽIŪRAI**, full of traditional wooden houses, their window frames carved into swirls and arabesques. The walk between Žiūrai and Marcinkonys, a two-hour trot along logging roads, is as atmospheric a woodland trek as you'll find. Whether you attempt the whole trail or not, be sure to make a short detour to forest-engulfed **BIŽAI**, a tiny village, 1.5km due south of Žiūrai; it's only accessible by dirt track and has a compelling end-of-the-world feel.

Margionys and Musteika

Heading southwest from Marcinkonys along the Druskininkai road brings you after 10km to **MARGIONYS**, a pretty village famous for the funeral laments sung by the villagers around a bonfire on All Souls' Day. More importantly for the casual visitor, it stands at the southern end of the disarmingly beautiful valley of the Skroblus, a stream which S-bends its way through wildflower-laden meadows. The downstream stretches of the Skroblus are in an off-limits nature reserve and therefore not accessible, but the banks of the stream around Margionys and the hamlet of Kapiniškės, 1.5km north, are well worth a wander.

In the woods 9km south of the Marcinkonys–Druskininkai road, **MUSTEIKA** is one of the more traditional villages in the area, a nest of timber houses lurking behind grey-brown picket fences. Trails lead south of the village into a captivating landscape of forest and marshland, where you stand a good chance of seeing cranes, grouse and even elk.

Druskininkai and around

Lying just beyond the western boundaries of the Dzūkija National Park, the spa resort of **DRUSKININKAI** is a strange mixture of modern town and rural getaway, its concrete buildings set incongruously in thick pine forest. The name of the town comes from the Lithuanian for salt (*druska*), a reference to the mineral-rich spring waters to which the town owes its health-retreat reputation. As well as being used in all kinds of physiotherapy, the waters are used to treat ailments ranging from arthritis to heart disease, bronchitis and asthma. Although the curative powers of the local waters had been well known to the locals for centuries (and King Stanisław August Poniatowski of Poland-Lithuania issued a decree recognizing this in 1794), Druskininkai's history as a spa really begins with the nineteenth-century craze for rest-cures. The first sanatorium was built here in 1838, and Druskininkai soon became the favoured summer retreat of Vilnius society – a status which to a large extent it still enjoys. During the Soviet period, when spa treatment was free to anyone who could talk a doctor into giving them the requisite sick-note, Druskininkai's sanatoria were receiving over 100,000 guests a year from all over the Soviet Union. These numbers went into steep decline after the Soviet Union's collapse, but Druskininkai is still the health resort of choice

ACCOMMODATION

Aqua Medūna	A
Dalija	G
Druskininkai	I
Druskininkų kempingas campsite	K
Europa Royale	E
Galia I	B
Galia II	D
Medūna	F
Regina	C
Spa Vilnius	J
Violeta	H

RESTAURANTS, CAFÉS & BARS

Alka	8
Dangaus skliautas	3
Kolonada	2
Medūna	G
Senasis Nemunas	6
Šicilija	4
Širdelė	1
Sūkurys	5
Švežios bandelės	7
Vido malūnas	9

DRUSKININKAI

0   200 m

for ailing Lithuanians – alongside a growing contingent of free-spending tourists who want to luxuriate in the resort's range of wellness and beauty treatments.

Served roughly hourly by **bus** from Vilnius, Druskininkai is just about do-able as a day-trip from the capital, although you'll need a night or two to allow its uniquely soothing, forest-shrouded ambience to take effect. There's plenty to see in the immediate surroundings, with the collection of Soviet-era sculptures at **Grūtas park** and the Baroque church at **Liškiava** both a short trip away.

Arrival, information and accommodation

Druskininkai's **bus station** lies a ten-minute walk south of the town centre at Gardino 1. The train station just beyond it is currently unused because the Vilnius–Druskininkai line – very popular in Soviet times – now runs through a corner of Belarus.

The main **tourist office** (the grandly named Tourism and Business Information Centre or Turizmo i verslo informacijos centras) is just southeast of the bus station building at Gardino 3 (Mon–Fri 8.30am–5.15pm; ☎8-313/60800, ⓦwww.druskininkai.lt), and it also operates an information booth on the corner of Dineikos and Čiurlionio (daily 10am–6.45pm; ☎8-313/51777). Both places can book you into bed-and-breakfast **accommodation** (①–③) in Druskininkai and outlying villages. There's a wide choice of hotels in Druskininkai, including plenty of sanatoria that cater for patients referred to the resort by Lithuania's health system, as well as tourists pure and simple – rooms are generally comfy and good value so don't be put off by the institutionalized air of some of these places. The year-round Druskininkų kempingas **campsite** at Gardino 3A (☎8-313/60800; ⓦwww.druskininkai.lt), run by the tourist office, incorporates a neat WC/shower block, electric power points for caravans and laundry facilities.

There are plenty of marked bike trails leading out of town and into the forest: you can **rent bikes** at a number of ad hoc outlets around town – check the tourist office for the latest details.

Hotels and guesthouses

Aqua Medūna Vilniaus alėja 13 ☎8-313/59195, ⓦwww.aquameduna.lt. Located in one of the circular buildings comprising Druskininkai Water Park (see p.386). Standard singles and doubles come with classy furnishings and flat-screen TVs, while apartments boast fireplaces and Jacuzzi-style baths. A pizzeria in the central lobby, decorated with fake boulders and palm trees, also serves as the breakfast room. ⑥

Dalija Vasario 16-osios 1 ☎8-313/51814, ⓔdalijahotel@one.lt. Homely eleven-room hotel in a historic building opposite the Orthodox church, offering functional, en-suite rooms with mix-and-match furnishings. Each room comes with sink, kettle and a set of cutlery, so at least you can prepare basic snacks (if not exactly Sunday lunch). No breakfast. ①–③

Druskininkai Kudirkos 43 ☎8-313/52566, ⓦwww.hotel-druskininkai.lt. Chic rooms with the full range of four-star comforts. There's a range of roomy suites on the fifth floor and a spa centre with massage and beauty treatments in the basement. Standard rooms ⑤–⑥, suites 320–500Lt

Europa Royale Vilniaus alėja 7 ☎8-313/42221, ⓦwww.europaroyale.com. Converted nineteenth-century mansion offering well-appointed rooms with thick carpets and flat-screen TVs. A covered

corridor leads directly to the next-door *Gydykla* (spa-treatment centre; see box, p.387). Two rooms have been adapted for wheelchair users. Ask about weekend or seven-day packages including half-board and spa treatments. Standard rooms ⑥, apartments from 500Lt

Galia I Maironio 3 ☎8-313/60511, ⓦwww .is.lt/galia. Modernized rooms, good service and an intimate feel in a centrally located villa. There's more of the same at *Galia II* and *Galia III*, round the corner at Dabintos 3 and 4 respectively. ③

Medūna Liepų 2 ☎8-313/58033, ⓦwww .meduna.lt. Resembling a traditional Lithuanian house but with one wall comprised entirely of glass – so you can admire the nearby Orthodox church as you make your way up and down the stairs – this hotel offers a range of en suites: "mini" doubles are cosy affairs with sloping attic ceilings, while regular doubles offer more in the way of storage and desk space. ③–④

Regina T. Kościuškos 3 ☎8-313/59060, ⓦwww .regina.lt. Modern, medium-sized hotel offering top-quality accommodation in a central location. Rooms are decked out in warm colours and feature sizeable bathrooms with tubs. Standard rooms ⑤, snazzy suites ⑦

Spa Vilnius Dineikos 1 ☎8-313/53811, ⓦwww .spa-vilnius.lt. Former sanatorium recently refitted

as a comfy spa hotel. Regular rooms come with en-suite shower, TV and small balcony, while the roomier apartments offer loungey furnishings and a full-size tub. Spa facilities on site (see box opposite); ask about accommodation-plus-spa packages. ⑤
Violeta Kurorto 4 ⓣ8-313/60600 & 60602, ⓦwww.violeta.lt. Characterful building in the style of a nineteenth-century spa pavilion, offering spacious rooms with modern bathrooms. Three rooms have fantastic views of the Nemunas; if you don't get one of these you can still enjoy the same panorama from the plant-filled lobby bar. Fitness room, Jacuzzi pool and Turkish steam bath in the basement, plus a massage centre. One room is wheelchair-accessible. ⑥

The Town

Although mostly made up of straight boulevards lined with modern buildings, Druskininkai can still muster some elegant reminders of the Tsarist era. There's a cluster of attractive wooden villas on or near **Laisvės aikštė**, a central roundabout where traffic trundles around the nineteenth-century **Orthodox church** (Stačiatikių cerkvė) in the middle of the central reservation. Sprouting a forest of blue spires capped with purple-coloured domes, it's arguably the most extrovert building in the country. The interior, covered in what looks like Victorian wallpaper, conveys a strong sense of period.

The Jacques Lipchitz Museum

Just south of the square, at Šv Jokūbo 17, a one-storey house with intricately carved verandah screens now serves as the **Jacques Lipchitz Museum** (Žako Lipšico muziejus; mid-May to mid-Sept Tues–Fri noon–5pm; 2Lt), honouring the Druskininkai-born Lithuanian-Jewish artist with a modest display of mementos and period furnishings, as well as photographs of Druskininkai's once-thriving Jewish community. Born in 1891 to a family of architects, Lipchitz attended art school in Vilnius before heading for Paris, where he lived in the so-called "Beehive" – a famously buzzing artists' colony that also included fellow emigrés from Russia's western provinces, Chaim Soutine and Marc Chagall. Lipchitz (1891–1973) made his name during World War I with a series of what he called "abstract architectural sculptures" – thrusting geometric forms which look like scale models of yet-to-be-built skyscrapers.

The Pump Room and the Water Park

East of Laisvės aikštė, the pedestrianized Laisvės gatvė leads eastwards to the historical centre of the resort, where you'll find a handsome collection of Neoclassical spa buildings holding the **Spa Centre** (*Gydykla*). Tacked on to the *Gydykla* is the bright, modern **Pump Room** (*biuvetė*; daily 8am–7pm), its minimalist, marble-effect interior providing a suitably clinical ambience in which to sample one of two local spa waters, the eggy-tasting Dzūkija and the bitter, brackish Druskininkai – the latter has a higher mineral content and is especially effective in treating the digestive system (and also goes down a treat as a hangover cure). North of here lies a futuristic grey tangle of concrete buildings built in the 1970s to serve as a spa treatment centre and expensively modernized in 2004–06. Now re-named the **Druskininkai Water Park** (Vandens parkas; Mon–Thurs 10am–10pm, Fri–Sun 10am–11pm; 37Lt/2hr; half-day and day tickets also available), the centre offers mineral water-fed swimming pool, huge, spiralling water slides, Jacuzzi-style jet baths and kiddies' paddling areas. A separate ticket (from 60Lt/2hr) gives you access to the Alita bath complex, where you can book a sauna, a Roman bath, or a steam bath – or drink cocktails in the wet bar.

The Town Museum and the Čiurlionis Museum

Heading south from the Pump Room along the flowerbed-lined **Vilniaus gatvė**, you come to the red-brick neo-Gothic **Church of the Virgin Mary of the Scapular** (Šv Mergelės Marijos Škaplierinės bažnyčia), before meeting up with Čiurlionio gatvė, which borders the kidney-shaped **Lake Druskonis**. Occupying a turreted, *belle époque* holiday home known as the Villa Linksma ("Happy Villa"), the **Town Museum** (Miesto muziejus; Mon–Sat 11am–5pm; 3Lt) at Čiurlionio 78, displays a marvellous collection of engravings showing nineteenth-century spa-town life, alongside views of Druskininkai in old postcards.

A few doors down at Čiurlionio 35, the **M.K. Čiurlionis Memorial Museum** (M.K. Čiurlionis memorialininis muziejus; Tues–Sun 11am–5pm; 4Lt) provides a fascinating insight into the life of the painter and composer (see box, p.366) who spent his early years in Druskininkai, and returned every summer in adulthood to brainstorm and brood. These seasonal visits certainly made an impression on the young Jacques Lipchitz (see opposite), who recalled later that he would watch Čiurlionis "passing like a shadow, always in deep thoughts... and I would dream to be like him." The exhibition begins with a modern pavilion filled with sepia photographs of Čiurlionis and family; behind it, the pastel-painted wooden house purchased by Čiurlionis's piano-teacher father in 1896 is crammed with nineteenth-century domestic knick-knacks. The focus of attention in the parlour is the piano presented to Čiurlionis by his patron, the Count Ogiński, on the occasion of the former's graduation from the Warsaw Conservatoire in 1899. A second house immediately next door was purchased by the family so they could rent holiday flats to tourists, although one room was kept aside as Čiurlionis's summer studio, preserved pretty much as he left it, complete with easel, writing desk and a couple of his paintings – devotional works intended for the family home, they reveal nothing of the Symbolist style for which he's famous.

The Jonynas Gallery and Lake Druskonis

A few steps west of the Čiurlionis Museum, the **Vytautas Kazimieras Jonynas Gallery** (Vytauto Kazimiero Jonyno galerija; Tues–Sun 11am–5pm) remembers the work of Vytautas Kazimieras Jonynas (1907–97), another local artist, who taught at Kaunas art school prior to World War II, designed stamps for the West German postal services in the late 1940s, and went on to create stained glass and devotional sculptures for Catholic churches throughout the US. The gallery displays a broad cross-section of Jonynas's work in a succession of chic, light-filled spaces. From here you can descend to Lake Druskonis, where there are **rowing boats and pedalos** for rent. On the far side of the lake, asphalted foot- and cycle-paths present plenty of opportunities for exploring the forest.

Taking the cure

The easiest way to benefit from Druskininkai's health-giving waters is to drink a drop of the stuff at the **Pump Room** (see opposite) or wallow in the pools of the **Water Park** (opposite). A range of more involved spa treatments is also available to the general public: mineral-water baths, massages and aromatherapy are among the services offered by the central **Spa Centre** (*Gydykla*) and many of the posher hotels. One of the most effective ways to reinvigorate weary muscles and bones is to take a Druskininkai mud bath, which basically involves a twenty-minute soak in a tub filled with peat from the Dzūkija forest floor.

Mud baths and other treatments can be booked at the reception desks of the spa centres listed below. A brief medical consultation or blood-pressure test may be required before you're allowed to take the treatment, although for most people of average health this is a mere formality.

Druskininkai Spa Centre (Druskininkų gydykla) Vilniaus alėja 11 (℡8-313/60508, ⊛www.gydykla.lt). Spa centre in the heart of the resort, offering mineral baths from 15Lt and mud baths from 26Lt. Also herbal bubble baths, and a plethora of mineral-bath-plus-body-scrub-plus-massage packages.

Spa Vilnius Dineikos 1 (℡8-313/53811, ⊛www.spa-vilnius.lt). Modern, relaxing spa centre in the hotel of the same name (see p.385), with a mineral water-fed pool and a host of treatments. These include mineral baths from 20Lt, mud baths from 30Lt, an array of beauty treatments and pretty much every variety of massage so far invented.

The Echo of the Forest

About 1.5km east of the town centre, the **Echo of the Forest** natural history museum (Girios Aidas) at Čiurlionio 116 (Wed–Sun 10am–6pm; 4Lt) occupies a purpose-built wooden house of almost fairytale appearance, with door posts in the form of giants and spindly balustrades carved into fir-branch shapes. It was constructed to replace an even odder original construction, which was suspended in the fork of a huge tree – both house and tree burnt down in 1992. The museum is divided into sections, each devoted to a particular tree typical of the region, with a display of the tools and furnishings traditionally made from it and information on its animal and bird life – unsurprisingly, there are a lot of stuffed pine martens. There are also some live ponies and deer out the back.

Eating and drinking

Druskininkai's eating and drinking scene is increasingly lively, with plenty in the way of Lithuanian meat-and-potato stodge and an increasing array of international options too.

Alka Čiurlionio 113a. A characterful wooden hut on the edge of the forest, with tables and chairs made from oddly shaped tree-trunks. Food is of the mundane Lithuanian pork-chop variety, although the salads and pancakes serve very well as light meals. Don't go after dark unless you enjoy stumbling home along ill-lit forest lanes. Noon–midnight.

Dangaus Skliautas Kurorto 8. A chic café-restaurant with a wonderful terrace overlooking the River Nemunas, serving up some excellent salads and soups as well as more substantial fish dishes, at prices slightly higher than elsewhere, but deservedly so. The adjoining late-night disco (Thurs–Sat 9pm–3am) attracts top Lithuanian DJs and live rock-pop acts. 11am–midnight.

Kolonada Kudirkos 22 ⓦ www.kolonada.lt. Parkside pavilion filled with potted palms, serving up good-quality international food, passable pizzas, and fancy cocktails. Frequent live jazz or pop-rock music, when there may be a cover charge. 10am–2am.

Medyna Liepų 2. Cosy, intimate restaurant squeezed into a corner of the *Medyna* hotel, with traditional meat and fish dishes given a stylish modern European twist. The weekday set lunches are a steal. Mon–Fri noon–11pm, Sat & Sun 1–11pm.

Senasis Nemunas Fonbergo 7. Hidden away in an unexciting courtyard behind the Maxima supermarket, this old, wood-panelled house serves up Lithuanian favourites *koldūnai* and *cepelinai*, and also offers salads made with the local marinated

mushrooms. The Vilkmerges draught beer makes a nice change from the mass-market varieties on offer elsewhere. Daily 10am–11pm.

Sicilija Taikos 9. A café-restaurant in a chic, modern pavilion offering tasty, thin-crust pizzas, as well as traditional Lithuanian stomach-fillers – including some divine potato pancakes drenched in sour cream. Sun–Thurs 10am–11pm, Fri & Sat 10am–midnight.

Širdelė Maironio 22. A rather old-fashioned café in a delightful wooden villa attached to the Dainava sanatorium, with simple pork and chicken dishes, cheap prices and a home-from-home atmosphere. The walls are covered with photographs of Lithuanian poets – a reference to the poetry festival hosted by the town each autumn (see opposite). Mon 11am–9.30pm, Tues–Sun 11am–11pm.

Sūkurys M.K. Čiurlionio 51 ⓦ www.sukurys .lt. Popular bowling alley with pool tables, whose adjacent lounge-style bar is a worthy drinking destination in its own right, with an inexpensive menu of hot food. Sun–Thurs 11am–midnight, Fri & Sat 11am–2am.

Svežios bandelės Čiurlionio 63. A bakery-cum-café churning out fresh pastries, croissants and muffins. The perfect place for breakfast or a take-away snack. Daily 9am–7.30pm.

Vido malynas Veisiejų 4. Atmospheric pub-restaurant in an old mill, with the rushing waters of a nearby stream providing the aural backdrop. The reasonably priced menu takes in pancakes, *koldūnai* and pretty much everything in the pork-chop line. Daily 10am–11pm.

Entertainment

Piano recitals are given at the Čiurlionis Museum every Sunday in summer, with performers tinkling away indoors while the audience sit on benches in the garden, watching and listening through a large open window. There's also a **Theatre Festival**, held at various venues in town, in late July/early August – contact the tourist office for details. The **Druskininkai Autumn Poetry Festival** (Poetinis Druskininkų ruduo) is a must for literati from all over the country – English-language writers are occasionally included in the programme.

Grūtas park

Three kilometres northeast of Druskininkai on the Vilnius road, just outside the village of Grūtas, **Grūtas park** (Grūto parkas; daily: May–Sept 9am–8pm; Oct–April 9am–5pm; ⓦwww.grutoparkas.lt; 10Lt) is the last resting place for many of the Soviet-era statues which were uprooted from town squares all over the land in the days and weeks following the collapse of the Moscow Coup in August 1991. The park is the private initiative of mushroom magnate Viliumas Malinauskas, who has earned a fortune from exporting the local fungus since setting up shop here in the late 1980s. Malinauskas began buying up discarded Soviet-era statues in the mid-1990s, hoping to establish a park that would tell the story of Lithuania in the second half of the twentieth century. The fact that he also saw the collection as a commercial tourist attraction was, however, regarded as a sign of insensitivity to Lithuanian sufferings by many observers. Malinauskas's plan to include a train ride in cattle trucks similar to those used in the deportations of Lithuanians to Siberia in 1941 and 1949 had to be dropped when critics complained that he was creating a "Soviet Disneyland". Officially opened in spring 2001, the park has swiftly become the number-one tourist draw in southern Lithuania – a status particularly valued by the hoteliers and restaurateurs of nearby Druskininkai, a town of which Malinauskas's son is currently mayor.

Grūto parkas is an extensive site that takes a good hour to walk around, with the **statues** themselves scattered throughout a superbly laid-out park landscaped with shrubs and streams. Each statue is accompanied by a plaque in both Lithuanian and English explaining its significance, ensuring that the park functions both as enjoyable history lesson and *plein-air* sculpture gallery – not all Soviet-era statuary was as bad as you might think. Among the instantly recognizable pieces on display here are a Stalin that once stood outside Vilnius railway station, and numerous Lenins in all shapes and sizes – including the one which dominated the capital's Lukiškių aikštė until ceremonially hauled away by crane in August 1991 (note the join just below the knee – the lower legs were sliced off by demonstrators unable to detach the statue from its pedestal).

△ Soviet statues in Grūtas park

Look out, too, for the stern visage of Felix Dzerzhinsky, the Vilnius-educated Polish communist who founded the Cheka (forerunner of the KGB) in 1918, and has been something of a pin-up for secret policemen the world over ever since. There are also plenty of statues honouring specifically Lithuanian revolutionary heroes, including one of Vincas Mickevičius-Kapsukas, who led the short-lived Lithuanian Bolshevik dictatorship of 1919, and an ensemble piece depicting Požela, Greifendingeris, Giedrys and Čarna – the underground communist leaders who were shot in Kaunas in 1926 and commemorated with this angular monument some fifty years later. In the middle of the park stands a projection hall where you can watch boy-meets-tractor propaganda films and examine a range of old photographs, newspapers and agitprop posters – including one with a primary-school slogan that reads "Love the Party, child, as you love your own mother!"

Getting to Grutas is fairly easy, with **bus** #1A trundling from central Druskininkai to the park seven times a day. There's a good café-restaurant just beyond the park entrance, offering everything from potato pancakes to roast duck.

Liškiava

Perched on a bluff overlooking the River Nemunas, **LIŠKIAVA** occupies the extreme western corner of the Dzūkija National Park. Its main draw is the eighteenth-century **Church of the Holy Trinity** (Šv Trejybės bažnyčia), a pastel-pink structure crowned by a stately grey-green dome, built to serve a now-defunct Dominican monastery. The interior is one of the few examples of the florid Rococo style in Lithuania, with swirling ceiling frescoes overlooking a show-stopping line-up of seven gilded altars, each decorated with expressive statues. Once you've seen this you can tour the remains of a nearby fourteenth-century hill-fort, commanding views of the majestic sweep of the river.

Liškiava is usually approached from the Druskininkai direction – from where it's an easy nine-kilometre bus or cycle ride along the riverbank. It's also the target of popular **river cruises**, which set off from a jetty just east of Druskininkai town centre every afternoon in season (June–Sept; timings and tickets from the tourist office).

Šiauliai and around

Although **ŠIAULIAI** (pronounced "Shyow-*ley*") is Lithuania's fourth-largest city and the administrative centre of the northwest, its historical origins remain something of a mystery. It's thought to have taken its name from a battle fought hereabouts in 1236 and known in German chronicles as the Battle of the Sun ("Saulės mūšis" in Lithuanian), when a Lithuanian-Žemaitijan army inflicted a crushing blow on the crusading army of the Knights of the Sword. Certainly by the mid-sixteenth century, Šiauliai had established itself as an important market town midway along the Königsberg–Rīga road – a position which also facilitated the arrival of successive waves of Swedish and Russian invaders. Emerging as a handsome and prosperous provincial centre under the Tsarist Empire, Šiauliai was so pummelled by Soviet artillery in World War II that it had to be almost completely rebuilt in the aftermath, and today's gridiron of concrete buildings is the result. However, there's an enjoyable clutch of **offbeat museums** to explore, and one of Lithuania's most important cult sights, the **Hill of Crosses**, lies just beyond the northern outskirts. The city also serves as a convenient stepping-stone if you're journeying west towards the Žemaitija National Park (see p.418) and the Baltic coast. **Trains** on the Vilnius–Klaipėda line pass through Šiauliai twice a day, and there are plenty of **buses** from Vilnius, Kaunas, Panevėžys and Rīga.

Arrival, information and accommodation

Šiauliai's main points of reference are the dead-straight Tilžės gatvė, which slices through the town on a northeast–southwest axis, and the pedestrianized Vilniaus gatvė, which cuts across Tilžės at right angles. The bus station is on Tilžės, about 500m southwest of Vilniaus, while the train station is slightly further out in the

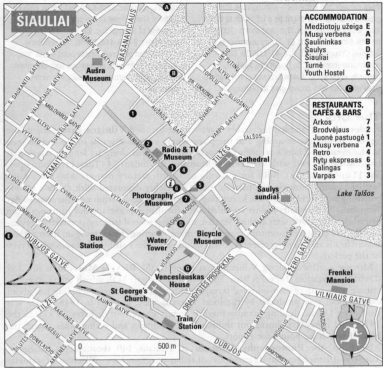

ACCOMMODATION

Medžiotojų užeiga	E
Musų verbena	A
Saulininkas	B
Šaulys	D
Šiauliai	F
Turnė	G
Youth Hostel	C

RESTAURANTS, CAFÉS & BARS

Arkos	7
Brodvėjaus	2
Juonė pastuogė	1
Musų verbena	A
Retro	4
Rytų ekspresas	6
Salingas	5
Varpas	3

same direction, at the southwestern end of Draugystės prospektas. The **tourist office**, Vilniaus 213 (Tues–Fri 9am–6pm, Sat 10am–5pm, Sun 10am–4pm; ☎8-41/521105, ⊛www.siauliai.lt), has plenty in the way of friendly advice and free town maps, and can reserve accommodation on your behalf. The town has a **youth hostel** (☎8-41/523992; 18Lt per person), located at Rygos 36, which is it's clean, though basic; there are no English-speaking staff.

Hotels

Medžiotojų užeiga Dubijos 20 ☎8-41/524526, ⊛www.medziotojuuzeiga.lt. Some way southwest of the centre on the far side of a major traffic intersection, but still just about within walking distance of the sights, this modern business-class hotel has a lofty, light-filled atrium stuffed with hunting trophies, and reasonably spacious rooms with all the creature comforts. Standard rooms ❹, deluxe rooms ❻

Saulininkas Lukausko 5A ☎8-41/436555, ⊛www.saulininkas.com. A medium-sized place on a quiet street beside the town park, offering functional en suites and a pair of "super-luxe" studio apartments with plush orange sofas and

laminate floors. There's a sauna in the basement (90Lt/hr) and a gym. Standard rooms ❸, super-luxe rooms ❹

Musų verbena Žemaitės. An attractively restored inter-war house just opposite the park with four rooms, each boasting pine floorboards, solid wooden beds and wardrobes, and embroidered linen pillows – alongside contemporary comforts such as TV and modern bathrooms. Room no. 2, with glass-enclosed balcony, is the best of an altogether charming bunch. ❹–❻

Šaulys Vasario 16-osios 40 ☎8-41/520812, ⊛www.saulys.lt. Stylish city-centre hotel centred on a nineteenth-century brick building to which various new bits have been added. Rooms feature deep carpets and bathtubs – although the slime-green colour scheme might be a bit much to take after a night on the tiles. Gym and sauna (100Lt/hr) on site. Standard rooms ⑤, luxury apartments ⑥

Šiauliai Draugystės 25 ⑦ 8-41/437333. Grey, multistorey monument to Soviet-era tourism, currently undergoing a slow process of renovation. Drab en suites with brown-grey furnishings on

some floors, pricier, thick-carpeted rooms with TV on others. Great views of the city from the west-facing side of the building. ①–③

Turnė Rūdės 9 ⑦ 8-41/500150, ⑩ www.turne .lt. Central, but on a reasonably quiet street, this is a modern hotel with an intimate feel, attentive staff and simply furnished en suites in muted shades. ④

The City

Explorations of Šiauliai inevitably start with flagstoned **Vilniaus gatvė**, the prime venue for daytime shopping and the place where everyone wants to see and be seen in the evening. There's an absorbing array of museums along its length, starting at its southeastern end with the **Frenkel Mansion** at Vilniaus 74 (Tues–Fri 10am–6pm, Sat 11am–5pm; 6Lt). Built for a family of Jewish factory owners who ran a huge leather-tanning business, the palace's rooms are richly decorated with delicate wood-panelling and florid stucco work, running the gamut of styles from neo-Baroque to Art Nouveau. The upstairs rooms are filled with furniture, porcelain and paintings from erstwhile aristocratic seats around Šiauliai, including several striking portraits of seven-teenth- and eighteenth-century magnates – many sporting the extravagant moustaches, shaved heads and flowing oriental gowns favoured by the Polish-Lithuanian aristocracy of the period.

Moving northwest along Vilniaus, you come to the **Bicycle Museum** at no. 139 (Dviračių muziejus; Tues–Fri 9am–5pm, Sat 11am–4pm; 3Lt), which offers an enter-taining round-up of two-wheeled transport throughout the ages, including just about every model ever produced by the local Vairas factory. Formed in 1948, Vairas was the Soviet Union's leading manufacturer of trendy chopper-style bikes for kids in the 1970s, and nowadays churns out thousands of mountain and racing bikes a year, the bulk of which are bound for export.

Next up, the **Photography Museum** at Vilniaus 140 (Fotografijos muziejus; Tues–Fri 10am–6pm, Sat 11am–4pm; 3Lt) has an impressive collection of cameras through the ages and a thorough round-up of the work of famous Lithuanian-based photographers, beginning with Józef Czechowitz's pioneering pictures of Vilnius in the 1870s. The seasonal exhibitions of contemporary work hosted by the museum's first-floor gallery are usually of the highest quality. A few doors down, the **Radio and Television Museum** at no. 174 (Radijo ir televizijos muziejus; Tues–Fri 10am–6pm, Sat 11am–4pm; 3Lt) was inaugurated to celebrate the output of local TV firm Tauras, although there's a lot else here besides, from old record players with enormous horns, to Art Deco radiograms from the inter-war years, and – if you needed proof that consumer-oriented gimmickry wasn't entirely a Western invention – a portable radio in the form of a toy robot, made by a Rīga firm in 1980. A modern concrete structure at the southeastern end of Vilniaus harbours the **Šiauliai Art Gallery**, Vilniaus 245 (Šiaulių dailės galerija; Tues–Fri 10am–6pm, Sat 11am–4pm; 2Lt), a good place to catch contemporary art shows.

A block away to the northeast, the gloomy corridors of the **Aušra Museum**, Aušros 47 (Aušros muziejus; Tues–Fri 9am–5pm, Sat 11am–4pm; 3Lt), are enlivened by a colourful display of folk costume from all over the country and a powerful collection of traditional sculpture, including a crowd of stern-faced saints and a riveting *Pietà*. Down at the southeastern end of Aušros, the junction with Tilžės gatvė is dominated by the **Cathedral of SS Peter and Paul**. Built in 1625, it burnt down along with just about everything else in the city in 1944. The current edifice dates from 1954, but is a faithful replica of the original, with a single white belfry (Lithuania's highest) rising up beside a supporting cast of tiny turrets – sug-gesting that it was originally intended as a fortified church capable of withstanding attacks by Swedes or Russians. Inside, all is light and purity, with a balustraded gallery overlooking a white-painted interior.

A short eastbound stroll along Aušros takas will bring you face to face with the **Archer** (Šaulys), a gilded, bow-wielding statue on top of a twenty-metre-high concrete pillar. Built in 1986 to celebrate the 750th anniversary of the Battle of Saulė, the monument also functions as a huge sundial – the flagstoned expanse beneath it is marked out with lines denoting the hours of the day. From here, a short walk south along Ežero gatvė brings you back to the eastern end of Vilniaus.

A block or two south of Vilniaus, the **Venclauskis House** at Vytauto 89 (Venclauskių namai; Mon–Thurs 9am–5pm, Fri 10am–4pm; 3Lt) originally served as the opulent home of prominent nineteenth-century lawyer Kazimieras Venclauskis (1880–1940), who served as mayor of Šiauliai in the immediate aftermath of World War I. His house is now given over to temporary exhibitions on local folklore and culture, alongside a memorial room commemorating Venceslauskis himself, together with his theatre-director wife Stanislava Jaskevičiutė.

Eating and drinking

Most of Šiauliai's eating and drinking venues are ranged along Vilniaus gatvė or just off it. The establishments along this strip have a tendency to go in and out of fashion at an alarming speed, but at least there are plenty of places to choose from. Šiauliai is not as a rule a big-spending city, and prices are generally reasonable.

Arkos Vilniaus 213. Roomy red-brick cellar with lots of cosy nooks and crannies, popular for quick lunches as well as more extended evening feasts. Lots of meat-and-potato main courses, plus pan-fried fish and a couple of veggie options. Also a good place just for a drink – especially at the weekend when there's live music and a cover charge. Daily 10am–midnight.

Brodvėjaus Vilniaus 146. Hedging its bets by offering both pizzas and pork-and-potatoes fare, Brodvėjaus is an unexciting place to eat but a great place to drink, with the staid bar-restaurant on the ground level leading to an animated downstairs bar, where fake leopard-print sofas and pop-rock sounds draw a loyal clientele of local youth. Sun–Thurs 10am–11pm, Sat & Sun 10am–midnight.

Juonė Pastuogė Aušros 31A. In an alleyway midway between Aušros and Vilniaus, this barn-like venue with wooden-bench seating and a beamed attic ceiling makes for one of Šiauliai's more cosy and convivial venues. Lithuanian staples such as *cepelinai*, pork chops and potato pancakes help to fill out the menu. It's a popular venue at weekends, with live country and western – Lithuanian style. Daily 11am–11pm.

Musų verbena Žemaitės. Charming teahouse on the ground floor of the *Musų verbena* B&B (see p.391), which serves traditional Lithuanian herbal teas alongside more familiar Indian and Chinese

varieties. Full menu of main meals as well. Daily 11am–10pm.

Retro Vilniaus 146 (entrance round the corner on Varpo gatvė). This relaxing basement café-restaurant just about earns its name, thanks to an antique gramophone and the odd vintage clock. The wide-ranging menu takes in plenty of fish and vegetarian options, alongside the usual cuts of pork and chicken. Daily 11am–11pm.

Rytų ekspresas Vilniaus 138. An unassuming doorway leads to a pair of candle-lit basement rooms (one blushing pink, the other minty green), with candles on the tables. A good place to sample standard Lithuanian café food (pork, pork and more pork) in more atmospheric than usual surroundings. Mon–Thurs 10am–10pm, Fri & Sat 10am–midnight.

Salingas Tilžės 168. This Chinese restaurant in an intimate basement setting is your only chance of finding a genuinely spicy meal in Šiauliai. There aren't too many surprises on the menu, but standards are solid and prices reasonable. Daily 11am–11pm.

Varpas Vilniaus 154. Another basement café-restaurant, this time with a vaguely Art-Nouveau interior which embraces plush red couches and ornate wooden chairs. Strong on pork- or chicken-based main meals, the menu also offers a page of pancakes and a good choice of desserts. Sun–Weds 9am–11pm, Thurs–Sat 9am–midnight.

Hill of Crosses

Twelve kilometres north of Šiauliai, just off the main road to Rīga, the **Hill of Crosses** (Kryžių kalnas) sums up the Lithuanian character more than any other single sight in the country. Combining evidence of profound Catholic piety, a deep appreciation for the simple forms of folk art and a fondness for contemplating the mysterious, it's a genuinely unique and strange attraction, and one that you should on no account leave out of your itinerary.

Like many similar mounds dotting the Lithuanian countryside, the hill may have been associated with various forms of ancestor worship in the pre-Christian era, evolving naturally (with pagan totems replaced by crosses) as the centuries wore on. Tradition maintains that the rebellions of 1831 and 1863 – and the need to commemorate the fallen in some way – was what turned the hill into a major focus of remembrance, with locals planting crosses out here in the countryside because the Tsarist authorities wouldn't have tolerated such an open display of national sentiment in an urban setting. It was certainly known as a focus of patriotic pilgrimage by the 1950s, when another round of cross-planting was undertaken by Lithuanians keen to preserve the memory of those who had died or disappeared as a result of the mass deportations to Siberia. Determined to discourage any further manifestations of religious or patriotic

△ Hill of Crosses

sentiment, the Soviet authorities had the site bulldozed repeatedly in the 1960s – each time, the locals responded by planting new crosses. A visit by Pope John Paul II in September 1993 helped to propel the hill into the premier league of pilgrimage destinations, with the construction of a brand-new Franciscan monastery just north of the site in 2001 serving to underline the place's growing spiritual stature.

Approaching the hill along an avenue of lime trees, it's initially difficult to work out what the bristling brown mass rising out of the flat green landscape actually is. It's only when you hit the coach-packed car park that you begin to pick out individual pilgrims and the strange collection of monuments they've come to visit. A cross presented by the Pope stands at the foot of the hill, its base inscribed with the words "Thank you Lithuanians for this Hill of Crosses, which testifies to the nations of Europe and the whole world the faith of the people of this land." Behind it, a towering wooden statue of Jesus, arms outstretched, seems to be ushering pilgrims onto the hill itself. More of a mound than a hill, it's an undeniably impressive site, with every inch of ground planted with crosses of every conceivable size. There are even tiny crosses hanging by metal chains around the crosspieces of the larger ones – the jangling sound they all make when the wind gets up is unearthly indeed. Among the crosses are some marvellous examples of Lithuanian wood-carving, with totem-like pillars adorned with images of various saints, and numerous examples of the Rupintojėlis, or Sorrowful Christ.

Getting to the hill is fairly easy. If you're driving, head out of town on the Rīga road and turn right when you see the sign for Kryžų kalnas about 6km beyond the city limits. By bus, seven daily Šiauliai–Joniškis services and four daily Šiauliai–Rīga services drop off and pick up right beside the Kryžų kalnas turn-off, from where it's a two-kilometre walk to the hill itself – Šiauliai tourist office might be a more reliable source of English-language timetable information than the bus station.

Travel details

Buses

Anykščiai to: Biržai (1 daily; 2hr); Kaunas (10 daily; 2hr 30min); Panevėžys (8 daily; 1hr); Vilnius (Mon–Thurs & Sat 4 daily; Fri & Sun 5 daily; 2hr 30min).

Druskininkai to: Kaunas (7 daily; 2hr 15min); Vilnius (8 daily; 2hr).

Kaunas to: Anykščiai (10 daily; 2hr 30min); Biržai (3 daily; 3hr 30min); Druskininkai (7 daily; 2hr 15min); Klaipėda (12 daily; 3hr 30min); Kėdainiai (hourly; 1hr); Panevėžys (13 daily; 2hr 30min); Šiauliai (7 daily; 2hr 30min); Vilnius (every 15–30min; 1hr 30min).

Kėdainiai to: Biržai (4 daily; 3hr 30min); Kaunas (hourly; 1hr); Panevėžys (12 daily; 1hr 20min); Šiauliai (8 daily; 1hr 30min); Vilnius (3 daily; 2hr 20min).

Panevėžys to: Anykščiai (8 daily; 1hr); Biržai (16; 1hr 20min); Kaunas (13 daily; 2hr 30min); Kėdainiai (13 daily; 1hr 20min); Šiauliai (11 daily; 2hr).

Šiauliai to: Kaunas (7 daily; 2hr 30min); Panevėžys (11 daily; 2hr); Vilnius (8 daily; 4hr).

Vilnius to: Biržai (4 daily; 3hr 40min–4hr 20min); Druskininkai (8 daily; 2hr); Kaunas (every 15–30min; 1hr 30min); Panevėžys (10 daily; 1hr 50min–3hr); Šiauliai (8 daily; 4hr).

Trains

Kaunas to: Klaipėda (2 daily; 6hr); Vilnius (12 daily; 1hr 30min).

Vilnius to: Ignalina (6 daily; 2hr); Marcinkonys (3 daily; 2hr); Šiauliai (2 daily; 4hr); Zervynos (3 daily; 1hr 50min).

International buses

Druskininkai to: Grodno (3 daily; 2hr); Kaliningrad (1 daily; 9hr); Warsaw (1 daily; 7hr).
Kaunas to: Rīga (3 daily; 5hr 20min).
Šiauliai to: Rīga (4 daily; 3hr 15min).

3.3

Western Lithuania

The undulating landscape of forests and lakes that characterizes much of western Lithuania rolls all the way to the Baltic Sea, where it culminates in a golden ribbon of sand backed by fragrant pines. With its seemingly limitless stretches of beach, towering dunes and church-topped hills, this part of Lithuania incorporates many of the country's most characteristic holiday-postcard images and is one of its most visited areas. The presence of a thriving resort culture along the seaboard ensures that there's plenty in the way of accommodation and entertainment, although you're never too far away from semi-abandoned beaches and tranquil, woodland paths. Strong folk art traditions survive in the villages: wooden farmsteads and fishermen's cottages sport intricately carved gables (the twin horse-head motif known as the *žirgelis* being one of the most typical designs), while totemic shrine-poles topped with statues of saints are commonly seen in gardens.

The region's unofficial capital is **Klaipėda**, a work-hard-play-hard port city with a medieval, German-flavoured Old Town at its heart. A short ferry ride away lies the **Curonian Spit** (also known as Neringa), an offshore sand bar boasting dense pine forests, rippling sand dunes and picturesque fishing villages, of which **Nida** is the most celebrated. Completely different in atmosphere is **Palanga**, just north of Klaipėda, a candyfloss-and-cocktails beach resort popular with families and fun-seeking youngsters in equal measure. South of Klaipėda, the rustic, reed-fringed villages of the **Nemunas Delta** provide the perfect getaway from the holiday-resort crush, and offer plenty of bird-watching opportunities in spring and autumn. The main attraction inland is the **Žemaitija National Park**, where you can enjoy boating on tranquil Lake Plateliai or walking and cycling around the region's pretty villages.

Getting to the coast **by road** usually involves a less-than-inspiring 275-kilometre journey (3–4hr if driving; 4–5hr by bus) along the Vilnius–Kaunas–Klaipėda highway, a dual carriageway that passes through an unchanging landscape of arable fields and pasture. A more scenic alternative is to take the Kaunas–Jurbarkas–Šilutė–Klaipėda road, which for much of its length runs alongside the stately Nemunas River, although it will add between two and three hours to your journey. The Vilnius–Klaipėda **rail line** loops northwards via Šiauliai before passing through **Plungė**, the main gateway to the Žemaitija National Park.

Some history: Žemaitijans, Curonians and Prussians

Western Lithuania is made up of two distinct areas: **Žemaitija** (sometimes called Samogitia in Western sources), which covers the rolling terrain in the northwestern corner of the country, and **Lithuania Minor** (Mažoji Lietuva), comprising the lowlands around the Nemunas delta in the southwest and the whole of the coastal strip. Žemaitija is named after the Žemaitijans, one of the original tribes that came to the Baltic around four thousand years ago, providing the ethnic bedrock from which the Lithuanian nation emerged. The Žemaitijans held on to their tribal identity much longer than other Lithuanians, however, remaining independent of the medieval Lithuanian state that came into being in the thirteenth century. They joined Lithuanian ruler Mindaugas in defeating the Teutonic Knights at Šiauliai in 1236, but remained only loosely allied to Lithuania until the fifteenth century, when they were formally absorbed into the Grand Duchy. They missed out on Lithuania's conversion to Christianity in 1389, remaining

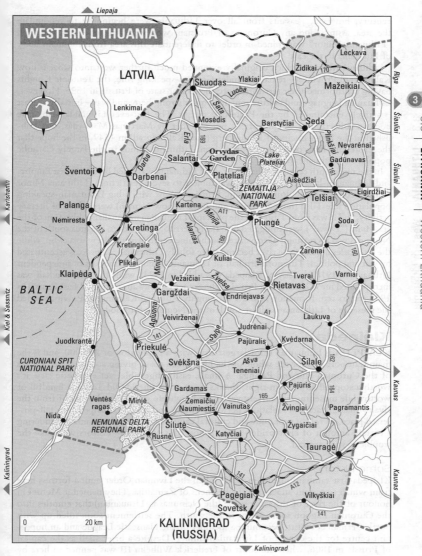

pagan for a further half-century – as a result, Žemaitija is still regarded as a repository of ancient, pre-Christian, Lithuanian traditions.

In the southwest were two other Baltic tribes: the **Curonians** (Kurši) on the coast and the **Prussians** (Prusai) on the banks of the Nemunas River. Both of these peoples were conquered by the Teutonic Knights in the thirteenth century and were either extermi-nated or driven into exile (the name "Prussia" survived though as a geographical label). The Teutons deliberately turned the whole of the seaboard into a wasteland, believ-ing that this would deter attacks by the Žemaitijans and Lithuanians. By the fifteenth century, however, peasants from all over Lithuania were beginning to repopulate the area, assimilating any Curonians or Prussians who were still left – and the term "Lithuania Minor" was coined in order to differentiate this area from the main body of Lithuania to the east.

Lithuania Minor – which originally extended much further west into what is now Kaliningrad Province – remained under German-speaking rule, the Teutonic Knights having transformed their territories into the secular state of Prussia in 1525. However, Lithuanian language and culture remained quite strong here, and was – initially at least – actively encouraged by the Protestant clergy. The first-ever Lithuanian-language book, a collection of religious texts put together by Martynas Mažvydas, was published in the Prussian city of Königsberg (now Kaliningrad) in 1547, in the hope that the Protestant faith could be exported from Lithuania Minor to the largely Catholic populace of Lithuania proper.

In the nineteenth century, when the rest of Lithuania was ruled by the Tsarist Empire, and Lithuanian-language publishing was subject to severe restrictions, Lithuania Minor enjoyed comparative cultural freedom. Prussian towns with a big Lithuanian-speaking population like Tilsit (now Sovyetsk) and Ragnit (now Neman) were a hive of literary activity, and it was from Tilsit that the principal Lithuanian nationalist publication of the era, *Aušra* ("Dawn"), was smuggled into tsarist territory. However, the area south of the Nemunas was increasingly Germanized as the nineteenth century drew to a close, while the territories north of the river became more solidly Lithuanian – a process accentuated by war and politics. This northern half of Lithuania Minor became part of independent Lithuania in 1918 (the city of Klaipėda was added in 1923), while the southern half was incorporated into German East Prussia. The Soviet Union's absorption of East Prussia in 1945 and its transformation into the thoroughly Russified Kaliningrad Province ended the presence of Lithuanian culture south of the Nemunas for good.

Klaipėda

KLAIPĖDA is Lithuania's third-largest city, with a population of 200,000, and is the main transport hub for the whole of the Lithuanian coast, giving access to the beaches of the Curonian Spit and Palanga. A small, easily digestible, yet energetic city, it's worth a stop-off in its own right, thanks to an atmospheric Old Town, a handful of worthwhile museums and a lively year-round nightlife scene. Standing aloof from the rivalry that characterizes relations between Vilnius and Kaunas, Klaipėda is a self-possessed place, its role as economic and cultural capital of western Lithuania engendering a certain amount of civic pride – which soon rubs off on any visitors who take the trouble to stick around.

Some history

Klaipėda first came into being in 1252, when the Livonian Order built a fortress here from which to mount attacks on the heathens of Žemaitija. They named it **Memel** in honour of the river of the same name (the Nemunas in Lithuanian) that empties into the Curonian Lagoon some 40km to the south. The settlement soon filled up with north German colonists, becoming a member of the Hanseatic League and an important centre for the export of Lithuanian timber. Despite a brief spell as the capital of Prussia in 1806, when the court of Frederick Wilhelm III was penned in here by Napoleon's armies, Memel's real period in the political limelight didn't come until the end of **World War I** when, evacuated by German troops, it was claimed by the newly independent state of Lithuania. Although surrounded by Lithuanian-speaking villages, the city itself was predominantly German, and the Great Powers assembled at the Paris Peace Conference didn't really know what to do with it. The French troops sent to garrison it turned a blind eye when the Lithuanians took matters into their own hands, seizing Memel by force in January 1923. The Lithuanians had already lost Vilnius to the Poles, and many in the international community saw their smash-and-grab raid on Memel as some form of compensation.

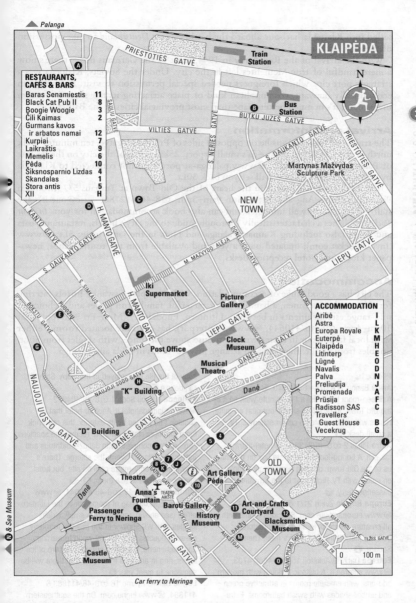

▲ Palanga

KLAIPĖDA

N

Train Station

Bus Station

3

3.3 | **LITHUANIA** | Western Lithuania

PRIESTOTIES GATVĖ

Ⓐ

RESTAURANTS, CAFÉS & BARS

Baras Senamiestis	11
Black Cat Pub II	8
Boogie Woogie	3
Čili Kaimas	2
Gurmans kavos ir arbatos namai	12
Kurpiai	7
Laikraštis	9
Memelis	6
Pėda	10
Šikšnosparnio Lizdas	4
Skandalas	1
Stora antis	5
XII	H

BUTKU JUZES GATVĖ

VILTIES GATVĖ

SAULIŲ GATVĖ

S. NERIES GATVĖ

PRIESTOTIES GATVĖ

S. DAUKANTO GATVĖ

Martynas Mažvydas Sculpture Park

NEW TOWN

Ⓑ

Ⓒ

Ⓓ

H. MANTO GATVĖ

K. DONELAIČIO GATVĖ

LIEPŲ GATVĖ

S. DAUKANTO GATVĖ

KANTO GATVĖ

M. MAŽVYDO ALĖJA

Iki Supermarket

Picture Gallery

ACCOMMODATION

Aribė	I
Astra	L
Europa Royale	K
Euterpė	M
Klaipėda	H
Litinterp	E
Lūgnė	O
Navalis	D
Palva	N
Preliudija	J
Promenada	A
Prūsija	F
Radisson SAS	C
Travellers' Guest House	B
Vecekrug	G

Ⓔ

Ⓕ

Ⓖ

Ⓗ

S. ŠIMKAUS GATVĖ

PUODŽIŲ

BOKŠTŲ GATVĖ

NAUJOJI UOSTO GATVĖ

VYTAUTO GATVĖ

NAUJOJI SODO GATVĖ

LIEPŲ GATVĖ

KARŠUJOS GATVĖ

DANĖS

DANĖS GATVĖ

Post Office

Clock Museum

Musical Theatre

"K" Building

"D" Building

Danė

▲ IV & Sea Museum

❹

❺

TURGAUS GATVĖ

TILTŲ GATVĖ

OLD TOWN

BANGŲ GATVĖ

Theatre

Anna's Fountain

❻ ❼ Ⓚ Ⓙ

Ⓘ Ⓑ

AUKŠTOJI GATVĖ

TEATRO AIKŠTĖ

ŽVEJŲ GATVĖ

TEATRO GATVĖ

❽ ❾ ❿

i

Art Gallery Pėda

Baroti Gallery

History Museum

DIDŽIOJI VANDENS

SUKILĖLIŲ GATVĖ

DARŽŲ

Ⓜ

❶❶

❶❷

Art-and-Crafts Courtyard

Blacksmiths' Museum

KURPIŲ

KŪLIŲ VARTŲ GATVĖ

TILŽES GATVĖ

TAIKOS PR.

Passenger Ferry to Neringa

Castle Museum

PILIES GATVĖ

GALINIO PYLIMO GATVĖ

Ⓞ

0   100 m

Ⓘ

▼ Car ferry to Neringa

Renamed **Klaipėda**, the city retained its German population, and both German and Lithuanian were the official languages in local government. The two communities got on reasonably well until the 1930s, when local Nazis – emboldened by the aggressive foreign policy of Hitler's Germany – began to demand the city's reunification with the Reich. Unable to stand up to the Germans on their own, the Lithuanians decided not to put up a fight. On March 23, 1939, the Führer himself sailed into Klaipėda harbour aboard the battle cruiser *Deutschland* to take possession of the city.

With the arrival of the Red Army in 1944, most of the Germans fled – there's now a mere handful of true Memelites left in the city. Under the Soviets, Klaipėda was a strategic port city which foreigners needed special permission to visit. Nowadays an economically buoyant, cosmopolitan kind of place attracting its fair share of foreign investment, it's in much better shape than most provincial cities in the Baltics.

Arrival and information

The **train and bus stations** lie on opposite sides of Priestoties gatvė, ten minutes' walk north of the Old Town. Klaipėda's small airport, 25km north of the city on the far side of Palanga (℡8-460/52020, ⊛www.palanga-airport.lt), is not connected to Klaipėda by public transport – a taxi will set you back 30Lt.

Klaipėda's **tourist office** is in the heart of the Old Town at Turgaus 5/7 (Mon–Fri 9am–6pm; June–Aug also Sat & Sun 9am–3pm; ℡8-46/412186, ℮tic@one.lt); the staff is particularly well informed and can also book accommodation for you. *In Your Pocket* publishes a characteristically thorough guide to the city's hotels, restaurants, bars and shops (also including Kaunas, Palanga and Nida in the same issue; 5Lt; ⊛www .inyourpocket.com), updated once a year and available from the tourist office, newspaper kiosks and hotel reception desks.

Accommodation

The city has a good range of accommodation, with a couple of swanky **hotels** catering for Western businessmen, a handful of characterful, family-run places and a choice of mid-range establishments in between. Litinterp, Puodžių 17 (Mon–Fri 9am–6pm, Sat 10am–4pm; ℡8-46/410644, ⊛www.litinterp.lt), has centrally located **rooms**, either with local families or in their own guesthouse above the office, with singles from 80Lt, doubles from 140Lt; they can also arrange private rooms in Nida and Palanga.

Hotels

Aribė Bangų 17A ℡8-46/490940, ⊛www.aribe.lt. A fifteen-room hotel just a five-minute walk east of the Old Town, *Aribė* offers simple but neat en-suite rooms with creamy-brown colour schemes, TV and a small desk. ❹

Astra Pilies 2 ℡8-46/313849, ℮hotel-astra@takas.lt. A boring-looking concrete box on the fringes of the Old Town, offering surprisingly swanky en suites with TV. Right next to the Smyltinė-bound passenger ferry. ❺

Europa Royale Žvejų 21/1 ℡8-46/404444, ⊛www.europaroyale.com. Spacious rooms with all creature comforts in a tastefully restored building just off the Old Town's main Theatre Square. ❼

Euterpė Daržų 9/Aukštoji 15 ℡8-46/474703, ⊛www.euterpe.lt. A historic building with modern add-ons, with en-suite rooms in attractive green and amber shades with swish bathrooms. Extra-snug rooms on the top floor have attic skylight windows, while some deluxe doubles have wood floors and subdued colours, and tubs in the bathrooms. If you're wondering why a Klaipėda hotel should end up being named after the muse of lyric poetry, it's because a Renaissance-era ceramic tile bearing her likeness was found on this spot – a copy of the tile is displayed in the lobby. Standard ❺, deluxe ❻

Klaipėda Naujoji Sodo 1 ℡8-46/404372, ⊛www.klaipedahotel.lt. Another hotel that shouldn't be judged by its exterior, this red-brick lump harbours classy en-suite rooms. The spacious "lux" rooms, complete with Jacuzzi-bathtubs and flat-screen TVs, are worth the splurge. There's a gym and twenty-metre pool on site, but hotel guests pay extra to use them. ❺–❻

Litinterp Puodžių 17 ℡8-46/410644, ⊛www .litinterp.lt. Mixed bag of rooms above the Litinterp office (see above), ranging from small, airless singles with WC/shower in the hallway to roomy en-suite doubles with natural wood furnishings and kitchenette. If arriving outside Litinterp office hours, ring in advance to be sure that there will be someone to meet you. ❸

Lūgnė Galinio pylimo 16 ℡8-46/411883 & 411884, ⊛www.lugne.com. On the southeastern fringes of the Old Town, the *Lūgnė* is grey on the outside, but unimpeachably chic on the inside, with smart, bright and comfortable en suites aimed at an international business clientele. Standard doubles ❸, two-room suites ❺

Navalis Manto 23 ℡8-46/404200, ⊛www.navalis.lt. Business-class comforts in a medium-sized, charmingly intimate place, housed in a handsome, nineteenth-century building. Handily located midway between train/bus stations and the Old Town. ⑥

Palva Smyltinės plentas 19 ☎8-46/391155, ⓦwww.palva.lt. Homely 17-room hotel just south of the passenger ferry dock, offering impressive views back across the lagoon toward Klaipėda's crane-studded shore. En suites feature minibar, TV and fabrics in primary colours. With bike hire available to guests, it is both a good base for the Curonian Spit and within commuting distance of central Klaipėda. ③

Preliudija Kepėjų 7 ☎8-46/310077, ⓦwww.preliudija.com. Snug six-room B&B in a restored Old Town house. The en-suite rooms come in a variety of shapes and sizes – including a couple of L-shaped doubles that are quirkily cosy. Most have wooden floors, muted colour schemes and either a sofa or extra desk space. ⑤

Promenada Šiaulių 41 ☎8-46/403020, ⓦwww.promenada.lt. Medium-sized contemporary building on a quiet street at the train-station end of town, offering spacious en suites decked out in warm colours. Contemporary Lithuanian paintings and graphics in the hallways lend an arty character to the place. ⑤

Prūsija Šimkaus 6 ☎8-46/412081. A family-run pension offering cosy little en suites with colour-clash decor, most of which come with a simple

TV. Only eight rooms, so arrive early or ring in advance. ④

Radisson SAS Šiaulių 28 ☎8-46/490800, ⓦwww.radissonsas.com. Ten minutes' walk north of the centre, with comfortable, modern, well-equipped rooms decorated in a vaguely nautical theme. ⑦

Vecekrug Juros 23 ☎8-46/301002, ⓦwww.vecekrug.lt. Modern hotel a short walk north of the centre on the edge of the container-port part of town, offering smart rooms with mostly grey-green colour schemes. Most come with showers – if you fancy a Jacuzzi-style tub in your bathroom, ask for one of the roomy deluxe doubles. The rooftop summer terrace is an interesting spot to drink and gaze at Klaipėda's crane-scape. ⑥

Hostel

Travellers' Guest House Butkų Juzės 7–4 ☎8-685/33104, ☎8-46/211879, ⓦwww.lithuanianhostels.org. Friendly backpacker-oriented hostel in a residential block just round the back of the bus station. With two cramped but neat bunk-bed dorms sharing a couple of toilets and a shower, and with a little kitchen, it's a bit like sleeping over at a friend's flat. It also rents out bikes and organizes trips to western Lithuanian historic sites, including Plokštine rocket base (see p.422). No breakfast, but with *Café-Pizzeria Pipita* only two minutes' walk away, this shouldn't be a problem. 44Lt per person.

The City

Tucked into the right angle formed by the River Danė and the Curonian Lagoon, Klaipėda's **Old Town** (Senamiestis) boasts the kind of cobbled streets and half-timbered houses reminiscent of a provincial German town – which is essentially what Klaipėda was until 1944. Many of the buildings, however, were damaged in World War II and rebuilt in not quite authentic style, giving the centre a rather untidy, fragmented air. The medieval, gridiron street plan still survives though, and reminders of the trades once practised here live on in street names such as Kalvių (Blacksmiths'), Kurpių (Cobblers') and Vežėjų (Undertakers').

North of the River Danė, the **New Town** (Naujamiestis) is a predominantly nineteenth-century district which nowadays serves as the city's business and commercial centre.

The Old Town

At the heart of the Old Town is cobbled **Theatre Square** (Teatro aikštė) named after the ornate Neoclassical theatre on its northern side. Hitler spoke from its balcony in March 1939 after Germany had annexed Klaipėda in its last act of territorial aggrandizement before the outbreak of war. In front of the theatre is **Anna's Fountain** (Anikės fontanas), a replica of a famous pre-war monument to the German poet Simon Dach (1605–59), depicting the heroine of his folksong, *Ännchen von Tharau*.

Running northeast of the square, **Turgaus gatvė** was once Klaipėda's main market street and retains many of its fine pre-twentieth-century town houses. One way of exploring the interior of one of these houses is to delve into **Art Gallery Pėda** at Turgaus 10 (entrance round the corner in the alley; Mon–Fri 10am–7pm, Sat 11am–5pm;

△ Half-timbered houses in Klaipėda Old Town

Ⓦwww.peda.lt; free). One of the older privately run galleries in the city, Pėda features the distinctive stone-and-metal sculptures of local artist Vytautas Karčiauskas, together with the pendants, necklaces, paintings and graphics made by his extended family.

Southeast of the square lies a mixed area of nondescript modern buildings and picturesque, half-timbered warehouses. An imposing 200-year-old example of the latter, at Aukštoji 3, now houses the **Baroti Art Gallery** (Mon–Fri 11am–6pm, Sat 11am–4pm; free), a commercial space with contemporary paintings and sculptures spread across three floors of atmospheric, timber-beamed rooms.

Just around the corner from the Baroti Gallery at Didžioji vandens 6, the **History Museum of Lithuania Minor** (Mažosios Lietuvos istorijos muziejus; Ⓦwww.mlimuziejus.lt; Wed–Sun 11am–7pm; 3Lt) presents a comprehensive chronological account of the region's history, including plenty of archeological interest, notably a scale model of a Lithuanian pagan sanctuary which once occupied Birutė's Hill, a well-known landmark in nearby Palanga (see p.413). The arrangement of the sanctuary reveals a high degree of astronomical knowledge, with the placing of totem-like poles dictated by the positions of the planets throughout the year, and the main axis of the ensemble aligned with the rays of the setting sun on April 23. The later, Christianized inhabitants of Lithuania Minor were obviously a sober, serious-minded bunch if the costumes on display here are anything to go by – greys and blacks predominate, with delicately embroidered belt-purses providing the only splash of colour. Finally, look out for photographs of Lithuania's seizure of Klaipėda in 1923, and a 1939 snap of Adolf Hitler riding down Manto gatvė in a motorcade, greeted by ranks of local Brown Shirts.

Immediately southeast of the museum, just beyond the junction of Daržų and Auklštoji streets, the so-called **Arts-and-crafts Courtyard** (Ⓦwww.artin.lt) harbours a string of workshops where local craftspeople make and sell domestic knick-knacks and fashion accessories which mix modern design with traditional folk art. In the same courtyard is the gallery of the **Klaipėda Cultural Communication Centre** (Klaipėdos kulturū komunikacijų centras, Ⓦwww.kulturpolis.lt), a small but stimulating space devoted to cutting-edge contemporary art.

A few steps northeast at Šaltakalvių 2 is the **Blacksmiths' Museum of Lithuania Minor** (Mažosios Lietuvos kalvystės muziejus; Wed–Sun 11am–7pm; 3Lt), based on the private collection of blacksmithery enthusiast Dionizas Varkalis, who made it his personal mission to collect and restore the neglected wrought-iron crosses found in graveyards across the region. These crosses are a traditional Lithuanian folk art form, frequently featuring intricate sun-ray motifs that point to a degree of pre-Christian, pagan inspiration. Domestic oddities, including irons, kitchen tools and doorknobs, round off a fascinating collection.

The Castle Museum

Southwest of the Old Town, an area of shipyards and docks marks the site of the original fortress built by Memel-Klaipėda's Teutonic founders. Although largely destroyed, two of the fortress's towers have been restored to house the **Castle Museum** (Pilies muziejus; Tues–Sat 10am–6pm; 4Lt), which tells the history of the city through a motley collection of exhibits – from mannequins dressed in medieval costumes to Renaissance ceramics and a scale model of sixteenth-century Memel. A section on the eighteenth-century timber trade makes mention of the Scottish merchant John Simpson, who served as mayor of Memel between 1758 and 1774. A wall of twentieth-century photographs includes an intriguing picture of a Red Army soldier hastening off with a (presumably) looted penny-farthing bicycle in 1945.

The museum is quite difficult to find – you have to walk through the gates of Klaipėda shipyard (roughly opposite Daržų gatvė), passing a kiosk selling museum entrance tickets, before crossing a yard bordered by decaying warehouses.

The New Town

Klaipėda's largely twentieth-century **New Town** (Naujamiestis) is best accessed by crossing the bridge across the River Danė at the northeastern end of Tiltų gatvė. On the opposite side stands a modern, arch-shaped memorial symbolizing the reunification of Lithuania Minor with the rest of the country in the wake of World War II. Looming to the east, on the far side of the *Klaipėda* hotel, are two prominent symbols of contemporary Klaipėda – a huge red-brick office block in the shape of the letter K, standing beside a structure in the shape of a D. Completed in 2006, and clearly visible to those approaching Klaipėda by sea, the buildings are intended to provide modern-day Klaipėda with an instantly recognizable visual trademark.

Running northwest from the river Danė is the New Town's principal artery, the shop- and café-lined **Manto gatvė**. More interesting, though, is **Liepų gatvė**, which runs parallel to the river and on which stands Klaipėda's splendid, red-brick, Gothic-revival **post office** (no. 16). Built between 1883 and 1893, it's a vivid reminder of German civic pride, not least because of the 48-bell carillon that rings out from the clock tower at noon every Saturday and Sunday. The post office is also famous for being the workplace of telephonist Erika Rostel, awarded the Iron Cross for staying at her post (and giving a running commentary on events to the German General Staff) when the Russian army raided the city in March, 1915 – most of the other civilians had taken to the Curonian Lagoon in boats.

A few doors along at Liepų 12, the **Clock Museum** (Laikrodžių muziejus; Tues–Sat noon–6pm; Sun noon–5pm; 4Lt) is stuffed with timepieces from the earliest candle clocks onwards. As much as anything else, the display provides a fascinating overview of changing fashions in clock design, with some magnificently over-the-top seventeenth- and eighteenth-century creations, and the odd Art Nouveau grandfather clock bringing up the rear. The nearby **Klaipėda Picture Gallery** at Liepų 33 (same hours as Clock Museum; 3Lt) has a small collection of twentieth-century Lithuanian paintings, and puts on challenging seasonal exhibitions by contemporary artists. More contemporary art is on display northeast of here at the **Martynas Mažvydas Sculpture Park** (Martyno Mažvydo skulptūrų parkas), peppered with all manner of abstract creations. Sixteenth-century priest and pub-licist Mažvydas provides the inspiration for several of the works here – although local sculptor Algirdas Bosas's characteristically angular portrayal of the man looks more like a football star seen through the eyes of Pablo Picasso than a distinguished literary figure. Standing at the park's northern end is a megalithic memorial honouring the Soviet war dead.

Eating, drinking and entertainment

There's no real distinction between eating and drinking venues in Klaipėda: bars and pubs usually offer a full menu of palatable food, while restaurants frequently serve as fun places in which to knock back a few beers. There's a decent selection of places to chose from, many of which are concentrated on or around the New Town's main thoroughfare, Manto gatvė, and its Old Town continuation, Tiltų gatvė. You can pick up food supplies from the Iki supermarket, on the corner of Mažvydo and Šiaulių (daily 8am–10pm).

Klaipėda's main cultural flagship is the **Drama Theatre**, Teatro 2 (Dramos teatras; box office Tues–Sun 10am–2pm & 4–6pm; ⓦwww.kldteatras.lt), although you'll encounter less of a language barrier at the **Musical Theatre** (Muzikinis teatras; box office Tues–Sun 11am–2pm & 3–6pm; ⓦwww.muzikinis.teatras.lt), which hosts chamber concerts, musicals and occasional visits by Vilnius's symphony orchestras.

Old Town cafés, restaurants and bars

Baras Senamiestis Bažnyčių 4/10. Unpretentious café-restaurant in a half-timbered house which mixes original wooden interior features with what looks like Seventies' lounge furniture. The vaguely studenty clientele contribute an arty vibe, while the basic pork-chop-and-fries menu keeps undemanding bellies well satisfied. Daily 11am–midnight.

Black Cat Pub II Žvejų 21/1. Smart but atmospheric expat-patronized pub, boasting plenty in the way of red-brick walls, subdued lighting and dark wood-panelled booths. Guinness on tap, and generous portions of food – with steaks and fish fillets the standout dishes. Daily 10am–midnight.

Gurmans kavos ir arbatos namai Fridriho pasaža, just off Tiltų gatvė. Refined two-storey café in the characterful alleyway that is Friedrich's Passage, offering excellent coffee, properly brewed tea and a hard-to-resist selection of salads and light meals, cakes and cookies. You can also stock up on speciality teas, freshly ground coffee and pipe tobacco from the retail counter. Mon–Fri 8.30am–11pm, Sat 9am–11pm, Sun 10am–10pm.

Kurpiai Kurpių 1A. Something of a Klaipėda legend: a cosy brick-and-timber pub with good food, regular live bands (mostly jazz, but also rock-pop covers; check the schedule at the door) and a regular crowd of easy-going punters. Tues–Sat noon–2am, Sun & Mon noon–midnight.

Laikraštis Turgaus 3. Right on the Old Town's main street, the "Newspaper" is a comfy, wood-floored, timber-panelled bar with a journalistic theme – note the pictures of local politicians, sportsmen and celebrities lining the walls. There's an extensive menu of main meals – and relatively early opening times make it a good spot for a breakfast fry-up. Mon–Sat 7am–midnight, Sun 10am–midnight.

Memelis Žvejų 4. A beautifully restored red-brick warehouse on the banks of the Danė River with hearty meat and fish fare, beer brewed on the premises, and late-night drinking and dancing in the Pabo Latino club on the top floor. Tues–Thurs noon–2am, Fri & Sat noon–4am, Sun noon–midnight.

Pėda Turgaus 10. Subterranean café beneath the Pėda art gallery (see p.403), offering mundane Lithuanian food, but well worth a visit due to its status as something of a Klaipėda landmark. Designed by the people from the Pėda art gallery, it features a warren of nooks and crannies, small-scale sculptures, deep-sea-divers' helmets, and other oddities that sometimes feature in glossy interior design magazines. Daily 11am–11pm.

Šiksnosparnio Lizdas Tiltų 5 (entrance round the corner on Jono gatvė). A popular subterranean eating and drinking venue offering meaty Lithuanian favourites, with live pop-rock bands on occasion. Daily noon–midnight.

Stora antis Tiltų 6 ☎8-46/493910. A cosy brick cellar whose arches are so low they're equipped with padded forehead buffers to save the skulls of those who stagger into them, the "Fat Duck" offers a lengthy menu of dishes from the Slavonic countries of Europe. It's best to stick to Russian and Ukrainian dishes like pelmeni (stuffed pasta parcels), potato pancakes, blini and various types of borscht, rather than plumping for the "Croatian" or "Bulgarian" options – which don't have a great deal to do with the cuisines of their alleged countries of origin. Daily noon–midnight.

New Town restaurants and bars

Boogie Woogie Manto 5. This over-designed fun-pub with enjoyably chintzy decor still attracts a classy crowd of enthusiastic drinkers at weekends. Full menu of food, including pizza, salads and steaks. Sun–Thurs noon–midnight, Fri & Sat noon–2am.

Čili Kaimas Manto 11. For a family-oriented evening out, Lithuanian-style, look no further than this place, with its folksy wooden furniture, wicker-basket lampshades and even a small stream gurgling its way through the middle of the dining room. *Cepelinai*, handsomely proportioned slabs of pork and other local staples form the backbone of the calorie-stuffed menu. Sun–Thurs 10am–midnight, Fri & Sat 10am–2am.

Skandalas Kanto 44. Spacious, enduringly popular bar-restaurant some twenty minutes' walk northwest of the Old Town, worth investigating for its broad choice of international beers and lengthy menu of heavy-duty steaks, BBQ ribs and quality seafood. With human-sized effigies of the Statue of Liberty, a Native American and a US traffic cop, there's a strong Uncle Sam theme to the decor, although the vintage adverts covering the walls seem to have been plucked from all corners of the English-speaking world. Daily noon–1am.

XII top floor, *Klaipėda hotel*, Naujoji Sodo 1. Cocktail bar-cum-restaurant decorated in snazzy amber shades, with grilled steaks prepared in an open kitchen and loungey window-side seating offering fantastic views of the city. Mains around 30–35Lt. Daily noon–2am.

Listings

Airlines FlyLAL Daukanto 20 ☎8-46/310488.
Bus station ☎8-46/411547.
Car Rental Avis, Nidos 22 ☎8-46/311111, ⓦwww.avis.lt; Budget, Šilutės 32 ☎8-46/342690, ⓦwww.budget.lt; Hertz, *Hotel Klaipėda*, Naujoji Sodo 1, ☎8-46/310737, ⓦwww.hertz.lt; Litinterp, Puodžių 17, ☎8-699 41994, ⓦwww.litinterp.lt; Unirent, Pievų takas 15 ☎8-46/312613, ⓦwww .unirent.lt.
Hospital Red Cross Hospital (Raudonojo kryžiaus ligoninė) Nėries 3 ☎8-46/410 739.
International ferries Lisco, Perkėlos 10 ☎8-46/395050, ⓦwww.lisco.lt (ferries to Kiel and Sassnitz in Germany; also agents for the once-weekly DFDS ferry to Gdańsk); Scandlines (ferries to Aarhus and Aabenraa), *Hotel Klaipėda*, Naujoji Sodo 1 ☎8-46/310561, ⓦwww.scandlines.lt.
Pharmacy Vokiečių Vaistinė, Turgaus 22. Mon–Fri 9am–7pm, Sat 10am–5pm.
Post office Liepų 16 ☎8-46/315022. Mon–Fri 8am–6pm.
Train station ☎8-46/296385.
Travel agents Baltic Clipper, Turgaus 2, ☎8-46/312312, ⓦwww.baltic-clipper.lt; Krantas Travel, Teatro 5, ☎8-46/395111, ⓦwww.krantas.lt.

The Curonian Spit

A short hop by ferry from Klaipėda's port, the long, sandy promontory which makes up the **Curonian Spit** (Kuršių nerija; also known as "Neringa" after the sea goddess who allegedly built it) is one of the most exotic natural wonderlands in the Baltic. Formed over several millennia by deposits of wind- and wave-driven sand, the spit closed off the Nemunas delta from the open sea, forming the Curonian Lagoon in the process. Only the northernmost half of the 97-kilometre-long spit falls within the territory of Lithuania – the remainder belongs to Kaliningrad Province, part of German East Prussia until 1945, but now governed by the Russian Federation.

A sliver of land never more than 4km wide, the spit basically takes the form of an undulating line of huge, fifty-metre-high sand dunes, some looking starkly Saharan in their bareness, but most covered in a dense carpet of dark-green pines, stately silver birches and skinny, soil-starved limes. It's an impermanent landscape, with sea breezes driving sand up the western slopes of the dunes and over the other side, causing a gradual eastward drift of the spit's central ridge. Deforestation in the seventeenth century sped this process up so much that villages had to be moved from one generation to the next as homes were progressively swallowed up by the sands. Systematic replanting of pines and grasses over the last century or so has served to stabilize the dunes. On the eastern side of the spit lies a scattering of villages that traditionally relied on the fish-teeming waters of the lagoon for a living (nowadays the main industry is tourism), while the western shore is one long, silky stretch of beach.

The whole of the Lithuanian part of the spit has been placed under the protective wing of the **Curonian Spit National Park** (Kuršių nerijos nacionalinis parkas) in

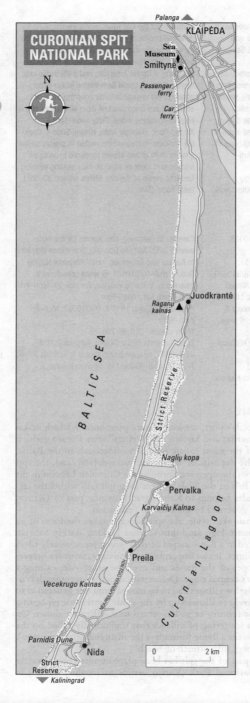

CURONIAN SPIT NATIONAL PARK

N

Palanga

KLAIPĖDA

Sea Museum
Smiltynė

Passenger ferry

Car ferry

Juodkrantė

Raganų kalnas

B A L T I C   S E A

Strict Reserve

Naglių kopa

Pervalka

Karvaičių Kalnas

C u r o n i a n   L a g o o n

Preila

Vecekrugo Kalnas

Parnidis Dune

406

Nida

0   2 km

Strict Reserve

Kaliningrad

order to preserve the pines-and-dunes environment and ensure the survival of the species for whom it is home. The northern and central parts of the promontory are nesting grounds for herons and cormorants, while some of the deeper forests still harbour a handful of elk, an animal described by novelist and local holiday-cottage-owner Thomas Mann – clearly an awestruck city boy – as "a cross between cow, horse, deer, camel and buffalo, and with very long legs". Although most of the park is accessible to the public, some areas of dune have been designated "strict reserves", closed to visitors in order to prevent erosion of the dunes.

The best way to explore the spit is by bike or on foot: there's an extensive network of **forest trails** and surfaced **cycle paths**, as well as plenty of signboards with maps – the visitors' centre at the northern end of the spit (see below) can help with further information.

Ferries from Klaipėda arrive at **Smiltynė** at the northern end of the spit, the site of a hugely popular aquarium. However, the best of Neringa's scenery lies well south of here, around neat, timber-built resort villages like **Juodkrantė** and most of all **Nida**, which allows access to the most spectacular of the dunes. Although Nida is do-able as a day-trip from Klaipėda, it makes sense to stick around – the village has an invigorating, Vilnius-by-the-sea feel in summer, and the surrounding sands-and-pines landscape is a joy to explore.

Getting there and information

Getting to Neringa involves taking one of two **ferries** from

Klaipėda. The smaller one, mainly for foot passengers (1.50Lt), departs from the Old Castle Port (Senasis pilies uostas), just outside the Old Town, every half-hour. A larger ferry (and the one to aim for if you're taking a car) leaves from the New Port (Naujasis uostas), 2km south of the Old Town, operating hourly in winter and half-hourly in summer (foot passengers 1.50Lt; cars 20Lt). The ferry from the Old Castle Port arrives in Smyltinė, handy for both the Sea Museum (see below) and the bus stop – from here frequent **minibuses** run the length of the spit as far as Nida. The ferry from the New Port ends up a good 2km south of Smyltinė, convenient if you're driving straight down the spit. All visitors who come with a vehicle have to pay a national park **entrance fee** (20Lt/car, 7Lt/motorbike) at the road barrier 5km south of Smyltinė – keep the receipt for the return journey. The speed limit on the spit is 40km/hr.

The **National Park Visitors' Centre**, just north of the passenger ferry landing at Smiltynės plentas 11 (May–Sept Tues–Sun 10am–6pm; ☎8-46/402257, ⓦwww .nerija.lt), offers rudimentary **maps** and friendly advice on how to explore the spit; otherwise the tourist office in Nida (see p.408) is your best source of information.

Smiltynė

Lying a ten-minute ferry hop across the lagoon from Klaipėda, **SMILTYNĖ** is not really a settlement as such, more of a rambling park, popular with Klaipėda folk as a recreation venue. Running along its eastern side is a promenade offering views of the merchant ships and loading cranes that crowd Klaipėda's port, while over to the west lies the start of the Curonian Spit's unbroken line of beach. Ranged between the two there's a respectable clutch of attractions, beginning with the **Fishermen's Farmstead** (Žvejų sodyba; free), just north of the ferry landing, a quaint ensemble of nineteenth-century, wooden buildings – a reed-roofed dwelling house (occasionally open) accompanied by a sauna, a fish-smoking shed and a potato cellar.

Another five minutes' walk north, a gun battery built to beef up Klaipėda's defences in the mid-nineteenth century provides the setting for the Lithuania's most visited tourist attraction, the so-called **Sea Museum** (Jūrų muziejus; May–Sept Tues–Sun 11am–7pm; Oct–April Sat & Sun 11am–6pm; 10Lt; ⓦwww.juru.muziejus.lt) – which is really an aquatic zoo with a few history-related displays tacked on for good measure. Resembling an enormous red-brick doughnut and surrounded by huge earthen ramparts, the former fortress is now garrisoned by all manner of water-dwellers – personable penguins and seals loll around in the inner moat, while the circular central enclosure accommodates everything from Black Sea sturgeon to piranha fish. Across the central courtyard, a display of nautical artefacts and model ships is less memorable than the atmospherically lit powder magazines in which it is housed. In summer, sea lions perform in an outdoor pool round the back of the main building – you'll need a separate ticket for the show (12Lt). An eternally popular annexe to the Sea Museum is the **Dolphinarium** (May–Sept shows at noon, 2pm & 4pm; Oct–April shows at noon & 3pm; 15Lt), a modern circular building next door to the fortress where Black Sea bottlenose dolphins are put through the hoops. Even if you don't arrive in time for a show, you can observe the dolphins swimming around from a large below-water-level window in the Dolphinarium's entrance hall. To get to Smiltynė's delicious, fine-sand **beach**, simply follow paths through the forest just west of the ferry landing – you'll hit it in ten minutes.

Juodkrantė and beyond

Fourteen kilometres south of Smiltynė, **JUODKRANTĖ** was the favoured resort of well-to-do Germans from Klaipėda during the inter-war years and still has an air of gentility about it, with its trim, big-balconied, wooden villas, well-tended gardens and seafront park. At the southern end of the resort are a few rows of wooden fishermen's houses, watched over by a red-brick church, the strange, twisting spire of which looks as if it was designed to drill holes in the sky. Immediately opposite, a **gallery** (Tues–Sun 10am–6pm; free) belonging to the Lithuanian Art Museum hosts exhibitions of art and photography in a fragrant, pine-beamed interior.

From the centre of Juodkrantė a path winds up onto **Witches' Hill** (Raganų kalnas), a forested ridge dotted with wooden sculptures made by contemporary folk artists from all over the country and depicting sprites and demons from Lithuanian folklore. There are lots of sculptures of the sea goddess Neringa and her fisher-lover, although the most attention-grabbing work on display is a muscular St George slaying an intricately chiselled, fish-scaled dragon. Trails lead on further into the forest, continuing over the ridge towards the spit's western coast, where – after a good twenty-minute walk – you'll find Juodkrantė's **beach**.

The coast around Juodkrantė is famous for being one of the prime Baltic nesting grounds for **cormorants**; they gorge themselves on the Curonian Lagoon's marine life – much to the chagrin of local fishermen.

Practicalities

Smiltynė–Nida **minibuses** pick up and drop off on Rėzos, Juodkrantė's single main street. The **tourist office** is at no. 54, inside the *Ąžuolynas* **hotel** (⑦8-469/53310, ⓦwww.hotelazuolynas.lt; ⑤), a concrete place with comfy en suites in four large accommodation blocks and a small swimming pool on site. More intimate is the *Kuršių Kiemas*, Miško 11 (⑦8-469/53004, ⓦwww.neringatravel.lt; ❸), a nicely renovated old building near the northern entrance to the village, offering neat en suites with TV and minibar. The smartest place to stay is the *Vila Flora*, at the northern end of the village at Kalno 7A (⑦8-469/53024, ⓔvilaflora@takas.lt; ⑥), a modern building in the style of a traditional, wooden villa, with smart rooms. There are also a number of private rooms (❷) available around town, bookable through the tourist office.

The *Vila Flora* boasts the most varied **restaurant** menu, although the locally caught fish on offer at *Žvejonė*, Rėzos 30, tastes all the better for being served up in a delightful flower-filled garden. You can tuck into cheap Lithuanian staples like *cepelinai* at *Pamario takas*, Rėzos 42.

South of Juodkrantė

Beyond Juodkrantė the southbound road heads inland and follows the spit's central wooded spine. Parking spaces have been strategically placed along the route so you can pull over and admire the tawny-coloured dunes off to the left; most of these fall within one of the national park's strict reserves, so you can't actually get up close to them on foot.

After 15km, a turn-off heads east to the village of **PERVALKA**, a sleepy place consisting of a few (largely modern) holiday cottages and the odd café, and also marking the northern end of the Nida–Preila–Pervalka cycle route (see p.411).

Nida

The ancient fishing village of **NIDA**, 35km or so south of Smiltynė, has been the main focus for tourism on the spit ever since the mid-nineteenth century, when the first German visitors were drawn here by the promise of unspoilt seaside rusticity. The Germans were quick to rediscover the place in the early 1990s, and it's now the country's most cosmopolitan resort, attracting a healthy cross-section of Lithuanians and outsiders. Despite some ugly Soviet architecture at its heart, it still possesses an impressive stock of traditional timber houses, many of their reed-thatched roofs sporting the wooden, horse-head crosspieces characteristic of Curonian homes.

Arrival and information

Minibuses arrive at the tiny bus station in the centre of the village. The **tourist office**, inside the cultural centre on the main square at Taikos 4 (mid-June to mid-Sept Mon–Sat 10am–8pm, Sun 10am–5pm; mid-Sept to mid-June Mon–Fri 9am–1pm & 2–6pm, Sat 10am–3pm; ⑦8-469/52345, ⓦwww.visitneringa.com), can help with all kinds of information.

Numerous adhoc establishments offering **bike rental** (*dviračių nuoma*) sprout up in the centre during the summer.

△ Traditional fisherman's cottage, Nida

Accommodation

The tourist office can book you a **room** in a private house (②) for a 6Lt fee. Litinterp in Klaipėda (see p.400) can also book rooms in advance, but at a slightly higher rate.

Nidos kempingas (Nida Camping; Taikos 45A ☎8-469/52045, ⓦwww .kempingas.lt) is a pine- and birch-shaded **campsite** 2km southeast of Nida, near the main Smyltinė–Kaliningrad road and handily placed for the beaches on the west side of the spit. There's an on-site café, sauna, swimming pool and limited cooking and clothes-washing facilities; tent 10Lt, car 10Lt, camper van 15Lt. It also offers apartments (see below).

Hotels

Auksinės Kopos Kuverto 17 ☎8-469/52212. A large, modern building near the main road with its own swimming pool, offering rather basic en-suite rooms with TV. Handy for the beaches on the western side of town. Open May–Oct. ⑤

Banga Pamario 2 ☎8-469/51139 and 8-686 08 073, ⓦwww.nidosbanga.lt. A thatched-roof cottage with fairytale exterior and some simple but comfortable en-suite rooms inside. Top-floor apartments feature kitchenette, sitting room and fabulous lunette windows. Breakfast is included. Two- to four-person apartments from 350Lt, standard doubles ④

Miško namas Pamario 11–2 ☎8-469/52290 and ☎687 36 902, ⓦwww.miskonamas.com. Charming B&B in a traditional-style house on the northern fringes of the centre. Rooms come in subdued browns and greens; those on the top floor boast sloping ceilings and skylight windows, while most of those lower down have small balconies. ④

Naglis Naglių 12 ☎8-469/51124 and ☎8-699 33 682, ⓦwww.naglis.lt. Waterfront cottage decked

out in Nida's traditional maroon and blue colour scheme, containing some small but stylish en-suite doubles in the attic and a brace of bright, kitchenette-equipped apartments, one of which boasts fireplace and sauna. Breakfast available. Two- to four-person apartments from 350Lt, standard doubles ⑥

Nidos kempingas Taikos 45A ☎8-469/52045, ⓦwww.kempingas.lt. Luxurious two- or four-person apartments above the registration building of Nida's campsite (see above), all boasting swanky minimalist decor and modern bathrooms with tub. Some have a groovy split-level layout, others boast small balconies; a limited number come with kitchenette. Breakfast available for an extra charge. Apartments 180–460Lt depending on size.

Vandėja Naglių 17 ☎8-469/52742 and ☎8-614 67 197, ⓦwww.forelle.com. Centrally located family house set in a neat garden, offering bright and spacious en suites with satellite TV. Breakfast available on request. ⑤

Vila Elvyra Purvynės 2 ☎8-469/51152 and ☎8-620 64 060, ⓔvarunas.balcytis@gmail.com.

B&B in an attractive two-storey lagoon-side house at the northern end of Nida, about twenty minutes' walk from the centre. Choose between compact en-suite doubles and roomy apartments with lounge space. May–Sept only. Two- to four-person apartments from 300Lt, standard doubles ❹

The village

Some of the prettiest of Nida's houses are to be found just south of the main square, along narrow streets like Lotmiškio and Naglių. Here you'll find neat lines of wooden fishermen's houses, attractively painted in a variety of maroons, yellows and blues, their tidy, picket-fenced gardens crammed with flowers and fruit trees. One of the best examples, at Naglių 4, is now the **Fishermen's Ethnographic Homestead** (Žvejo etnografinė sodyba; June to mid-Sept daily 10am–6pm; mid-Sept to May Mon–Sat 10am–5pm; 4Lt), a plain, wooden structure set end-on to the road. The reconstructed interior provides a fascinating insight into the domestic life of Curonian fishermen in the nineteenth century. Oblong dwellings such as this were designed to accommodate two households, one at each end, each with their own kitchen, sitting room and bedroom. Curonian families were very much into colour-coordinated interiors if the furnishings on display here are anything to go by – wooden chests, wardrobes and bedsteads are painted the same bright blue as many of the house exteriors. Walls were left bare except for uplifting religious mottoes, neatly embroidered and framed.

East of the main square lies Lithuania's most fashionable yacht marina, the starting point of a seaside path that heads north past well-tended lawns and flowerbeds. Cutting inland and ascending Pamario gatvė takes you towards Nida's ruddy-coloured **parish church**, its bell tower sprouting ten mini-pinnacles resembling pine cones. The nearby graveyard contains a fair number of traditional wood-carved crosses (*krikštai*) many fashioned into abstract, thistle-like forms, a symbol of rebirth that goes back to pre-Christian times.

Five minutes' walk further up Pamario, the **Neringa History Museum** at no. 53 (Neringos istorijos muziejus; June to mid-Sept daily 10am–6pm; mid-Sept to May Mon–Sat 10am–5pm; 4Lt) contains a colourful and well-labelled local-history display. Scale models of traditional water-borne craft include the sail-powered sledges once used for crossing the lagoon in winter, and the *kurėnas*, a fishing boat particular to the region, characterized by a tall, oblong main sail and big lee boards like the gills of a fish. There's a large collection of the metal weather vanes that have decorated local fishing vessels ever since 1844, when new laws specified that each boat had to display a sign showing which of the Curonian fishing villages it belonged to. Originally this consisted of a simple two-colour design rather like a flag, but with time, fishermen began to add pictorial details – shapes representing buildings, trees, lighthouses, churches and horses – hence the highly stylized weather vanes still made today. Looking more like something out of a horror film are the inter-war photographs of villagers laying nets to catch crows, swarms of which descended on the spit every autumn. Tasting a bit like wild pigeon, the crows were prized as a delicacy by the locals – and giving a crow as a present was considered a special way of saying thank you. Once caught, they were killed by administering a swift bite to the neck. You might be relieved to know that crow no longer forms part of the local diet.

Thomas Mann's House

Carrying on up Pamario and bearing right into Skruzdynės brings you after ten minutes to the most famous of Nida's wooden houses, **Thomas Mann's House**, at no. 17 (Tomo Manno namelis; May–Sept Tues–Sun 10am–6pm; 4Lt), a thatched cottage of almost fairytale loveliness, where the writer spent his summers from 1930 to 1932. The rather disappointing museum within contains a few photos of Mann and family and various editions of his books, including *The Story of Jacob* (1933), and *Young Joseph* (1934), both of which were largely written here. Mann first visited Nida in 1929 on an excursion from the nearby summer resort of Rauschen (now Svetlogorsk in Kaliningrad Province), and was immediately enchanted by the landscape and its people –

3.3 LITHUANIA | Western Lithuania

whom he described as "not exactly good-looking, but friendly". He engaged Klaipėda architect H. Reissmann to build a summer house straight away, ready for his return the following year. When he arrived to take up residence in July 1930, the locals lined the streets to greet him, an event recorded by press cuttings on show in the museum.

The dunes

The highlight of any trip to Nida are the **dunes**, which begin just south of the village. From the southern end of Naglių a shore path runs to a flight of wooden steps that forges up past wild raspberry bushes onto the shoulder of the fifty-metre-high **Parnidis Dune** (Parnidžio kopa), one of the biggest that Neringa has to offer. The summit is marked by a modern **sundial** in the form of an imposing obelisk decorated with rune-like inscriptions. Struck from its pedestal by lightning in 1999, it has been only partially reconstructed, and now looks like the mysterious remnant of some ancient civilization.

From the summit extends a rippling sandscape of semolina-coloured dunes, their flanks mottled with patches of grey-green moss and purplish thistle flowers. The eastern, lagoon-facing sides of the dunes are roped off in order to prevent subsidence, although you can strike out southwards for about 1.5km before coming up against the boundary of a strict nature reserve – a glorious pale-sand wilderness into which you are not permitted to venture, stretching as far as the Russian border some 2km beyond.

You can walk west from the sundial – or indeed take any of the paths leading westwards from Nida – to reach the **beach** on the spit's far shore, where you'll find a handful of food-and-drink shacks. It's a glorious place for a stroll even on bad-weather days, when gunmetal seas roll in under glowering skies. Running parallel to the strand and handy for exploring the woods just behind the beach is a north–south foot- and cycle-path.

The Nida–Preila–Pervalka cycle route

One of the best ways to explore the Curonian Spit's tranquil woodland is to follow the **Nida–Preila–Pervalka cycle route** (dviračių takas Nida-Preila-Pervalka), a sixteen-kilometre-long asphalted path that leads through the mixed birch and pine forest on the eastern side of the spit. As popular with walkers as it is with cyclists, it provides access to a wonderfully serene landscape, with numerous opportunities for climbing up and down trail-side dunes.

Leaving Nida via the *Skalva* hotel at the northern end of the village, the path forges inland for the first few kilometres, running beneath the forest-blanketed western slopes of the spit's central ridge. After about 5km you'll catch sight of Vecekrugo kalnas – at 67m high, the park's highest point. The pine-covered dune gets its name ("Old Pub Hill") from an inn that used to stand at its foot, catering to a local population whose villages have long since vanished under the sands. After another 3km the trail rejoins the shores of the lagoon, running alongside the reedy Preila Bay before entering Preila itself, a single street of lush-lawned, seaside suburbia, harbouring a couple of simple snack bars. From here it's another 6km to Pervalka, passing another lofty dune, Karvaičių kalnas, en route. Somewhere under the dune's western slopes lies the village of Karvaičiai, abandoned in 1797 owing to shifting sands, but still very much remembered as the birthplace of Liudvikas Rėza (1776–1840), the Königsberg-educated poet and publisher who kick-started the process of cultural revival in Lithuania Minor.

Eating, drinking and entertainment

For **eating and drinking**, try the wonderfully relaxing garden café of the *Sena sodyba*, Naglių 6, which serves up omelettes, pancakes and potato dishes in a miniature orchard. A modern pavilion with a thatched-roof makeover, *Ešerinė*, Naglių 2, offers less in terms of atmosphere, but has a satisfying range of main courses and is an enjoyable place for a beer. *Seklyčia*, Lotmiško 1, is Nida's fanciest eatery, a big wooden villa with lots of seating both inside and out; the fish dishes are excellent and you can still get cheap staples like *cepelinai*. *Senasis uostas*, Naglių 18a, is a bit lacking in character but serves up good grilled and pan-fried fish.

A handful of kiosks near the bus station and on the waterfront serve smoked fish (*rūkyta žuvis*), very much a local speciality and well worth trying. The fish is usually served whole, complete with head and bones, and you are supposed to eat it with your fingers. An appealingly tangy snack, it makes the perfect accompaniment to a glass or two of beer.

The cultural centre on the main square hosts films and concerts throughout the summer season, and serves as the main venue for the **Thomas Mann Cultural Festival** in July (Ⓦwww.mann.lt), featuring solo recitals, chamber music and Mann-related literary symposia.

The Nemunas delta

Roughly opposite Nida, on the eastern side of the Curonian Lagoon, the River Nemunas divides into several branches before emptying into the sea. The lush green flatlands of the delta are prone to seasonal flooding, producing a distinctive landscape of water meadows (grazed by dairy herds when dry), bogs and riverside marsh. Rich in fish and insects, the delta supports a large population of white storks, cranes and cormorants, and is an important stopping-off point for migrating species in September and October – when literally millions of birds pass along the shores of the Curonian Lagoon. The **Nemunas Delta Regional Park** (Nemuno deltos regioninis parkas; Ⓦwww .nemunodelta.lt) operates a small visitors' centre near Rusnė in the middle of the delta, while the ornithological station at **Ventės ragas** on the northern side of the delta provides great views of the Curonian Lagoon and its wildlife. The inland market town of **Šilutė** is the delta's main service centre, and there is plenty in the way of B&B accommodation in local villages. Public transport is meagre, so you'll need a car or long-distance-cycling stamina to get around.

Šilutė, Ventės ragas and around

Fifty-five kilometres south of Klaipėda, the pleasant one-street town of **ŠILUTĖ** is home to the regional **tourist office**, Lietuvininkų 10 (Mon–Fri 8am–noon & 1–5pm; Ⓣ8-441/77785, Ⓦwww.siluteinfo.lt), which sells maps of the region and can book you into B&B **accommodation** (❷) in local farmsteads throughout the delta.

Heading northwest from Šilutė via the village of Kintai brings you after 19km to **Ventės ragas** ("Ventė Horn"), a stubby peninsula which protrudes over the northern side of the delta. Ventės ragas is the perfect place from which to observe the comings and goings of the Curonian Lagoon's birdlife, and has become something of a cult destination among birdwatchers as a result. An **ornithological research station** (*ornitologijos stotis*) has been operating here since 1901, employing huge funnel-shaped nets to capture migrating birds – which are then tagged by researchers and released. The ornithological station holds a small display of stuffed birds (daily 10am–5pm; 1Lt), and allows access to the neighbouring lighthouse for a sweeping panorama of the Lagoon. Whether you're interested in birds or not, fine views of the Curonian Spit to the west more than justify the trip.

The Ventės ragas area is a beautiful and restful place **to stay**, with the shore-side *Ventainė* tourist complex 3km to the north of the cape (Ⓣ8-441/68525 and 8-686 70490, Ⓦwww.ventaine.lt) offering a fully equipped **campsite** and an attractive small **hotel** (❹) with comfortable en-suite rooms and great lagoon views. The verandah of the *Ventainė*'s restaurant is the perfect place from which to observe the sun setting over the Spit. A further 2km northeast, the 🌿 *Sturmų švyturys* hotel (Ⓣ8-687 97 756 and Ⓣ8-650 29 420, Ⓦwww.sturmusvyturys.lt; ❺) is one of the most romantic spots on the Lithuanian coast, offering rooms with pine furnishings and nautical blue-and-white colour schemes – the family-sized triples and quads include child beds in the shape of fishing boats. The **restaurant** (open daily in summer, weekends in winter) serves up freshly-caught fish baked on an open grill.

Some 5km inland from Ventės ragas and accessible via gravel roads from Kintai, the village of **MINGĖ** straddles both banks of the (so far bridge-less) Minija River – locals still get around by boat, earning the place the unlikely sobriquet of "Lithuanian Venice". Providing you don't expect Mingė to live up to such comparisons it's an undeniably pretty spot, featuring some lovingly restored fishermen's houses and a busy little yacht marina.

Rusnė

Some 7km southwest of Šilutė lies the island of Rusnė, a croissant-shaped piece of lowland no more than 10km from north to south which is enclosed by the Curonian Lagoon on one side and the Atmata and Skilvutė branches of the Nemunas on the other. Made up of cow-grazed meadows and bird-infested marshes, Rusnė has bags of wild, untouched-by-modernity charm. Standing at the eastern edge of the island, the village of **RUSNĖ** boasts some lovely traditional timber houses, especially along either side of the Pakalnė River, the banks of which are popular with local strollers. There's plenty of **farmstead accommodation** (❶–❷) in and around the village; book through the tourist office in Šilutė (see opposite). The tiny settlement of Pakalnė, 5km beyond Rusnė village, boasts a small **Nemunas Delta Regional Park Visitors' Centre** (Lankytojų centras; ☎8-44158154; Mon–Thurs 8am–5pm, Fri 8am–3.45pm), where you can pick up maps of the island and ask directions to the birdwatching tower at the end of a track 4km to the north, the perfect vantage point from which to observe goings-on in the coastal reed-beds. On the riverside just beyond the Visitors' Centre, there's a **tent-pitching site** (*stovyklavietė*), equipped with simple earth toilets.

At the northern end of the island, the sleepy hamlet of **UOSTADVARIS** is the site of an attractively stumpy red-brick lighthouse, and a nineteenth-century pumping station built to serve Rusnė's irrigation channels. With bleak coastal marshes on either side, it's a fittingly atmospheric place at which to wind up your tour of the delta.

Palanga and around

A short drive up the coast from Klaipėda, **PALANGA** is Lithuania's favourite beach resort and summertime playground, a self-contained empire of ice cream and candy floss visited by everyone from bucket-and-spade-wielding families to drink-fuelled party animals. On summer evenings you can see all of them parading up and down the bar-lined central strip, Basanavičiaus.

This erstwhile fishing village was first developed as a resort by Polish-Lithuanian aristocrat Jozef Tyszkiewicz (1835–91), who invited the doyen of wooden architecture, Stanislaw Witkiewicz, to Palanga to build a Kurhaus, and though the building no longer stands, Witkiewicz's trademark style – all spindly balustrades, pointy gables and fanciful turrets – can still be seen in many of the town's older villas. Originally patronized by well-to-do Poles, Palanga became the resort of choice for Lithuanians after World War I; it was cheaper than Juodkrantė and Nida, which tended to be monopolized by the Klaipėda Germans.

Aside from the beach and the fast-paced nightlife, ample reason to visit is provided by the lush and leafy **Botanical Gardens**, laid out by Jozef Tyskiewicz's son Felix, and an absorbing **Amber Museum** in the Tyskiewicz Palace. Tyskiewicz's **Winter Garden** at nearby **Kretinga** is an easy half-day excursion from town.

Palanga is served by regular municipal **buses** from Klaipėda bus station, though these tend to stop at every minor halt en route; it's best to take one of the faster minibuses, also from Klaipėda bus station; these run from 7.30am to 10.30pm and depart when full. There's a handful of direct services from Vilnius and also four daily buses from and to Liepāja in Latvia (some of these are based in Kaliningrad, so destination boards will be in the Cyrillic script).

Arrival and information

Palanga's **bus station** is just off Vytauto gatvė, the main street running north–south through town. The **tourist office** (Mon–Fri 9am–1pm & 2–6pm; June–Sept also Sat

& Sun 9am–1pm & 2–4pm; ☏8-460/48822), at Kretingos 1, is right in the bus station forecourt.

Bikes can be hired from most hotels, whether you're a guest or not.

Accommodation

The tourist office can book you into a **private room** (❶). The Litinterp office in Klaipėda (see p.400) offers the same service, but charges slightly more (❷). If you're prepared to search yourself, you'll turn up rooms at even cheaper rates – there are plenty of *kambarių nuoma* ("rooms for rent") signs in the suburban streets northwest of the bus station; beware, though, that this can be a time-consuming business and not all hosts speak English.

A few unrenovated, Soviet-era hulks aside, Palanga is well stocked with modern, snazzily designed **hotels**. Owing to the resort's popularity, however, prices are high in peak season (June–Sept). Outside this period, rates may be thirty to fifty percent cheaper than those quoted below.

Infohotel Kretingos 52 ☏8-460/40011, ⓦwww.feliksas.lt. Functional but chic rooms in a contemporary, box-like building on the eastern approaches to town – but still only fifteen minutes' walk from the seafront. Rooms feature cheerful, bright-orange carpets; the larger rooms have fold-down sofas and can sleep four at a pinch. ❻

Kerpé Vytauto 76 ☎8-460/52379, ⓦwww
.kerpehotel.lt. Modern, medium-sized hotel offering
rooms with subtle, green-brown colour schemes,
contemporary furnishings and big windows. The
top-floor, split-level suites are perfect if you want
to spread yourself out. Standard rooms ⑤–⑥
depending on size, suites ⑥

Palanga Birutės alėja 60 ☎8-460/41414, ⓦwww
.palangahotel.lt. Elegant, crescent-shaped contemporary building near the sea, with rooms offering
bold modern furnishings, ample desk space, swish
bathrooms and balconies. The apartments on
the upper floors have invigorating treetop views.
Saunas (free in the mornings, 80–150Lt/hr afterwards), a small indoor pool and a heated outdoor
pool complete the picture. One room is adapted
for wheelchair-users. Standard doubles ⑦, deluxe
doubles from 800Lt, apartments from 1200Lt

Palangos Vétra Daukanto 35 ☎8-460/53032,
ⓦwww.palangosvetra.lt. Boasting a casino and
beauty centre on the ground floor, and saunas in the
basement, this hotel is perfect if you want a host of
holiday-resort facilities under one roof. The standard
rooms are bland but comfortable, but there are some
spectacular top-floor suites with balconies or bay
windows. Handily located right beside the Botanical
Gardens. Standard rooms ⑤, suites ⑥–⑦

Pušų Paunksnéje Dariaus ir Giréno 25 ☎8-
460/49080, ⓦwww.pusupunksneje.lt. An
apartment-hotel, with self-catering units suitable
for couples or families of three or four, owned
by basketball superstar Arvydas Sabonis. The
furnishings look as if they've come straight out
of an upmarket design magazine, and there's a
fully equipped gym at guests' disposal. The name
means "in the shade of the pines" – a reasonably
accurate description. Two-person apartments from
700Lt, four-person apartments from 800Lt.

Rąžé Vytauto 74 ☎8-460/48265, ⓔpalturas@is.lt.
Smallish B&B in a traditional timber-clad building,
offering homely en suites with TV and fridge, in a
supremely central location. Sauna and dipping pool
on site. ④–⑤

Vandenis Birutés alėja 47 ☎8-460/53530,
ⓦwww.vandenis.lt. The floorboards are a little
creaky at this twenty-room hotel but rooms are
bright and comfortable, with pale, creamy colours
predominating. Conveniently near the seafront,
and also home to one of Palanga's most popular
live music clubs, this hotel is ideal if you're not the
early-to-bed type. ④

Žalias namas Vytauto 97 ☎8-460/51231,
ⓦwww.zaliasnamas.lt. Cheerful B&B offering functional, neat en suites with TV, minibar and plenty of
wardrobe space. ④

Žydroji Liepsna Gintaro 36 ☎8-460/52441,
ⓦhotelzliepsna.lt. Medium-sized hotel occupying
a downtown block just north of the bus station.
Inside are spacious en suites decorated in bold colours, and some slightly frumpier fourth-floor rooms
which nevertheless have the added snugness of
sloping attic ceilings. ⑤

The Town

Palanga is made up of an easily navigable grid of broad avenues lined with lime trees
and pines. The main reference point is the pedestrianized **Basanavičiaus**, the resort's

△ Palanga beach

premier promenading ground, lined with a garish succession of amusement arcades, cafés and bars. At its western end is the simple, wooden **pier** (jūros tiltas), which stretches out to sea for almost half a kilometre – a stroll to the end of it is considered an essential part of the Palanga experience, and does at least provide you with a wide-angle view of the dune-backed beach, which stretches as far as the eye can see in either direction.

Once you've cast an eye over the seascape, you really need to make a beeline for Count Felix Tyszkiewicz's **Botanical Gardens**, a huge expanse of parkland that drapes itself across the southern end of town. Comprising clipped lawns, a myriad of different tree species and untamed forest, the park was laid out in 1897 by much-travelled Frenchman Edouard André, whose landscaped gardens can be seen in locations as diverse as Sefton Park in Liverpool and Evksinograd in Bulgaria. Over on the northeastern side, beyond a bow-shaped lake, the **Orangery** (Oranžerija; Tues–Sat 10am–6.30pm; 2Lt) houses a diverse collection of cacti, umpteen varieties of begonia and fig, and spectacular, exploding-firework bromelias. In the centre of the park, the Neoclassical **Tyszkiewicz Palace** hosts orchestral concerts on its colonnaded portico, and the tastefully refurbished interior harbours an enjoyable **Amber Museum** (Gintaro muziejus; Tues–Sun: June–Aug 10am–9pm; Sept–May 10am–5pm; ⓦwww.pgm.lt; 7Lt). It's a real tour de force, presenting the natural history of the substance in easily digestible style, before bombarding the visitor with an array of examples, as well as prehistoric insects trapped in pieces of amber, and roomfuls of amber jewellery.

Just southwest of the palace, a Christmas pudding-shaped mound known as **Birutė's Hill** (Birutės kalnas) is associated with the story of pagan princess Birutė, who was keeper of the hill's pagan shrine until forcibly abducted by her suitor, Grand Duke Kęstutis. It's said that Birutė's heart softened during the journey to Kęstutis's capital, Trakai (where they were married and Birutė gave birth to the future Grand Duke Vytautas the Great), but she returned to her hilltop shrine in Palanga after Kęstutis's death to keep pagan traditions alive in a country slowly turning to Christianity. Despite

Amber

According to Lithuanian folklore, amber came into being when king of the gods Perkūnas discovered that Jūrate, queen of the Baltic Sea, was having an affair with mortal fisherman Kastytis, despite being betrothed to water-god Patrimpas. Perkūnas showed his displeasure by zapping Jūrate's undersea palace with a thunderbolt, scattering numerous golden-coloured fragments across the Baltic.

The scientific version of events is rather different, maintaining that amber is essentially the fossilized resin of fifty-million-year-old pine trees, deposited on the Scandinavian side of the Baltic, and washed up on the shores of Lithuania, Latvia and Estonia. Taking the form of translucent, orange-brown nuggets, amber is usually clear, although it sometimes includes pine needles or insects caught in the resin before it solidified, allowing today's scientists the chance to study creepy-crawlies that may have died out millennia ago.

Valued as an ornament ever since Neolithic times, amber provided the ancient Baltic tribes with an important means of exchange, putting them at the supply end of trade routes that extended south to Rome, Byzantium and beyond. Although amber can still be found all along the Baltic coast, the richest deposits are in the Russian province of Kaliningrad – as much as ninety percent of the world's amber is thought to lie underneath the town of Yantarny, where it is mined on an industrial scale.

In all three Baltic states, charms, bracelets and necklaces made from amber remain the principal diet of souvenir stalls and gift shops. It can also be picked up in its raw form on Baltic beaches if you're lucky – fragments of the stuff are usually washed up after storms, when you'll see lots of people, gimlet-eyed, earnestly searching the sands.

Birutė's status as a standard bearer for the old gods, both she and Kęstutis are pictured in the stained glass that adorns the octagonal nineteenth-century chapel at the hill's summit. Following paths due south from here will bring you after ten minutes to a small and easily-missed **Jewish Genocide Memorial** (Žydų genocido vieta), marking the spot where the bulk of Palanga's Jews were murdered by German troops and Lithuanian auxiliaries in the summer of 1941. A simple granite block rears up out of the grass, bearing a Star of David and an inscription so worn that it's now illegible – the figure of 105 (the number of victims) is all that can be made out.

Returning from the park towards central Palanga along Vytauto gatvė will take you past the **Dr Jonas Šliūpas Memorial House** at no. 23 (Dr Jono Šliūpo memorialinis namas; Tues–Sun: June–Aug noon–7pm, Sept–May 11am–5pm; 2Lt), a charming nineteenth-century dwelling which honours one of Palanga's former mayors. The Šiauliai-born Dr Šliūpas began his political career in the 1890s with the clandestine distribution of Lithuanian-language magazine *Aušra*, an epoch-defining publication which brought together all the leading intellectuals of the day. Escaping Tsarist persecution, he emigrated to the US, where he began to canvass international support for the Lithuanian national movement. Old photographs recall the man and his times. Other snaps record the motorcade bearing a bemused Lord Baden Powell through the streets of Palanga in 1933 – as one of the few internationally known personalities who bothered to set foot in inter-war Lithuania, he was accorded the status of a visiting head of state.

A block west of here, at Daukanto 16, the **Antanas Mončys Museum** (Antano Mončio muziejus; Tues–Sun: June–Aug 10am–9pm; Sept–May noon–5pm; 6Lt) celebrates the work of émigré sculptor Mončys (1921–93) with an impressive display of his anguished, skeletal creations. The gallery space downstairs is dedicated to seasonal exhibitions by contemporary Lithuanian artists.

Eating and drinking

Pretty much everything you need is on or near the two main streets, Vytauto and Basanavičiaus; there are innumerable snack stalls selling hot dogs and *čeburekai*, and probably more pizzerias than in the rest of Lithuania put together. Many eating and drinking venues feature live music in summer – if you're lucky you'll be treated to classy jazz or pop-rock covers, although more often than not be prepared for Lithuanian techno or medallion-man balladeering.

1925 Basanavičiaus 4. Currently one of the classier places on the main strip: a little yellow wooden house with an intimate, if slightly ersatz, rustic-style interior. The Lithuanian food (with the accent more on meat than fish) is well presented and includes plenty of tasty salads; a good place for a civilized meal or drink. Daily 10am–midnight.

Feliksas Vytauto 116. Smart café-bar with dark-wood interior and street-side outdoor seating. Hosts frequent live jazz, easy-listening crooners or piano-tinklers on summer evenings. There's a full menu of main meals and plenty in the way of desserts, making it a popular stop-off for coffee-and-cake addicts in the afternoon. Sun–Thurs 8am–midnight, Fri & Sat 8am–2am.

Klubas Ramybė Vytauto 35 ⓦ www.klubasramybe .lt. A cosy bar which also functions as a mildly wacky cultural centre, this is a fantastic alternative to the mainstream café-restaurants lining Basanavičiaus. Year-round programme of live gigs, literary readings, film evenings and other events; check the website for schedule details. Daily 7pm–2am or later.

Palanga Birutės alėja 60. Upscale restaurant in the hotel of the same name, with floor-to-ceiling windows allowing you to commune with the surrounding pine trees. The international cuisine is first-rate (this is one place where you can order a Caesar Salad and not be disappointed), with exotic seafood and exquisite desserts standing out. Expensive but well worth the splash-out. Daily 11am–midnight.

Ramybė Vytauto 54. On the ground floor of the *Villa Ramybė* B&B, this café is slightly more laid-back than some of the places along Basanavičiaus, with jazzy sounds on the stereo and jazzy clientele laying into the scrumptious pancakes. Mon–Sat 9am–midnight, Sun 11am–11pm.

Vandenio muzikos klubas Birutės alėja 47. Café-restaurant occupying one wing of the *Vandenis* hotel (see p.415), specializing in jazz and the classier end of the pop-rock spectrum. Gigs take place almost every day in summer and at weekends during the rest of the year. 9am–2am or later.

Žuvinė Basanavičiaus 37A. A contemporary structure built in traditional Palanga style – with the exception that one side of the building is entirely glass, giving it the look of a huge dolls' house. Fish is the speciality here: choose from an array of delicious marinated-herring starters, baked halibut or cod, and grilled trout. With mains in the 35–40Lt

region, a meal here is an affordable treat. Daily noon–midnight.

Žvaigždė Daukanto 6. Ukranian-themed restaurant just off Basanavičiaus, with folksy textiles and equally folksy dishes – the borscht is something of a local lunchtime favourite. Also worth trying are the Ukranian *pelmeni* (pastry parcels) stuffed with potato, and the inevitable Chicken Kiev – accompanied by several varieties of *horilka* (Ukranian vodka). Daily 10am–10pm.

Kretinga

Occupying hilly ground 12km east of Palanga, **KRETINGA** is visited primarily for its Winter Garden and perhaps its monastic heritage. It has been one of the most important monastic centres in the country since 1602, when a community of Bernardines established themselves here under the patronage of the Grand Hetman (supreme military commander) of Lithuania, Jan Karol Chodkiewicz (Katkevičius in Lithuanian). Closed down by the communists in 1945, the monastery was re-founded by the Franciscans in 1993 and is flourishing once more. The lean-spired **monastery church of the Annunciation** still dominates the spacious town square, Rotušės aikštė.

Heading north past the church brings you after ten minutes to **Tyszkiewicz Palace** (Wed–Sun 10am–6pm; 4Lt), an outwardly undistinguished mansion built by Jozef Tyszkiewicz in the 1890s and now mostly occupied by an agricultural college. Nowadays, visitors flock here from their coastal hotels to see Jozef Tyszkiewicz's **Winter Garden**, a narrow, glass-enclosed chamber packed with palms, ferns, cacti and climbing plants, and overlooked by three elegant tiers of cast-iron balcony. The centrepiece at ground level is a fountain, surrounded by Greco-Roman pillars that have been encrusted with pebbles to provide a grotto effect. A handful of the palace's ground-floor rooms have been opened up for visitors: in the Blue Room a frieze of haughty-looking gryphons makes more of an impression than the collection of anonymous-looking nineteenth-century paintings, while the Red Room (which originally served as the music room), is filled with photographs of the whiskery Czech musicians imported by Jozef to play in his private brass band.

Practicalities

In summer, minibuses shuttle between Palanga bus station and Kretinga's main square from about 7.30am until 10.30pm. Regular services from Klaipėda use Kretinga bus station, just west of the centre on the opposite side of the river.

There's a small **tourist office** at Rotušės aikštė 3 (Mon–Fri 9am–5pm; ☎8-458/51341, ✉itc@kretinga.omnitel.net). Most people visit Kretinga as a day-trip from Palanga, but if you want to stay try the *Gelmė*, Žemaičių 3 (☎8-258/76931; ❶), just off the southeastern corner of Rotušės. *Pas Grafą*, the **café-restaurant** inside the Winter Gardens (open until 10pm), is a wonderful place to indulge in coffee, cakes or main-course meat or chicken dishes among the palm branches.

The Žemaitija National Park and around

Lying in a gently rolling landscape of glacier-smoothed uplands, 50km east of Palanga, the **Žemaitija National Park** is one of the country's smallest, most compact conservation areas, comprising the placid waters of Lake Plateliai and the belt of pastureland, forest and bog that surrounds it. Barely 5km from north to south and 2km across, Lake Plateliai is one of the more attractive bodies of water in this part of Lithuania – its eastern shore is smooth and sandy, while the western shore is broken up by a confusion of tree-smothered promontories. Around 30 percent of the park's territory is made up of agricultural land and 45 percent woodland – largely spruce and pine, although there's a sufficient number of deciduous trees (mostly birch, ash,

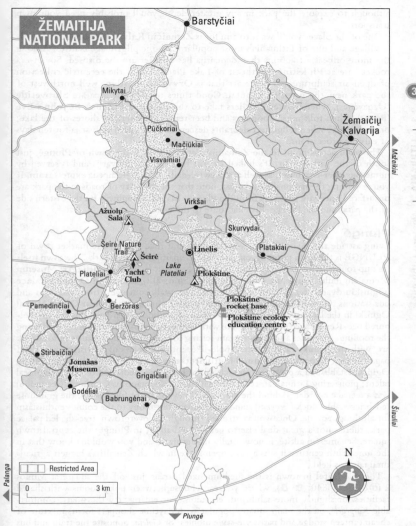

ŽEMAITIJA
NATIONAL PARK

Barstyčiai

Mikytai

Pūčkoriai

Mačiūkiai

Visvainiai

Žemaičių
Kalvarija

Virkšai

Skurvydai

Ažuolų
Sala

Platakiai

Šeirė Nature
Trail

Šeirė

Linelis

Yacht
Club

Lake
Plateliai

Plokštinė

Plateliai

Plokštinė
rocket base

Pamedinčiai

Beržoras

Plokštinė ecology
education centre

Stirbaičiai

Jonušas
Museum

Godeliai

Grigaičiai

Babrungėnai

Mažeikiai

Šiauliai

Palanga

Plungė

Restricted Area

0   3 km

N

alder and oak) to produce a much more varied range of greens than you might find elsewhere in Lithuania. Although there's only a handful of signed paths, the region's country lanes and dirt roads make it a wonderful environment for woodland walks and bike rides, while the waters of the lake are perfect for messing about in rowing boats or pedalos. In addition, there's a strong tradition of **folk art** in the area, with many a garden or driveway sporting a wayside shrine, often painted, with wooden figurines representing the Virgin, St George or other popular saints.

The village of **Plateliai** on the lake's western shore is the park's main service and information centre and most of the park's accommodation is in or near the village. You can access nearly all of Lake Plateliai's western side on foot or by bike from Plateliai, although to explore the park in any greater depth you'll probably need your own transport.

One of the places you'll want to aim for is **Žemaičių Kalvarija**, a blissfully bucolic village and one of Lithuania's most popular Catholic pilgrimage centres. Among the more offbeat attractions that Žemaitija has to offer are the disused, Soviet-era rocket base at **Plokštinė**, southeast of Lake Plateliai, and the eccentric collection of open-air sculpture and naive art that is **Orvydas's Garden**, well northwest of the park near the town of Salantai. Good times to visit the area are **Shrovetide** (Užgavėnės), when masked revellers take to the streets of Plateliai; **St John's Eve** (Rasos), when folk music, bonfires and beer tents take over the shores of the lake; or **early July**, when religious celebrants descend on Žemaičių Kalvarija for ten days of calvary processions.

The main access point to the Žemaitija National Park is the town of **Plungė**, just south of the park border. It's linked by **bus** to Žemaičių Kalvarija and is served by numerous inter-city buses, as well as the twice-daily Vilnius–Klaipėda express **train**. If you're visiting the national park by car, note that the majority of roads in the park are unsurfaced once you get away from the Plungė–Mažeikiai highway on the eastern side of the park, and the Plungė–Plateliai route to the west.

Plungė

Lying astride the main Klaipėda–Šiauliai rail and road routes, the market town of **PLUNGĖ** is the main jumping-off point for Žemaitija National Park. The town itself isn't up to much, but it's worth making time for a visit to the **Žemaitija Art Museum** (Žemaičių dailės muziejus; Wed–Sun 10am–5pm; 2Lt), housed in **Oginski Palace** (Oginskių dvaras) on Dariaus ir Girėno, a short walk southwest from the train and bus stations. Oginski Palace was built for Polish-Lithuanian aristocrat Count Michał Oginski in the late nineteenth century. Set amid landscaped gardens, this creamy-coloured neo-Renaissance pile – complete with Greco-Roman-style statues perched along the roofline – provides a suitably elegant setting for some superb examples of local folk art, with tree trunks carved, totem pole-like, into likenesses of Christian saints and pagan deities. A roomful of musical instruments recalls the days when keen arts patron Oginski established a private music school in the palace, dedicated to nurturing local talent; pioneering Lithuanian composer Mikalojus Konstantinis Čiurlionis (see p.366) was a teenage boarder. Behind the palace, and beyond a lily-filled pond, the grandiose red-brick stable block (*žirgynas*) stands in eloquent testimony to the count's enthusiasm for all things equine. Once you've strolled through the overgrown, tree-shaded palace park, there's not a great deal else to get excited about in Plungė: the central town square, Senamesčio aikštė, is now totally modernized, and you wouldn't know that in the nineteenth century it was a vast, open space in which Žemaitija's biggest agricultural fair was held.

The sole **hotel** in town is the medium-sized *Beržas*, just off the square at Minios 2 (☏8-218/56840; ❶–❸), where you can choose between poky rooms with shared facilities, or slightly more salubrious en suites. For **eating**, try the smart, comfortable *Katpėdėlė*, on the main square, popular with daytime shoppers for its mixture of cheap canteen stodge and patisserie-style nibbles; or *Galera*, opposite the train and bus stations, which doles out pork-and-potato standards and decent beer, and becomes a late-opening disco-bar at weekends.

Plateliai and around

Twenty kilometres north of Plungė, the lakeside village of **PLATELIAI** revolves around a sleepy main square. Just to the south is the wooden parish church dating from 1744, its freestanding bell tower resembling a fortress or a fire-station lookout. Behind the church, a small park surrounds a venerable tree known as **Witch's Ash** (Raganos uosis) – with a girth of 7m, it's thought to be Lithuania's stoutest example of the species. Across the road stands a beautifully restored **Granary** (Dvaro svirnas; ask the National Park Information Centre about access), now used for seasonal art exhibitions and a permanent display of local crafts, including a veritable crowd of wood-carved saints and examples of the devilish masks worn by Shrovetide revellers.

North of the main square, a surfaced road veers down towards the lakeside, where the Yacht Club (Jachtklubas) rents out **rowing boats** and pedalos (10Lt/hr); it's well worth venturing out onto the water to savour the superb landward views of the wooded bays and peninsulas that characterize the lake's western shore. North of the Yacht Club lies an enchanting area of virgin forest traversed by the **Šeirė Nature Trail** (Šeirės gamtos takas), a five-kilometre-long, figure-of-eight circuit whose starting point is marked by a national park information board on the Yacht Club access road, about 500m back from the lake. The trail passes through dark, dense forest before bridging a section of Gaudupis Bog (Gaudupio pelkė), a squelchy expanse of mosses punctuated by the odd stunted pine, and culminating at Piktežeris, a beautiful, spruce-encircled lake, marking the northernmost extent of the trail.

From the southern end of Plateliai, it's an easy two-kilometre walk to the next village, **BERŽORAS**, site of another eighteenth-century wooden **church**, resembling an enormous stable with wonky crosses perched on its roof. Just east of the village lies a small **beach**, picturesquely situated in a bay between the densely wooded Kreiviškių and Auksalės peninsulas. Southwest from Beržoras a dirt road leads across undulating pastures to the hamlet of **GODELIAI**, 5km distant, where local couple Regina and Justinas Jonušas have established a **Museum of Folklore and Ethnography** (Tautodailės ir etnografijos muziejus; enquire at National Park Information Centre about opening times; donation requested) in their farmstead. The main house holds examples of Justinas's own wood sculptures, as well as innumerable other pieces he's salvaged from decaying wayside shrines, while a barn across the way is packed with all manner of agricultural tools, wardrobes, hatboxes and handbags salvaged from local households.

Practicalities

The **National Park Information Centre**, on Plateliai's main square at Didžioji 8 (May–Aug Mon–Fri 8am–5pm, Sat 9am–5pm; Sept–April Mon–Fri 8am–noon & 1–5pm; ☎8-448/49337, ⊛www.zemaitijosnp.lt), sells maps, dishes out advice on what to see in the park and rents bikes (4Lt/hr). In addition, it can book **rooms** in local farmhouses (❶), most of which are in Plateliai or in the nearby village of Beržoras, and also runs the **hostel**-style *Dvaro svetainė* (35Lt), 200m south of the square at Didžioji 19. *Šaltinelis*, just north of the village on the way to the Yacht Club, is a **B&B** with plain but comfortable rooms. A step up in terms of comfort, 2km south of Plateliai in Beržoras, ⚒ *Marija Straukienė* (☎8-448/49152, 698/03485 or 612/74973; ❸) has a lakeside ensemble of reed-thatched **holiday houses** with ultra-swish, hard-floored interiors – you can opt for a double room (❷) or an entire house (❹) – and guests can rent bikes. Further afield (and a good 10km from Plateliai by road), the *Hotel Linelis*, on the opposite shore of the lake (☎8-448/49422; ❷), offers a choice between modernized rooms with pristine bathrooms and dinky balconies, or Soviet-era en suites with lino floors and weird wallpaper, and there's both a restaurant and a sandy beach on site – to get there, take the road to Žemaičių Kalvarija and turn right at the northeastern shoulder of the lake, when you see the sign for "Poilsiavietė".

If you don't mind rough **camping**, there's a handful of designated sites around Lake Plateliai where you can pitch tents and light fires – a national park warden calls round every day or so to empty rubbish bins and collect fees (5Lt for tent and vehicle). The nearest site to Plateliai is the *Šeirė stovyklavietė*, just north of the Yacht Club; also within striking distance is the *Ažuolų sala* site, 3km north –an idyllic lakeside spot well signed off the road. Over on the opposite side of the lake, the *Plokštinė* site occupies a part-sandy, part-forested spot, 2km south of *Hotel Linelis*.

For **eating and drinking**, try *Senas Ąžuolas* on Plateliai's main square, which has a full range of soups, potato pancakes and meaty main courses, and is also a reasonable place to drink, while *Šašlykinė*, a pavilion in the forest just off the Yacht Club access road, does a reasonable line in Caucasian-style, skewer-grilled kebabs.

Plokštinė rocket base

It's perhaps not surprising that the Soviet authorities should consider the sparsely populated wilderness of forests and bogs in the **Plokštinė** area, southeast of Lake Plateliai, to be the perfect place to hide a rocket base. Built in 1962, the facility at Plokštinė was one of the first such silo sites in the Soviet Union, housing four nuclear missiles capable of hitting targets throughout western and southern Europe. Closed down in 1978 and left to rot for over three decades, the base has now been reopened to the public as the so-called **Militarism Exhibition** (Militarizmo ekspozicija; May–Aug tours daily at 9am, 11am, 1pm, 3pm & 5pm; 4Lt; Sept–April advance booking required; contact the National Park Information Centre). It's accessible via a dirt road which leaves the Plateliai–Plungė road just south of Beržoras – to register for a tour and pick up a guide, head first for the National Park Information Centre in Plateliai.

There's not much to see on the surface, save for an unwelcoming family of grey domes, and it's only on descending into the facility's subterranean areas that the size of the base becomes apparent: a seemingly endless sequence of concrete-floored, metal-doored rooms, passages and stairways. It's rather like exploring a cave system in which the showpiece cavern is one of the silos themselves – a vast, metal-lined cylindrical pit deep enough to accommodate 22m of slender, warhead-tipped rocket. Peering into the abyss from the maintenance gallery can be a numbing experience – especially when you consider that most similar silos around the world are still very much in working order.

Žemaičių Kalvarija

Marking the northeastern corner of the park, about 20km out from Plateliai, the attractive village of **ŽEMAIČIŲ KALVARIJA** consists of a twin-towered hilltop church surveying a greeny-yellow collage of wooden houses, haystacks and fields of horses. It's also one of the most important Catholic pilgrimage sites in the country, thanks to a three-and-a-half-centuries-old tradition of calvary processions, which draw thousands of celebrants every year between July 2 and July 12.

The village owes its prominence to Jerzy Tyszkiewicz, Bishop of Žemaitija, who in 1644 invited the Dominicans to establish a monastery and a school here. They brought with them an image of the Madonna, whose supposed prayer-answering powers soon transformed the settlement into the most popular shrine in Žemaitija. They also started the construction of nineteen calvary chapels around the village, forming a five-kilometre-long processional route that has been the focus of religious ritual ever since. During the communist period local party bosses organized free folk festivals during the procession season in the hope that they would divert popular attention away from Žemaičių Kalvarija – a strategy that never met with more than limited success. Nowadays, people from all over the country throng to the village to take part in formal processions led by banner-wielding ecclesiastics, or to embark on a private circuit of the chapels, often approaching each chapel on their knees as a sign of devotion and sacrifice.

Scattered throughout the village, many of the chapels look like barns or outhouses and some are only recognizable from the wrought-iron crosses on their roofs. The chapel interiors, decorated with scenes from the Passion, are almost invariably closed outside the procession season, but the padlocked structures still provide an excellent excuse for a round-the-village stroll. Most of the chapels are concentrated on the hillocks around the church – there's an especially attractive cluster near the town graveyard due west, and an outer loop of chapels dotting the cornfields just off the road to Barstyčiai to the northwest. Žemaičių Kalvarija's gleaming-white, nineteenth-century church is always closed outside prayer times, although the local priest might open it up to show you the much-revered image of the Virgin on the high altar.

Žemaičių Kalvarija is 2km off the main Plungė–Mažeikiai road. There are only two **buses** a day from Plateliai, but about seven daily Plungė–Mažeikiai services trundle past the turn-off – some enter the village to pick up and drop off. A small **Žemaitija National Park Information Centre** stands just south of the church at Alsėdžių 3 (usually summer Mon–Fri 9am–5pm; ☎8-448/43200), although it's sporadically

△ Žemaitija National Park

staffed and less well equipped than the main one in Plateliai. There's a rudimentary **café** in the cultural centre opposite the church, and a couple of food shops on the main street nearby.

The Orvydas Garden

Twenty-five kilometres northwest of Plungė on the Skuodas road and well outside the territory of the national park, the undistinguished country town of Salantai would be a mere dot on the map were it not for its proximity to the **Orvydas Garden** (Orvydų sodyba; daily dawn till dusk; donation requested), an open-air sculpture park that ranks among the most offbeat and eccentric art collections in the whole Baltic region. It's located 2km southwest of Salantai on the Plungė road and is served by the four daily Plungė–Salantai–Skuodas buses. The garden is on the farm of **Vilius Orvydas** (1952–92), a self-taught sculptor who specialized in the larger-than-life, tree-trunk-sized statues of religious and mythical subjects typical of Lithuanian folk art. He also collected graveyard crosses, religious sculptures from wayside shrines and Catholic-related folk art in order to save them from an atheistic Soviet regime that either had them destroyed or left them to decay where they were. Orvydas arranged these objects in his own garden, adding landscape features such as ponds, pathways and rocks carved with strange, rune-style signs. During the last years of the Soviet Union, the garden became a cult site among Lithuanian intellectuals who saw Orvydas's magpie activities as a sign of defiance; since independence, Orvydas has been acclaimed as an outstanding practitioner of naive, non-academic sculpture and landscape art – and you'll see coffee-table books devoted to the man and his garden in Vilnius bookshops.

Still a private garden owned by Orvydas's descendants, the site has none of the touches, such as labelling or logical ordering, that you might expect to find in a state-run collection. Strolling around the garden is certainly a strange experience: like the Hill of Crosses (see p.393), its power rests in its seemingly unplanned, cluttered nature, with the presence of a Soviet-era rocket and a World War II tank adding to the junkyard feel.

Travel details

Buses

Klaipėda to: Kaunas (9 daily; 2hr 30min–3hr); Palanga (minibuses; every 30min–1hr; 30min); Šiauliai (3 daily; 3hr); Šilutė (5 daily; 1hr 20min); Vilnius (12 daily; 4–5hr).
Nida to: Juodkrantė (8 daily; 30min); Kaunas (1 daily; 4hr); Smiltynė (8 daily; 45min); Vilnius (1 daily; 6hr).
Palanga to: Kaunas (5 daily; 3hr 45min); Klaipėda (minibuses; every 30min–1hr; 30min); Kretinga (minibuses; every 30min–1hr; 20min); Šiauliai (3 daily; 3hr); Vilnius (7 daily; 5hr).
Plateliai to: Plungė (Mon–Sat 6 daily, Sun 3 daily; 25min); Žemaičių Kalvarija (2 daily; 40min).
Plungė to: Klaipėda (5 daily; 1hr 40min); Kretinga (9 daily; 1hr); Palanga (4 daily; 1hr 25min); Plateliai (Mon–Sat 6 daily, Sun 3 daily; 25min); Salantai (4 daily; 40min); Šiauliai (3 daily; 1hr 40min).
Smiltynė to: Juodkrantė (8 daily; 15min); Nida (8 daily; 45min).

Trains

Klaipėda to: Kaunas (1 daily; 6hr 30min); Plungė (5 daily; 2hr); Šilutė (2 daily; 1hr 30min); Vilnius (2 daily; 5hr).

Plungė to: Klaipėda (5 daily; 2hr); Šiauliai (4 daily; 1hr); Vilnius (2 daily; 3hr).

Flights

Palanga to: Vilnius (1 weekly; 45min).

International buses

Klaipėda to: Kaliningrad (3 daily; 5hr); Liepāja (4 daily; 2hr); Rīga (2 daily; 5hr).
Palanga to: Kaliningrad (1 daily; 5hr 30min); Liepāja (4 daily; 1hr 30min); Rīga (2 daily; 4hr 30min).

International ferries

Klaipėda to: Arhus (1 weekly; 45hr); Gdańsk (1 weekly; 10hr); Karlshamm (6 weekly; 16hr); Kiel (3 weekly; 21hr); Sassnitz (3 weekly; 20hr).

International flights

Palanga to: Billund (5 weekly; 2hr 25min); Copenhagen (2 daily; 1hr 10min); Dublin (1 weekly; 3hr); Hamburg (1 daily; 2hr 20min); Oslo (3 weekly; 2hr 25min); St Petersburg (3 weekly; 1hr 40min).

Contexts

Contexts

History..427

Baltic folk music 445

Books 455

History

H
istory is a serious business in a region that has seen more than its fair
share of conquests, foreign occupations and hard-fought independence
struggles. While there is much that all three Baltic States have in common
– most notably the shared experience of Tsarist rule in the nineteenth
century and Soviet occupation in the twentieth – there are equally long periods
when Estonians, Latvians and Lithuanians have pursued widely diverging desti-
nies. The very expression "Baltic States" is itself merely a convenient geographical label of twentieth-century invention – under the surface of which lie three
emphatically different cultures.

Estonia

The history of Estonia begins in the tenth millennium BC at the close of the last
Ice Age, when the retreat of the glaciers finally made the region fit for human
habitation. It's not known who first settled the area, but by 3000 BC they had
been either assimilated or displaced by the ancestors of today's Estonians, a **Finno-
Ugric** people closely related to the Finns – and more distantly, the Hungarians.
The Estonians, together with related Finno-Ugric tribes such as the Livs (see
p.233), originally occupied a much larger territory than they do today, but were
pushed back by the arrival of the Baltic peoples (forerunners of today's Lithuanians and Latvians) after 2000 BC – and Estonia has been a more-or-less stable
ethnic unit ever since.

The early Estonians were farmers and fishermen, practising an animist religion
of which little is known. There weren't really any villages or towns until the tenth
century, when a tribal society emerged, presided over by chieftains ruling from
stockade forts.

The Christian conquest of Estonia

Contacts with the outside world were limited until the tenth century, when the
Vikings established trading posts on the northern coast and the emerging Russian
towns of Pskov and Novgorod began sending mercantile and military missions
to the southeast. In the early thirteenth century, land-hungry Western rulers
persuaded the pope to authorize a crusade against the pagan peoples of the Baltic
region, and with the German-based **Brotherhood of the Sword** (subsequently
the Livonian Order) given free reign to invade what is now Latvia, rights to northern Estonia were granted to **King Valdemar II of Denmark**. Valdemar sent an
army in 1219, founded the fortress town of Tallinn to serve as a base for future
expansion and went on to build castles at Rakvere and Narva. Meanwhile, the
Brotherhood of the Sword, well established in Rīga since 1201 and eager to prevent the Danes from becoming the dominant power in the region, expanded into
Estonia from the south.

Although the Estonians put up fierce resistance, they were no match for their
heavily armed, technically superior adversaries, and by the 1230s the Danes and
the Brotherhood had succesfully carved up the country betwen them. The locals
were forcibly **converted to Christianity** and their land divided up among a new
ruling class of knights and bishops. While towns like Tallinn and Tartu filled up
with German-speaking immigrants drawn by the region's mercantile potential, the

Estonians themselves remained on the land, obliged as serfs to work on the feudal estates carved out by their conquerors – a situation which was to remain largely unchanged until the nineteenth century.

Feudal exactions in the Danish-controlled north provoked the so-called **St George's Night Uprising** of 1343, when Estonian peasants went on a rampage of violence, massacring landowners and burning monks in their monasteries. Worried by the cost of pacifying the countryside, the Danes sold all their possessions in northern Estonia four years later to the Brotherhood of the Sword's successor organization, the **Livonian Order**, for 19,000 silver marks. A geographical distinction between the southern and northern halves of the country remained: the south, together with northwestern Latvia, was known as Livland ("Livonia") and tended to look towards Rīga as its principal city; while the north, centred on Tallinn, was termed Estland ("Estonia") – a name which, centuries later, was to be applied to the whole country.

Under the Order, the gulf separating Estonian peasants from German-speaking landowners and priests grew wider. The towns in particular remained oases of German culture – even in the cosmopolitan port city of Tallinn, which attracted a growing Estonian community of domestic servants, boatmen and artisans from the fifteenth century onwards, total absorption into the German-language community was the prerequisite for social advancement.

Swedes and Russians

Estonian society under the Livonian Order was characterized by a slow-burning power struggle between the landed gentry, townsfolk and the Church. In the early sixteenth century, the cause of the **Reformation** (and especially its attack on ecclesiastical privilege and corruption) was enthusiastically taken up by aristocrats and burghers alike, transforming Estonia from a Catholic country into a bastion of Lutheranism almost overnight. Founded on medieval crusading ideals, the Order itself lost its *raison d'être*, producing a power vacuum eagerly exploited by neighbouring powers. In 1556, the **Swedes** captured Tallinn, using it as a base from which to expand across the whole of Estonia and northern Latvia. When the Russians invaded Estonia in 1558, the locals were glad of Swedish protection. The Swedes enlisted Polish support to throw the Russians back, beating them outside the Latvian town of Cēsis in 1578 and forcing them eastwards, and capturing Narva later the same year. In 1595, the Treaty of Tensina confirmed Swedish control over the whole of Estonia.

Estonians still refer to the seventeenth century as the "**Good Swedish Times**". Although the power of the German magnates remained largely intact, Swedish rule brought a degree of justice to rural courts (torture was outlawed in 1686) and extended primary education to an increasing number of rural towns. Local government was placed in the hands of a new breed of competent, enlightened administrators – most of whom were graduates of the newly established Tartu University, founded by Swedish King Gustav Adolphus in 1632.

This comparative golden age came to an end with the **Great Northern War** (1700–21), a titanic struggle between Swedes and Russians which laid waste to large parts of Estonia, left Tallinn and Tartu in ruins, and made Russian Tsar Peter the Great the undisputed master of the Baltic. Having incorporated Estonia and Livonia into his empire, Peter won the support of the German magnates by reconfirming their privileges and offering them top jobs in the imperial administration. Manorial estates flourished, encouraging their owners to build ever grander manor houses (such as those at Palmse and Sagadi; see pp.134 & 137), although conditions failed to improve for the Estonian peasants, for whom eighteenth-century feudalism increasingly came to resemble a system of forced labour. The abolition of serfdom (in Estonia in 1816, Livonia in 1819) actually led to impoverishment for many peasants, who, cut loose by the big manorial estates that once supported them, ended up working as seasonal labourers for meagre wages.

The Estonian National Awakening

At the start of the nineteenth century, there was little in the way of an Estonian national consciousness. Even those Estonians who had escaped from the countryside to make a career in the towns had thoroughly Germanized themselves in order to do so. However, an increasing number of enlightened Baltic Germans were becoming interested in Estonian language and folklore. The **Estonian Learned Society**, founded by Germans attached to Tartu University in 1838, promoted the study of local culture and soon welcomed educated Estonians into its ranks. One of these, **Friedrich Reinhold Kreutzwald**, used traditional folk-tale fragments as the inspiration behind his epic poem *Kalevipoeg* ("Son of Kalev"; 1857), the first large-scale piece of narrative fiction to be written in the Estonian language. Estonian journalism was taking off too, with **Johann Voldemar Jannsen** publishing the weekly *Pärnu Postimees* ("Pärnu Courier") from 1857, then moving to Tartu in 1863 to found the (still-flourishing) daily *Eesti Postimees*. It was Jannsen who organized the first-ever **All-Estonian Song Festival** in Tartu in 1869.

The Russian authorities increasingly came to see Estonian–German struggles as an inconvenience and by the 1890s had begun a programme of **Russification** in a belated attempt to build a pan-national sense of Tsarist patriotism. Use of Russian was imposed on the (previously German-speaking) University of Tartu and the ensuing disruption led to a fall in academic standards. The chief result of the Russification campaign was to radicalize the Estonian national movement. Local intellectuals who had previously seen the Tsarist bureaucracy as a potential ally against the Baltic Germans now realized that they had to challenge both at the same time.

In 1904, Estonian parties won a majority of the seats on Tallinn City Council, with Tartu-educated lawyer **Konstantin Päts** (1874–1956) becoming vice-mayor – form dictated that the post of mayor itself go to a Russian. Estonians enthusiastically supported the anti-Tsarist **Revolution of 1905** in the hope that it would result in further constitutional reforms; its failure was a serious setback – most national leaders were forced into exile (including Päts, who was condemned to death *in absentia*) before an amnesty in 1910 allowed them to return.

World War I and the Estonian War of Independence

With the outbreak of **World War I** in 1914, the outlook for the Estonian national movement was pretty bleak. Hopes were revived, however, when the **Russian Revolution** of February 1917 delivered the sudden collapse of the Tsarist system. The Estonian representative in Petrograd, Jan Tõnisson, persuaded the new regime to grant Estonia a good measure of autonomy, and an **Estonian Assembly** was established in Tallinn to take over administrative duties. November 1917 saw the Bolsheviks win power in Russia; they won control of Tallinn, too, in early 1918, but soon evacuated the city, leaving the coast clear for a newly constituted Estonian government under the leadership of Päts to declare **Estonian independence** on February 24. Encouraged by the Bolshevik withdrawal, however, the German army marched into town the next day and had Päts arrested. When Germany surrendered to the Western allies on November 11, 1918, Päts quickly reassumed control, declaring Estonian independence again on November 18. Resurgent Bolsheviks occupied Narva and Tartu, but were prevented from capturing Tallinn by a swiftly assembled defence force that included teenage schoolboys. With former Tsarist officer **General Laidoner** at the helm, Estonia's nascent army soon developed into an efficient, highly motivated unit. Supplied with arms by the British and supported by volunteers from Finland (drawn to Estonia by the close ethnic ties between the two nations), Laidoner swiftly rolled back the Bolsheviks, forcing them to accept peace terms by autumn 1919.

At the same time, the Estonians had to counter the threat of a Baltic-German army under General von der Golz advancing towards their southern borders from Rīga. In June 1919, Estonian troops, accompanied by Latvian volunteers, marched into northern Latvia, defeated the Germans at the **Battle of Cēsis** and chased them all the way back to Rīga before signing an armistice and returning home.

The inter-war years

The Constituent Assembly elected in April 1919 opted for an idealistic constitutional model, establishing a single-chamber parliament (Riigikogu) to be presided over by a head of state (Riigivanem, or "State Elder") who combined the duties of prime minster and president. Estonian democracy never functioned as perfectly as had been intended, however, and left-wing coup attempts in 1924 led to outlawing of the Communist Party and the execution of its leaders. The 1920s were good years for agriculture (Estonian tinned pork was a big hit in the UK), but post-independence prosperity was brought to an end by the Great Depression after 1929. Many of those who had fought in the 1918–19 War of Independence were now disillusioned with an Estonian state unable to provide them with the jobs and rising living standards they'd expected and voiced their discontent by joining the **VAPS** – a fascistic pressure group which called for the imposition of authoritarian rule. Konstantin Päts sidestepped the appeal of VAPS by carrying out an authoritarian coup of his own: parliamentary parties were banned in 1934 and the Fatherland Front (Isamaaaliit) was created to provide the country with a single, guiding ideological force. Päts appointed himself president and set about transforming Estonia into a corporatist state similar to Mussolini's Italy, although World War II intervened before his reforms bore fruit.

World War II

As a small state lying between powerful neighbours, Estonia never had much room for manoeuvre in international affairs, and its fate was sealed by the **Molotov-Ribbentrop Pact** of August 1939, a secret agreement between Germany and the USSR which placed the Baltic States firmly within the Soviet sphere of influence. Eager to press the advantage, the Soviets insisted on establishing military bases in Estonia in October 1939, going on to occupy the country outright in **June 1940**. Fixed elections produced a pro-Soviet parliament, which obediently declared Estonia's accession to the USSR. Hostility to the new order was widespread; the Soviet authorities tried to break the back of Estonian opposition by organizing mass **deportations** – on June 14, 1941, as many as 10,000 Estonians of all social classes were bundled into cattle trucks bound for the east.

Many young Estonians took to the forests at this time, fearing that further round-ups were on the cards. They formed partisan groups that helped kick the Red Army out when **Nazi Germany** declared war on the Soviet Union on June 22. Any hopes that the Germans would behave like liberators were soon disappointed, however, with the country being incorporated into the new protectorate of Ostland – which, ironically, fell under the aegis of the Tallinn-born Nazi Alfred Rosenberg, leading ideologue of Aryan superiority and no great friend of the Estonians.

The second Soviet occupation

By September 1944, the Germans had been thrown out of Estonia by the advancing Red Army and the country once more became part of the USSR. If anything, the **second Soviet occupation** was even harsher than the first: a hard core of Moscow-trained activists was brought in to run the local Communist Party and a second wave of **deportations** in March 1949 removed as many as 20, Estonians (2.5 percent of the total Estonian population) to camps in the east. Women, children and the elderly made up ninety percent of the total – suggesting that deportees were arbitrarily chosen to fulfil a pre-determined quota rather than being punished for any specific anti-Soviet beliefs. The bulk of deportees came from the countryside, leading to a collapse in agricultural production, only made worse by forced collectivization.

Thousands of young Estonians joined the anti-Soviet partisan movement known as the **Forest Brothers**, believing that the Western powers were bound to declare war on the USSR sooner or later. The British secret services trained Estonian exiles in London before shipping them across the Baltic Sea to join the Brothers, unaware that their movements had already been betrayed to the KGB by London-based moles. The movement had petered out by the early 1950s, by which time it was clear that no further help from the West was forthcoming. Amnesties in 1956–57 encouraged most surviving partisans to give themselves up, although the last known Forest Brother, August Stubbe, survived until September 1978, when he committed suicide to avoid capture by the KGB. Other pockets of **anti-Soviet resistance** included the Underground Committee of the Young Partisans of Estonia, who hoisted the Estonian tricolor from a church in Viljandi in 1954; and the Blue-Black-and-Whites, a group of idealistic high-school students who blew up a Soviet statue in Tartu in 1956.

Towards the "Singing Revolution"

Communist discipline was relaxed slightly during the post-Stalin thaw of the late 1950s, but expressions of Estonian patriotism were still viewed with displeasure by the party hierarchy. Things didn't really change much until the mid-1980s, when the policy of **Glasnost** ("Openness") initiated by Kremlin leader Mikhail Gorbachev gradually released long-repressed feelings of national resentment and outrage.

The first signs of change in Estonia came on August 23, 1987, when two thousand protesters met in Tallinn's Hirvepark to mark the anniversary of the Molotov-Ribbentrop Pact, followed by a three-thousand-strong demonstration in February 1988, to commemorate the anniversary of Estonia's 1918 declaration of independence. In April 1988, Tartu University history professor Edgar Savisaar called for the formation of a **Popular Front** during a TV phone-in, launching a mass popular movement at a single stroke. In September of the same year, over 250,000 Estonians converged on Tallinn's Song Grounds in a mass gesture of support for increased independence from the USSR. TV pictures of singing, flag-waving crowds were beamed around the world, and the Baltic push for independence has been known as the **"Singing Revolution"** ever since. On August 23, 1989, the fiftieth anniversary of the Molotov-Ribbentrop Pact was marked in all three Baltic nations with over 200,000 people joining hands to form a **human chain** from Tallinn to Vilnius.

Now controlled by Popular Front members and pro-independence communists, the Estonian Supreme Soviet adopted a cautious approach, pressing for increased autonomy rather than outright secession from the union. Despite abortive attempts to crush the independence movements in Lithuania and Latvia in January

1991, the Soviet regime held back from launching a similar crackdown in Estonia. In March 1991, the Estonians felt confident enough to hold a **referendum** on full independence from the USSR, with 65 percent voting in favour. With the **Moscow Coup** of August 1991 threatening a return to the bad old days of hard-line rule, the Estonian Supreme Soviet swiftly convened to make a full **declaration of independence**. On the collapse of the coup, international recognition of Estonian independence quickly followed.

From independence to the present

In September 1992, Estonia's first fully free elections in over sixty years were won by the right-of-centre Fatherland Party, whose youthful leader **Mart Laar** became prime minister. Despite numerous political realignments in the years that followed, the tone of post-independence politics has remained essentially the same, with a succession of cabinets – usually staffed by young technocrats untainted by involvement in Soviet politics – pursuing unabashedly free-market policies.

The speed of Estonia's transformation into a modern capitalist state made it an obvious candidate for membership of the EU. A referendum on accession in September 2003 received overwhelming support, paving the way for full membership in May 2004. Estonia joined NATO in the same year, confirming the country's position as a fully integrated member of the Western community.

One enduring aspect of the country's Soviet heritage is the continuing presence of a large Russian community on Estonian territory. Before the Soviet occupation, Estonia had been one of the most ethnically homogenous nations in Europe. After 1945, however, **Russian-speaking immigrants** from all over the USSR had been encouraged to move to Estonia – both to provide an industrial workforce and to engineer a new, less wholly Estonian, demographic profile. By 1990, Russian-speakers constituted about thirty percent of the population, concentrated especially in Tallinn, Narva and the oil-shale mining towns of the northeast. The introduction of a **citizenship law** that required non-Estonians to take a language test resulted in the exclusion of almost all of the non-Estonian population. Over a period of years, most Russian-speakers passed the test and became Estonian citizens – although an estimated 100,000 so-called "non-citizens" still remain. Whether citizens or not, many Russians are not fully integrated into Estonian national life, and their social and economic problems are often treated with indifference by the Estonian majority.

Bad feeling between the two communities came into the open in 2007, when the so-called Bronze Soldier, a monument to the Red Army war dead situated on Tõnismägi hill in the centre of Tallinn, became the focus of ad hoc demonstrations by both Russian nationalists and their Estonian opponents. Prime Minister Andrus Ansip of the right-of-centre Reform Party suggested moving the statue to an out-of-town location, ostensibly to take the heat out of the situation – although analysts were quick to point out that with general elections looming, Ansip stood to gain from an upsurge in Estonian national sentiment. On April 25, government workmen moved in to exhume the bones of thirteen Soviet soldiers buried beneath the monument, sparking Russian fears that the Bronze Soldier itself was about to be dismantled. Two nights of rioting followed, with ethnic Russian youths smashing city-centre windows and looting shops. The statue itself was spirited away to the Siselinna military cemetery south of the centre (where it has taken on a new life as an offbeat tourist attraction), provoking a storm of protest from the Russian government in Moscow. Most Estonian Russians distanced themselves from the rioters and the violence in Tallinn soon subsided. The dispute took on new shape, however, when Russian computer hackers successfully disabled commercial and banking websites on which an increasing number of Estonians relied to do their daily business. With Estonian–Russian relations at their lowest ebb since the dying days of the Soviet Union, the country looks set for some interesting times ahead.

Latvia

It's far from certain who the original inhabitants of Latvia were, and the history of the region doesn't really begin until around 2000 BC, when the **Baltic tribes** – the ancestors of today's Latvians and Lithuanians – migrated to the Baltic seaboard from their original home somewhere in west-central Russia. They soon coalesced into a handful of regionally based tribal units, with the Curonians (Kurši) in the west, the Zemgalians (Zemgaļi) in central Latvia and the Selonians (Sēļi) and Latgalians (Latgaļi) further east. Initially they had to share northern and central Latvia with remaining pockets of Livs, a Finno-Ugric people closely related to the Estonians, who lived around the Gulf of Rīga. None of these tribes had unified state structures based on capital cities, living instead in a network of loosely allied rural communities defended by stockade forts.

The Baltic Crusades

The pagan Latvians remained wholly outside the orbit of Western Europe until the twelfth century, when ambitious German clerics conceived the idea of converting the Baltic peoples to Christianity. First to make the arduous trip to Latvia's shores was Father Meinhard of Holstein, who built a church at Uexküll (Ikšķile) on the banks of the Daugava, east of present-day Rīga, and persuaded the pope to declare him Bishop of Uexküll in 1188.

Although Meinhard died soon afterwards and his followers were chased off by hostile locals, the publicity generated by his enterprise encouraged Pope Innocent III to declare a full-scale **crusade** against the Baltic pagans in 1198. Three years later the Bremen-based ecclesiastic, Albert of Buxhoeveden, led a fleet of ships to the mouth of the Daugava River and chose Rīga (formerly a Liv fishing village) as the site of his projected crusader capital. Albert's retinue of idealistic Christian knights and plunder-hungry freebooters formed themselves into the **Brotherhood of the Sword**, a military-religious organization, that (initially at least) enforced a strict, almost monastic code of behaviour on its members. The Brotherhood advanced from Rīga, conquering the Latvian communities one by one and confiscating their land – subsequently divided up between the Brotherhood's members. The social order established by the Brotherhood, in which a German feudal aristocracy ruled over a Latvian-speaking peasant majority, was to remain in place for the next seven centuries.

The Brotherhood didn't have things all their own way, encountering stiff resistance from the Zemgaļi and failing to extend their crusade south towards Lithuania as planned. Defeated by a combined Zemgalian-Lithuanian army near Šiaulai in 1236, the Brotherhood lost so many knights that it no longer had the numerical strength to carry on as a crusading organization. Its surviving members merged with the Prussian-based German Order to form a new grouping, the **Livonian Order**, which consolidated its rule over the Latvian lands, expanded northwards into Estonia and established the Livonian Confederation – to remain the dominant political force in the region for over three hundred years.

The archbishop of Rīga served as the Confederation's titular head, although he presided over a far from unified body politic: the Livonian Order and the Church were both major landowners and tended to be competitors for temporal power rather than spiritual partners, while the mercantile city of Rīga enjoyed privileges that increasingly made it hostile to both.

The end of the Livonian Order

It was the townsfolk of Rīga who spearheaded support for the **Reformation** in the early sixteenth century, seeing the new creed as a useful way of avoiding the financial demands made on them by the Catholic Church authorities. The Reformation also had unforeseen benefits for Latvian culture, with rural aristocrats funding vernacular translations of the gospels in order to popularize the new faith among their serfs.

The Reformation eroded the ideological certainties that had underpinned the crusading effort in the Baltic and a dissent-riven Livonian Order was incapable of defending its territories against ambitious neighbours. The region was devastated by the **Livonian Wars** of 1558–83, a three-way struggle involving Sweden, Russia and the Polish-Lithuanian Commonwealth. The Livonian Order was dissolved in 1562 by its last grand master, Gottfried Kettler, who appointed himself secular duke of Courland (see p.226) and placed himself under the protection of the Polish-Lithuanian crown – which also gained control of Latgale in the southeast. With Rīga and the northeast falling to the Swedes in 1621, the Latvian lands were effectively divided between two rival empires.

Latvia remained a target for Russian territorial ambitions, too, however, and in the **Great Northern War** (1700–21), Peter the Great kicked the Swedes out of the east and dragged the Polish-controlled west into the Russian sphere of influence. Full Russian control of Latvia was confirmed in 1795, when the so-called Third Partition finished off what was left of the Polish-Lithuanian state.

The Latvian National Revival

Despite these changes in sovereignty, little changed for the Latvians themselves, the vast majority of whom continued to work on agricultural estates owned by a German-speaking aristocracy. It was only in the mid-nineteenth century that a Latvian middle class began to emerge in Rīga and other towns, eager to develop indigenous language and culture. The Baltic Germans continued to regard the Latvians as second-class citizens who had to either abandon their culture or stay on the farm – an attitude best summed up by Rīga newspaper editor Gustav Keuchel, who declared that "to be both Latvian and educated is an impossibility".

Unsurprisingly, a rising generation of Latvian patriots increasingly saw German-language culture as an instrument of oppression that could only be overcome by encouraging the more widespread use of Latvian. The leader of these so-called **New Latvians** (Jaunlatvieši) was **Krišjānis Valdemars** (1825–91), who founded the first Latvian newspaper, *Pēterburgas avīzes* ("St Petersburg News"), in 1862, and helped set up a series of Latvian naval colleges that, it was hoped, would create an indigenous technocratic elite. Encouraged by Valdemars, **Krišjānis Barons** (1835–1923) embarked on the collection of folkloric materials in order to provide the Latvians with a sense of their own cultural history, in the process building up a remarkable archive of over one million *dainas* – four-line folk songs passed from one generation to the next, but never previously written down.

The New Latvians had always assumed that the Tsarist bureaucracy was their most likely ally in the struggle against the Baltic Germans – a delusion that it took the turmoil of the **1905 Revolution** to dispel. A pro-democracy uprising that spread from St Petersburg across the Russian Empire, the revolution was followed by a mercilessly authoritarian crackdown, and in Latvia a whole generation of nationalist activists were exiled or imprisoned.

War and independence

The outbreak of **World War I** in 1914 pushed national aspirations further into the background, and with the Russian Revolution leading to the eastern front's whole-sale collapse in 1918, Latvia fell to the Germans – who set about turning it into a protectorate of the Reich. However, Germany surrendered to the Western allies in November 1918 and a hastily convened Latvian National Council rushed to seize the initiative, meeting in Rīga's Russian Theatre (now the National Theatre) on November 18, 1918 to declare Latvia's independence. Lawyer and Formers' Union leader Karlis Ulmanis was appointed head of government and was to remain at the apex of Latvian politics for the next twenty years. Ulmanis's freedom of manoeuvre was limited by the fact that German troops were still in control of Latvia and had no intention of withdrawing. Indeed the British and French – neither of whom could spare the troops to garrison Latvia themselves – wanted the Germans to stay put in order to defend the region from Bolshevik Russia. In the event, both the Latvians and the Germans ended up fleeing Rīga in the face of the Bolsheviks, who captured the city on January 3, 1919, and established a Latvian Soviet Republic under veteran left-wing activist Pēteris Stučka.

Ulmanis and his government took refuge in the port city of Liepāja, where they remained virtual pawns of a more powerful German force led by the char-ismatic General Rudiger von der Goltz. Supported by the local aristocracy, von der Goltz dreamed of turning Latvia into a German-dominated statelet that would both stem the tide of Bolshevism and put the indigenous population in their place. The Ulmanis government formed a fledgling Latvian army (under Colonel Oskars Kalpaks) as a counterweight to von der Goltz's Germans, but this didn't prevent the latter from trying to depose Ulmanis in favour of a more malleable puppet in April 1919. Ulmanis was saved by the British, who installed him on a ship in Liepāja harbour and began delivering arms and sup-plies to his men. The Germans threw the Bolsheviks out of Rīga in May, but were themselves compelled to leave by a combined force of Estonians and Latvians – backed up by British and French warships. The British arranged for Ulmanis's return to Rīga in July, and after the failure of another German attack on the capital in October, the independent state of Latvia looked secure. The Bolsheviks, who still occupied parts of southeastern Latvia, were beaten off in the winter war of 1919–20 and the Latvian–Soviet treaty, signed on August 11, 1920, officially ended hostilities.

The inter-war period

Inter-war Latvian politics were characterized by the proliferation of small parties and a succession of short-lived coalition governments – although the presence of the Farmers' Union (and their leader Karlis Ulmanis) in all cabinets ensured a degree of continuity. During the 1920s, Latvia won export markets both for its dairy products and the consumer goods made by Rīga's VEF electronics fac-tory, but a period of steadily rising living standards was cut short by the onset of the **Great Depression** after 1929. The ensuing economic slowdown led to widespread disillusionment with parliamentary politics, and the emergence of anti-democratic (and often anti-Semitic) right-wing groups, such as **Perkonk-rusts** (Thunder Cross), persuaded Prime Minister Ulmanis to declare a **state of emergency** on March 16, 1934. Fearing that a return to democracy would render the country ungovernable, Ulmanis appointed himself president in 1936 and pro-ceeded to dismantle Latvia's liberal institutions, presiding over the construction of a corporatist state based on Mussolini's Italian model.

World War II

With the rise of Nazi Germany and consolidation of communist rule in Russia, the fragility of Latvian independence became increasingly apparent as the 1930s wore on. With the signing of the **Molotov–Ribbentrop Pact** on August 23, 1939, Germany and the USSR agreed to the establishment of spheres of influence in north-central Europe. Along with the other Baltic States, Latvia was designated part of the Soviet sphere. Latvia was forced to sign a mutual assistance pact with the USSR in October 1939, a prelude to the wholesale military occupation of the country on **June 17, 1940**. Deciding that armed resistance would be futile, President Ulmanis advised the nation to stay calm and adopt a wait-and-see approach, famously announcing in a live radio broadcast, "I'm staying where I am, and I want you to stay where you are." In the event, the Soviet invaders simply sidestepped Latvia's timorous political elite and did as they pleased; Stalin's trusted sidekick, Andrey Vishinsky, arrived in Rīga to oversee the country's painless incorporation into the Soviet Union. Under his guidance, stage-managed elections were held in July (most anti-Soviet candidates were barred from competing), and the resulting parliament, packed with Soviet puppets, voted to join the USSR. Ulmanis himself was exiled to Siberia, where he died in September 1942.

As the likelihood of war between the Soviet Union and Germany drew near, Stalin decided to tighten his grip on Latvia by **deporting** a large part of the country's intelligentsia to Siberia, and an estimated 16,000 people were rounded up and shipped east on the night of June 13–14, 1941.

The **German army** began its invasion of the Soviet Union on June 22, 1941, and were in total control of Latvia two weeks later. Although most Latvians initially greeted the Germans as liberators, they were soon disappointed by the realities of occupation, with Latvia becoming a marginal province in the new Nazi protectorate of Ostland. Special units arrived almost immediately to deal with Latvia's Jewish population, murdering an estimated 30,000 in the first six months of the war and a further 40,000 by 1945. The Germans were assisted in their butchery by a 12,000-strong Latvian auxiliary force led by local police chief **Viktors Arājs** – later sentenced to life imprisonment for war crimes after being unmasked in Germany in 1979.

Fears that Germany might lose the war and leave Latvia to the mercies of the Soviet Union encouraged more Latvians to sign up to the Nazi cause. A **Latvian Legion** was formed as an auxiliary to the SS in 1943 and led Latvia's defence against the advancing Red Army a year later. Rīga itself fell to the Soviets in October 1944 – thousands of Latvians were immediately conscripted into the Red Army and sent to fight their own countrymen in the Legion, who were still holding out in the northwest. As the war neared its end, as many as 200,000 Latvians **fled the country**, preferring life in West European refugee camps to the future offered by the Soviet Union.

Latvia under the Soviets

Resistance to the reimposition of communist rule was initially encouraged by the erroneous belief that the Western powers would sooner or later come to Latvia's aid. In the immediate post-war years, as many as 20,000 Latvians took to the countryside to join the anti-Soviet partisan movement known as the **Forest Brothers**. The Soviet security services responded by creating bogus partisan units of their own and using them to lure the real Forest Brothers into the open. The Soviet grip on the country was confirmed by a new wave of **deportations**, which saw the transport of over 43,000 Latvians to work camps in Siberia and beyond in March 1949.

Loyal Moscow-trained communists were imported to run the local party, and tens of thousands of workers were encouraged to emigrate to Latvia from other parts of the USSR in order to render the republic less ethnically homogenous. The death of Stalin in 1953 led to a gradual relaxation of ideological controls, but outright opposition to official Kremlin policy remained off the agenda. When leading Latvian communists **Berklavs** and **Krūmiņš** began openly to voice misgivings about the ongoing Russian emigration into Latvia, they were thrown out of the party by a specially convened central committee plenum in 1959 – Berklavs himself was exiled to Russia.

Denied political expression, patriotic Latvians threw their energies into the **cultural sphere**. In the 1970s and 1980s, folklore groups and choral societies blossomed: music was one of the few areas of Latvian life in which national sentiment could be expressed without provoking a clampdown by the Soviet state.

Latvians also prided themselves on being more culturally liberated than their conservative Soviet counterparts, and it's no surprise that the Soviet Union's first (and last) sex manual – psychotherapist Jānis Zālītis's *In the Name of Love* – was published here in 1981. After selling 100,000 copies, it was banned by party officials, scandalized by the explicit illustrations – a picture-free second edition went on to shift another 75,000 units.

The road to independence

The appointment of the reformist **Mikhail Gorbachev** as General Secretary of the Soviet Communist Party in 1985 began a gradual erosion of ideological certainties throughout the USSR. Latvian intellectuals were suddenly able to discuss subjects that had been taboo for years – notably the highly illegal nature of the Soviet Union's initial occupation of Latvia in 1940. In autumn 1988, Latvian communists tried to take control of the growing tide of anti-Soviet feeling by forming a **Popular Front** with themselves at the helm – they were soon outmanoeuvred by more genuine patriots. Swiftly growing into a broad-based mass organization, the increasingly confident Front called for the full restoration of Latvian independence in October 1989. Relatively **free elections** to the Latvian Supreme Soviet in March 1990 produced a pro-independence majority which immediately issued a Declaration of Restored Independence and announced the restoration of the 1922 Latvian Constitution.

Although many of Latvia's communists swung behind the independence drive, a pro-Moscow faction under Alfrēds Rubiks took control of the party in May 1990, and kicked pro-independence members out. Exploiting the fears of a sizeable ethnic Russian population made anxious by the implications of Latvian independence, the pro-Moscow lobby also launched a mass organization called **Interfront**, which attempted to storm Latvia's Supreme Soviet on May 14.

For the next nine months Latvia drifted in a strange limbo between independence and Soviet rule, with most people waiting on the outcome of the power struggle between Gorbachev, reformists and hardliners then unfolding in Moscow. In **January 1991,** Gorbachev sided with the hardliners, launching a military operation to seize key installations in the Lithuanian capital Vilnius. Fearing that the same would happen in Rīga, Latvians converged on the capital to mount a 700,000-strong pro-independence demonstration on January 13. Many of the participants stayed on to man barricades hastily erected around the Supreme Soviet, Telephone Exchange and TV Tower. On January 20, Soviet special forces attempted to gain control of the Latvian Interior Ministry, gunning down five innocents in the process. Stung by criticism from the international community, Gorbachev abandoned plans for a further Baltic crackdown and another period of uneasy stand-off ensued. When conservative communists tried to unseat Gorbachev in the **Moscow Coup** of August 1991, only to surrender power several days later, the Soviet Union entered its death throes. Latvia reiterated its independence declaration later the same month and international recognition soon followed.

Independent Latvia

The main issue facing Latvia's post-independence rulers was the question of how best to deal with the country's sizeable **non-Latvian population**. Of a population of 2.5 million, as many as forty percent were Russian-speaking – a direct result of the resettlement policies pursued by the Soviet regime. Latvian nationalists argued that full **citizenship** should only be granted to those descended from the pre-1945 population, attracting fierce criticism from an international community keen to promote a non-ethnic approach to civic rights. Latvian demographic angst was compounded by the fact that the country had one of the lowest birth rates in Europe and was therefore most unlikely to breed its way out of a population crisis. In the end, the Latvian government opted to bestow citizenship on post-1945 immigrants who had a "basic proficiency" in the Latvian language, while the European Union helped to fund language-study opportunities for those who wanted to qualify. Those who remained non-citizens retained the right to reside in Latvia, but couldn't vote and were barred from civil service jobs. In the early 1990s, there were an estimated 750,000 non-citizens in Latvia, a number that has now fallen to just under 400,000 – although this is due as much to outward migration and natural death as to any real improvement in language learning.

The other main theme of post-independence domestic politics was the transformation of a dysfunctional state-run economy into a free, consumer-driven market. This was achieved at miraculous speed, but at great social cost, with a minority making big bucks from the transition to pure and unfettered **capitalism**, while the majority eked out a living on meagre wages. The failure of successive governments to battle corruption and raise living standards for all produced a fluid political landscape in which few parties could count on consistent mass support. A succession of coalition governments, each made up of broadly right-of-centre parties, has come and gone without producing any leaders of real charisma or authority.

Latvia was ably represented on the world stage by President **Vaira Vika-Freiberga** (served 1999–2007), an internationally well-respected figure who spearheaded the country's drive to join both **NATO** and the **EU**. Since accession to the latter organization in 2004, Latvia has enjoyed something of an economic boom, and the work-hard, spend-hard city of Rīga has seen a dizzying rise in real-estate prices. High inflation has led to fears that the good times may not last, however, and the Latvian government's ambitious plans to join the Euro zone have been shelved indefinitely by EU financial bigwigs.

Lithuania

Along with the ancestors of the Latvians, the forebears of today's Lithuanians moved into the Baltic seaboard from western Russia from around 2000 BC onwards. These tribes originally lived in loose, clan-based units closely related by language, speaking a unique and ancient group of Indo-European dialects distinct from the Slav tongues of their near neighbours – indeed contemporary Lithuanian is said to be the closest of all living languages to Sanskrit. They also had a common religion, involving a pantheon of gods, of which Perkūnas (the thunder god) and

Laima (Fortune) were among the most prominent. There was also much nature-worship, with trees, lakes and glades accorded a sacred importance.

Protected by belts of forest and swamp, the early Lithuanians lived largely undisturbed by events elsewhere in Europe, preserving a village-based, Iron Age lifestyle, without a written language, until well into the Middle Ages. In the twelfth century, Lithuanian society came under increasing pressure from their German and Slav neighbours, and tribes in eastern Lithuania began to unite into something resembling a centralized state, with the fortresses of Kernavė, Trakai and **Vilnius** serving as its main strongholds. The absence of defendable frontiers meant that the nascent Lithuanian state could only ensure security by expanding, leading to the emergence of a highly mobile military machine which soon imposed its rule on Slav lands to the south and east.

The western Lithuanians (known as **Žemaitijans** and speaking a slightly different dialect, they were long considered to be a nation in their own right) were still divided into small tribes at this time, although they somehow managed to come together in inflicting a crushing defeat on Rīga-based crusaders the Brotherhood of the Sword at the **Battle of Saulė** in 1236. Other tribes closely related to the Lithuanians fared less well: the **Yotvingians** to the southwest and the **Prussians** to the west either died out or were assimilated by more powerful neighbours, although the name of Prussia was subsequently adopted by that region's German conquerors.

The rise of the medieval state

Little is known of Lithuania's rulers until the emergence of **Mindaugas** in the mid-thirteenth century, a powerful chieftain who had become master of the state by the 1240s and accepted Christianity in the hope of winning recognition from Western rulers. He was crowned King of Lithuania by a papal representative in 1253, only to be murdered ten years later by nobles eager to preserve Lithuania's pagan culture.

Lithuania's status as the last pagan state in Europe increasingly attracted the attention of Germany's crusading orders, with the Teutonic Knights raiding the country from the west and the Livonian Order mounting frequent attacks from the north. Many Western European knights volunteered to serve in these campaigns – Lithuania is mentioned by Geoffrey Chaucer as being one of the places where the Knight of *Canterbury Tales* fame saw action.

The experience of constant warfare against the crusaders helped forge Lithuania into a major military power. Prevented from making territorial acquisitions in the west, fourteenth-century ruler **Gediminas** (1271–1341) extended Lithuanian rule eastwards into Russia and Ukraine. Slav chieftains from the conquered territories were co-opted into the Lithuanian ruling elite, and a Slav dialect close to modern Belorussian became the official language used in court documents – the Lithuanians themselves still didn't have a written form of their own tongue.

Jogaila and Vytautas

By the late fourteenth century, Lithuania was a vast multinational empire, which, despite being demonized by Western propagandists for its continuing pagan sympathies, was an increasingly important player in Central European affairs. When King of Poland Louis of Anjou died without a male heir in September 1382, Polish nobles offered the hand of his daughter **Jadwiga** to Gediminas's grandson and current Lithuanian ruler **Jogaila** – henceforth known to history by the Polonized form of his name, Jagiełło. The Poles hoped that the marriage would provide them with a key ally in their struggles against the German crusading orders and facilitate a joint Lithuanian-Polish programme of expansion into Eastern Europe into the bargain. Jogaila jumped at the chance to internationalize his power base, forging a dynastic link between Lithuania and Poland that would endure for the next four centuries. Jogaila's part of the deal was to promise the **Christian conversion** of his country, bringing down the curtain on Europe's longest-enduring pagan culture.

The marriage took place in 1389, after which Jogaila was crowned King of Poland and went on to spend most of his time in Kraków. A large part of the Lithuanian nobility saw Jogaila as a traitor who had sold out to the Poles and supported a rebellion by his cousin Vytautas in 1392. Unable to control events in Lithuania, and fearful that his newly won inheritance might soon disintegrate, Jogaila offered Vytautas the position of Grand Duke of Lithuania, on condition that Lithuania would pass to Jogaila or his heirs after Vytautas's death. On July 15, 1410, Jogaila and Vytautas together led Polish-Lithuanian forces to victory at **Žalgiris** (called Grünwald in Poland; Tannenberg in Germany), a battle which destroyed the Teutonic Order as an effective military power. Vytautas went on to rule Lithuania as a virtually autonomous sovereign – a situation which suited Jogaila, because it demonstrated to the Polish nobles that Lithuania was still a powerful state with a will of its own. It was under Vytautas that Lithuania achieved its greatest territorial exent, stretching from the Baltic in the north to the Black Sea in the south – not surprisingly, Grand Duke Vytautas "the Great" has always been a bigger national hero in Lithuania than Jogaila.

The sixteenth and seventeenth centuries

After Jogaila's death, his descendants continued to rule in Poland while Lithuania remained an autonomous Grand Duchy. Sometimes the King of Poland appointed himself Grand Duke of Lithuania; at others he would award the title to a trusted son or cousin. Although technically separate from Poland, Lithuania was soon drawn into the Polish cultural orbit. The Polish language was the main vehicle by which Catholic ritual and Renaissance culture arrived in Lithuania, and by the sixteenth century almost all of the Lithuanian nobility was **Polish-speaking**. Leading magnates retained a sense of regional patriotism, however, and the defence of Lithuania's special status vis-à-vis the Polish crown remained a popular rallying cry.

By the mid-sixteenth century, Lithuania's eastern borders were increasingly threatened by an aggressively expansionist Russia. Fearful that their Polish counterparts would abandon Lithuania rather than assist in its defence, the Lithuanian nobles allowed themselves to be rushed into a more formal union between the two states. In 1569, the agreement known as the **Union of Lublin** created the so-called **Polish-Lithuanian Commonwealth**, in which the Grand Duchy retained certain self-governing rights but lost its wholly autonomous status.

The Grand Duchy's position on the eastern fringes of a large state centred on Warsaw didn't leave it immune to intellectual currents coming from the rest of Europe. Although the **Reformation** arrived here somewhat later then elsewhere, an estimated sixty percent of the aristocracy had turned Protestant by the late 1500s. The atmosphere of religious debate occasioned the first attempts at Lithuanian publishing, with Protestant nobles sponsoring the production of native-language prayer books and Counter-Reformers responding with texts of their own. The gradual re-Catholicization of the country was carried out without recourse to violence.

Among the beneficiaries of the Grand Duchy's reputation for cultural and religious tolerance were the **Jews**. Present in Lithuania ever since the Middle Ages, their numbers increased massively in the sixteenth century owing to an influx of Yiddish-speaking Jews from Germany. They soon became the dominant ethnic group in many provincial towns, with Vilnius serving as their spiritual and cultural capital.

Lithuania under the Tsars

Having taken control of most of Estonia and Latvia in the **Great Northern War** of 1700–21, Russia exerted an increasing amount of influence in the affairs of the Commonwealth and installed a succession of weak kings on the Polish throne. Russia, Austria and Prussia progressively helped themselves to more and more of the Commonwealth until wiping it off the map once and for all in the so-called **Third Partition of Poland** in 1795. The Grand Duchy of Lithuania was formally absorbed into Tsarist Russia and, carved up into lesser administrative units, ceased to exist as a territorial entity.

With Lithuania's aristocracy and intelligentsia thoroughly Polonized, any aspirations to independence were invariably tied to the idea of a resurrection of the Polish-Lithuanian Commonwealth. Lithuanian landowners, priests and peasants took an enthusiastic part in the **Polish Uprising of 1830**, liberating much of the countryside, until Tsarist troops arrived to restore order. Lithuanian participation in the **Polish Uprising of 1863** was even more widespread, provoking a brutal crackdown engineered by new governor-general Mikhail "the hangman" Muravyev. Muravyev's response to the threat of Polish-Lithuanian patriotism was to embark on a wholesale programme of **Russification**. Russian became the language of instruction in all but a handful of schools, and a ban on the printing of books in any script other than Cyrillic effectively put paid to any Lithuanian-language publishing.

The 1863 Uprising was the last occasion on which Lithuanians and Poles fought side by side for the restitution of a common state. A new generation of educated Lithuanians increasingly saw the dominance of Polish culture as a barrier to national self-realization. The main ideologue behind this new course was **Jonas Basanavičius** (1851–1927), who encouraged research into traditional folk culture and promoted fresh study of Lithuania's period of medieval greatness. From 1883 onwards many of these ideas found expression in the magazine *Aušra* (Dawn), printed over the border in Germany and smuggled into Tsarist Russia by a dedicated underground team of *knygnešiai*, or **"book-bearers"**. In 1904, the forty-year ban on printing Lithuanian in the Latin alphabet was rescinded, leading to a flowering of indigenous-language culture.

World War I

Lithuania represented a key line of defence for Tsarist armies on the outbreak of **World War I** in 1914, but within a year the whole country had been overrun by the Germans. The collapse of the Tsarist regime in 1917 persuaded Lithuanian national leaders that the time had come to make some kind of pro-independence statement, although they were extremely wary of upsetting either their German occupiers or the Western powers. In December 1917, the recently formed Lithuanian **Taryba**, or Council, declared Lithuania an independent state under the protection of Germany. On February 16, 1918, they reissued the declaration, this time cutting any explicit reference to the Germans. The Germans quietly ignored both declarations and the Taryba was left in limbo until November 1918, when Germany's unexpected collapse left surprised Lithuanian leaders in command of a newly independent country.

The inter-war years

It had always been assumed that the Lithuanian state would be centred on the old ducal capital **Vilnius**, an ethnically mixed city that was also claimed by Lithuania's neighbours. After an inconclusive three-way tug of war between Poles, Lithuanians and Bolsheviks, the city was finally seized by Polish General Żeligowski in 1920. The Lithuanian government took up residence in **Kaunas** instead, but refused to recognize the loss of Vilnius, declaring Kaunas to be only the "provisional capital" and freezing relations with Poland as a sign of their displeasure. Having failed to prevent the Polish seizure of Vilnius, the international community turned a blind eye when the Lithuanians themselves grabbed the German-speaking port city of **Memel** (**Klaipėda** in Lithuanian) in 1923.

The emerging nation's attempts to build a viable democracy were short-lived. In 1926, a left-of-centre government signed a treaty of friendship with the Soviet Union, enraging right-wing nationalists and encouraging the authoritarian-minded President **Antanas Smetona** to suspend parliament. A decade and a half of benign dictatorship followed, with the main opposition coming from radical right-wing groups such as Iron Wolf (Geležinis Vilkas), which peddled a modish mixture of anti-liberal, anti-Semitic ideas. On the international stage, Lithuania was the most isolated of all the Baltic States, distrustful of neighbours like Poland and Soviet Russia and in dispute with Germany over the status of Klaipėda – when Hitler reoccupied the city in March 1939, the Lithuanians had no choice but to meekly stand aside.

World War II

Lithuania was in no position to offer resistance when the **Soviet Union**, having grabbed the eastern half of Poland in autumn 1939, moved to occupy all three Baltic States in June 1940. Stage-managed elections produced a pro-Soviet Lithuanian parliament which voted for immediate incorporation into the USSR. With the threat of war with Nazi Germany looming, the Soviet Union tightened its grip on Lithuania with the **deportation** of a randomly chosen cross-section of its citizens to Siberia in June 1941.

The Germans launched **Operation Barbarossa** against the Soviet Union on June 22, 1941, overrunning Lithuania within days. Almost immediately, a murderous campaign of terror was launched against the country's 240,000-strong Jewish population. Special units known as Einsatzgruppen were sent to the Baltic to "deal" with the "Jewish problem" – thousands of Lithuania's Jews were taken to forest clearings and shot within weeks of the Nazi occupation. Many Lithuanians participated enthusiastically in round-ups and killings – it was widely believed that Jews were more likely than Lithuanians to harbour communist sympathies and therefore had to pay for the Soviet occupation of 1940–41. **Ghettos** were established in the cities of Vilnius, Kaunas and Šiauliai, where a semblance of Jewish life continued until summer 1943, when SS leader Heinrich Himmler ordered the deportation of their inhabitants to concentration camps, where the majority were murdered. About ninety percent of Lithuania's Jewish population was wiped out during the Holocaust, and many of the survivors emigrated to Israel or the US after the war. There are currently around 5000 Jews left in the country, most of whom live in Vilnius.

From occupation to independence

With the Red Army's advance into Lithuania in 1944, resistance to Soviet rule started up almost immediately, with various partisan groups joining forces to form the movement subsequently known as the **Forest Brothers**. Despite the KGB's success in infiltrating the organization, armed resistance continued for almost a decade, finally petering out after the arrest and execution of the Brothers' most senior leader, Jonas Žemaitis, in 1953. Meanwhile, in March 1949, another round of **mass deportations** had deprived Lithuania of much of its intelligentsia. The **Church** continued to provide a limited outlet for anti-Soviet sentiment, most notably in the person of Bishop Sladkievičius, who, despite being exiled to a rural village in 1959, organized the production and distribution of the underground dissident journal *Chronicle of the Lithuanian Catholic Church*. Sladkievičius later became archbishop of Kaunas and was made a cardinal by the pope in 1988.

The post-war political scene was dominated by **Antanas Sniečkus**, a trusted servant of Moscow who presided over a purge of "national communists" in 1959. A political thaw in the mid- to late 1960s led to a modest cultural revival, although Lithuanians had to wait until the Glasnost era of the 1980s before outright political dissent was allowed into the open. The first **anti-Soviet demonstration** in Lithuania, held on August 23, 1987, to demand the publication of the Molotov-Ribbentrop Pact (the secret Nazi-Soviet agreement which sealed the fate of the Baltic States in 1939), only attracted a crowd of a few hundred. Within a year, however, the opposition had mushroomed into a mass movement, with the openly pro-independence **Sąjūdis** ("Movement") organization holding its first congress in October 1988. The same year saw the Lithuanian Communist Party elect a new leader, Algirdas Brazauskas, who began to offer cautious support to the independence movement.

Elections to the Lithuanian Supreme Soviet in February 1990 produced a majority for the Sąjūdis camp, with professor of music **Vytautas Landsbergis** becoming its chairman. Landsbergis declared Lithuania's independence from the Soviet Union on March 11, 1990, the first Soviet republic to do so. The Kremlin responded with an economic blockade of Lithuania that led to severe shortages of food and fuel. Egged on by hardliners in Moscow, Mikhail Gorbachev authorized a military **clampdown** in January, 1991, which began with an attack on the Vilnius TV Tower by Soviet tanks. After the deaths of thirteen unarmed demonstrators (a further five hundred were injured), the operation was called off by a Soviet leadership fearful of causing a bloodbath. Kremlin hardliners remained eager to teach Lithuania a lesson, and on July 31, 1991, a special forces' detachment attacked a frontier post at Medininkai on the Lithuanian–BelOrussian border, killing seven Lithuanian border guards in the process. With the failure of the anti-Gorbachev Moscow coup of August the same year, however, Soviet power quickly evaporated, leaving Lithuania suddenly, and joyously, independent.

The political present

Although the nationalist-conservative Landsbergis remained the dominant figure in parliament during the first ten years of independence, he surprisingly lost the first presidential elections of 1992 to former communist and born-again Social Democrat **Algirdas Brazauskas**. Brazauskas was on hand to welcome Pope John Paul II to Lithuania in September 1993, the pontiff's visit serving as a powerful symbol of the country's break with the communist past.

The Conservative Party of Landsbergis provided much of the ideological impetus behind the wholesale switch to **free-market economics** that transformed Lithuania in the 1990s. The change was not without negative consequences, however, with the collapse of loss-making industries, rising unemployment and declining living standards for the majority. The Social Democrats of Brazauskas frequently emerged from elections as the largest group in parliament, although the balance of power was often held by a shifting constellation of pragmatic, centre-right parties whose popularity was often based on the personal charisma of their leaders rather than any coherent ideology.

One notable feature of post-independence politics has been the pro-Western orientation of the country's foreign policy, with successive administrations championing the cause of Lithuanian entry into NATO and the EU. A referendum on **EU membership** in May 2003 produced a huge majority in favour, signalling genuine popular excitement – a result which symbolized for many Lithuanians their extraordinary voyage from Soviet satellite to modern European state.

Baltic folk music

The characteristic Baltic song festivals – hugely popular events – played a significant role in the emergence to independence of Estonia, Latvia and Lithuania and have long been a focus for national consciousness. Now Baltic musicians explore and reinterpret not just global pop but music with roots closer to home.

Despite the considerable national and regional differences between (and within) the three countries, they share in the continuity of culture around the Baltic (including Finland and the Russian Baltic areas), reaching back thousands of years. All have folk song-poetry of the **runo-song** type and they have in common several traditional instruments, notably **Baltic zithers** variously called *kantele*, *kannel*, *kokles* or *kanklės*. As a result of historical domination, however, the Baltic States manifest Germanic and Slavic cultural traits not found in Finland.

Though inevitable changes in village life during and after the Soviet period have meant that the social contexts of much traditional song and dance have all but disappeared, there's still a great deal to be found in living memory. The **folklore movements** that sprung up in the 1960s and 70s saw urban enthusiasts making trips to the villages, and performing the material they found there. These attempts to reflect and celebrate still-living musical traditions paved the way for today's musicians: in all three countries bands are seeking to create music that uses traditional musical forms, but connects with the present day.

Estonia

Estonia's traditional culture, while distinct, has strong links with that of the linguistically and geographically close Finland, with **runo-songs** and its own variants of **Baltic zither**.

Runo-song

Estonian runo-song, *regilaul*, has the same basic form as the Finnish variety to which it is related. A large number of runo-song texts have been collected, largely from women, thus offering a female point of view. Typical subjects include work, rituals, spells, ballads and mythical stories, and the songs tend to a stoic sadness, or wry observation of life's realities, rather than extreme expressions of joy or love. The more ornamented **swing-songs** were sung while sitting on the big communal village swing whose movement made its own rhythmic demands.

Estonia's national epic **Kalevipoeg**, by folklorist **F. Reinhold Kreutzwald** (1803–82), was published in the 1860s, paralleling folklorist Elias Lonnröt's creation from runo-song sources of Finland's *Kalevala*, first published in 1835. **Armas Launis'** collection of melodies from the runo-songs from which *Kalevipoeg* had been constructed was published in 1930.

By the early twentieth century runo-song was largely overtaken by more European forms of rhyming folk song with wider-spanning tunes and occasional instrumental accompaniment. Nevertheless it survived in a few areas – notably in **Setumaa**, which straddles Estonia's Russian border, and also on the island of **Kihnu** and among Estonian-resident members of Ingria's repeatedly displaced population.

Setu song

The songs of the **Setu people** have considerably influenced contemporary roots singers, both in Estonia and in Finland. There's been a recent revival in Setu culture and the speaking of its dialect. Several villages, such as Värska, Kosselka, Helbi, Obinitsa and Uusvada, have established women's vocal groups that perform songs traditionally sung and danced while working or at social events, particularly the three-day wedding celebration. The eight-syllable runo pattern of these songs is often interrupted by extra syllables and refrains, and unlike other Estonian vocal traditions, they are sung polyphonically, the other singers taking the leader's line (the *torrõ*) and adding a lower part (the second *torrõ*), and a higher, penetrating single voice (the *killõ*) which often uses just two or three notes.

Kannels and zithers

The old pastoral wind instruments such as animal horns, wooden birchbark-bound trumpets, willow overtone whistles and bagpipes have lost their traditional herding context but are used to some extent by present-day folk-rooted musicians. The fiddle, the ever-popular accordion and the long-bellowed concertina are used in the playing of couple-dance tunes, the most prevalent form of which is the **polka**.

Polkas also feature, together with older music, in the repertoire of the **kannel**, the Estonian version of the Baltic zither, which, though it tends to have six strings rather than five, is of the same basic design as Finland's *kantele* – a carved, wedge-shaped box, with strings passing direct from pegs to a single attaching bar. Players died out during the twentieth century but the instrument itself survived (if only to hang on the wall) amongst the many exiles in North America – where the small *kannel* has had something of a revival. In Estonia itself, the formation of Soviet-style folkloric ensembles involved the creation of an "orchestral series" of bigger chromatic box-*kannels*. However, visits from contemporary Finnish *kantele*-players such as Hannu Saha and Antti Kettunen have helped to stimulate new interest in small *kannels*.

Setumaa has its own form of *kannel*, usually with a soundboard extended wing-like beyond the box rather like those found in eastern Latvia and parts of western Russia. This form is increasingly used, for example by Finnish *kantele* virtuoso Timo Väänänen. Leading Estonian *kannel* players include **Tuule Kann** and multi-instrumental ethnomusicologist **Igor Tõnurist**.

In Estonia, as in Latvia and Lithuania, folk players of a wide and ingenious range of **board-zither** or **chord-zither** can be found. These aren't true *kannels*/*kanteles* but are closer in design to the factory-made zithers, autoharps and other domestic multi-stringed instruments made largely in German factories and sold across northern Europe and North America. The bowed lyre, **hiiu-kannel** (called a **jouhikko** in Finnish) was played until the twentieth century in the Swedish enclaves of Estonian islands (relics of Sweden's fifty-year rule over Estonia from 1660 until 1710), particularly Runö, and is finding a role again today in some of the modern folk bands.

Festivals

During the 1960s, instructions were sent by Moscow to cultural organizers throughout the Soviet Union that supervised manifestations of genuine, living folk culture were to be encouraged, to demonstrate the government's support for the needs and expressions of the masses. In the Baltics, reluctant members of these 'masses' were researching these same living cultures, not in response to Moscow's wishes but in order to explore the distinctiveness of their own culture.

Performing ensembles fell into two groups: 'ethnographic' – which came from a particular area and specialized in local forms – and 'folkloric' – which drew on the whole country's traditions. The first of the 'ethnographic' type to appear in the more liberal climate of the 1960s was the Setu choir **Leiko** from Värska, formed in 1964. Of the 'folkloric' type, **Leigarid** (formed in 1969 to entertain tourists at Tallinn Open-air museum) soon turned away from the colourful folkloric spectacle approach towards a more authentic style rooted in village traditions. Regional ethnographic performance groups were formed, too, as were young city-based ensembles such as **Leegajus** (led by **Igor Tõnurist**) and **Hellero**.

In 1985, the conference of CIOFF (Conseil International des Organisations de Festivals de Folklore et d'Arts Traditionelles) was held in Estonia, and in 1986 the first **Viru Säru** folk festival took place. The **Baltica** festival, which moves each year to a different Baltic state, began in 1987, and Tallinn first hosted in 1989. These growing performance opportunities stimulated more groups and further cultural developments including the opening of a folk music department at the Cultural College in Viljandi in 1990. **Viljandi Folk Music Festival**, which concentrates on young Estonian folk bands, plus foreign guests mainly from neighbouring Baltic countries, began in 1993.

Estonia's most famous composer internationally, **Arvo Pärt**, doesn't show any obvious borrowings from traditional music, but some others have reflected it as inspiration or by incorporating it in their music. The best known of these is **Veljo Tormis**, most of whose big choral works are interpretations and expansions of folk songs.

The mass singing festivals continue: the All Estonian Song Festival, **Laulupidu**, which started in Tartu in 1869, is held every five years in Tallinn. It's still a huge event: there can be over 20,000 choir members and 100,000 in the audience. The Setu people have their own song festival, **Leelopäev**, a gathering of singing groups for performance and celebration with traditional food and costume, held every three years in the village of Värska.

Latvia

The land of amber has more Baltic zithers, as well as drone-based singing and a large body of traditional song-poetry – **dainas** – with strong pre-Christian symbolism and a lack of heroes.

The daina

The Latvian **daina** is a short song of just one or two stanzas, one or two lines in length, without rhyme, and largely in the same four-footed trochaic metre as runo-songs. *Dainas* feature mythological subjects and reflect most aspects of village life, but the stories and heroic exploits described in many countries' folk songs are notably absent.

The sun is a dominant image, often personified as **Saule**, and her daily course across the sky and through the year is linked metaphorically with human life. While the sun is female, **Mēness**, the moon, is male, and a frequent song theme is courtship between them or other celestial figures such as the twin sons of Dievs (God) and the daughter of the sun. The solstices were traditional occasions for celebration – in particular Jāņi (midsummer), whose central figure was Jānis, the archetypal vigorous, potent male with strong phallic associations. As the *ligotne* (midsummer song) "Jāṇa Daudzinajums" describes him:

Oh Jānis, the son of Dievs,
what an erect steed you have
The spurs are glittering through forests
the hat above trees
Jānis was riding all the year
and has arrived on the Jāņi eve;
Sister, go and open the gate, and let Jānis in.

Translation by Valdis Muktupāvels

The major collection of **dainas** was made by **Krišjānis Barons** (1835–1923); the six volumes of his *Latvju Dainas* were published between 1894 and 1915, and contain about 300,000 texts.

In keeping with other regions of the Baltics, newer song-forms spread during the nineteenth century, when chordal, fixed-scale instruments – such as the accordion – arrived. Thus **zinge** is a singing style with a strong German influence. The older forms remained, however: **dziesma** means a song with a definite melody, while **balss** means "voice" or "speech" and has no clearly defined melody, changing with the rhythm of the words. *Balss* was the style used in calendar celebrations, as well as during work. It usually follows a three-voice form: the leader sings a couple of stanzas of a *daina*, then the others repeat them. In some regions these repetitions are sung over a vocal drone – a distinctive feature not found elsewhere in the Baltics.

Instruments

Traditional Latvian instruments, used in *sadzīves* music – the dances and songs of the villages – include zither, bagpipe, whistle, hurdy-gurdy and, more recently, violin and accordion.

Of these, the instrument with the greatest national-symbolic status is the **kokle** or **kokles**, Latvia's version of the Baltic zither. Larger, heavier box-built *kokles* with more strings were developed for use in Soviet-style folkloric ensembles. These, fitted with screw-in legs and often ornamented with a central jewel of the locally abundant amber, are attractive in appearance and ensemble sound, but not very responsive as instruments, with musicians displaying a rather stiff playing style based on a Western classical approach.

Renewed interest in the traditional, smaller carved *kokles* began during the folklore movement of the 1970s. The instrument survived in the living tradition of only a few areas, most notably in Kurzeme in western Latvia and Latgale in the east. The strongest influence in this revival was **Jānis Porikis**, who made a couple of hundred *kokles* and organized workshops and performances. **Valdis Muktupāvels**, Latvia's leading player, learnt the style of the Suiti region from Porikis, and has gone on to champion the instrument.

A wide variety of interesting designs of **citara** (chord-zither) are found in Latvia. Most have large numbers of strings, some or all of which are tuned as ready-made chords. These are not principally related to Baltic zithers but rather to the mostly German, factory-made chord-zithers and autoharps sold since the nineteenth century across Europe and North America. Individual Baltic makers have made ingenious modifications, resulting in some very big instruments and a few that are cylinder-shaped. There are also hybrid forms between citara and *kokles*, known as **citarkokles**.

In the eastern province of Latgale, **hammered dulcimers** have been played since the early nineteenth century, a borrowing from nearby Belarus.

Festivals and performers

Latvia's national song festival has been taking place, usually at five-year intervals, since 1888. In 1990, the first after the country's return to independence, it reached its largest size with over 35,000 singers, dancers and instrumentalists. Latvia also takes its turn as host of the **Baltica** festival, and has a range of other folk-music-related festivals of varying regularity.

Like the other Baltic States, Latvia still has a large number of local and regional **folklore groups** and **ethnographic ensembles**, most of them largely vocal rather than instrumental; the website *folklora.lv* has a list of many of them. While what they do is a preservation, both of songs and of costume, it is nevertheless a community activity – they meet to rehearse, make costumes and so on – and these groups, often established many decades ago and with members of all ages, are in themselves a folk culture, and a living source of much traditional music.

Then there are the folk bands going deep into traditional music and its instrumentation, but using it in new configurations. Since they don't feel themselves to be folk musicians in the old sense of village culture, they dub their music 'post-folklore'. There have been a number of formative bands in this development but most influential have been those of ethnomusicologist, *kokles* player and bagpiper **Valdis Muktupāvels**, and of the band **Iļģi**, which since its formation in 1981 by singer and fiddler **Ilga Reizniece**, has developed from a quiet acoustic group to a strong performing and recording unit.

Iļģi's and Muktupāvels' albums, and most of today's other Latvian tradition-rooted music as well as some pop and jazz, are on the **UPE** label, owned and run by **Ainars Mielavs**. Mielavs had considerable pop success in Latvia as leader of the band Jauns Mēness, and is now a songwriter, traditional singer, bandleader and radio DJ. At a time when there were almost no recordings of Latvian traditional or post-folklore music available, and little money around to finance them, Mielavs gathered leading musicians on the post-folklore scene and began a series of elegantly recorded and well-packaged CD projects on UPE including the ongoing *Latvian Folk Music Collection*.

The shores of the gulf of Rīga are home to several Livonian folklore groups, the best known over the past three decades being **Skandinieki**, the vocal ensemble centred on the **Stalts** family. Having sung throughout her childhood in Skandinieki, in 1999 **Julgi Stalte** formed, with Estonian musicians, the Livonian-language folk-rock band **Tulli Lum** ("Hot Snow").

Lithuania

The largest Baltic state has a rich variety of folk forms, including layered **polyphonic music**, sung or played on reed instruments, flutes and – in common with its neighbours to the north – Baltic zithers.

Song

Thousands of Lithuanian traditional songs – **dainos** – have been collected. They deal with every aspect of life, and wedding and love songs feature particularly prominently. Some would be passed on as well-known songs, but others, such as lullabies, would be varied or improvised to suit the occasion. In the early twentieth

General Baltics compilations

Voix des pays Baltes: chants traditionnels de Lettonie, Lituanie, Estonie (Inedit, France). Field recordings, mostly made by Lithuanian Radio, from all three Baltic countries going back as far as the 1930s, including calendar songs, work songs and Lithuanian *sutartinės*.

Estonia compilations

Eesti Rahvalaule Ja Pillilugusid (Estonian Literary Museum, Estonia). Field recordings, most from 1957–67, of a variety of runo-songs, plus a few instrumentals. Assembled largely from the collections of ethnomusicologist Herbert Tampere, this album was originally released on vinyl in the 1970s.

Estonia: Olden Tunes (Ocora, France). Twenty-six tracks, mostly recorded by Estonian national radio, of performers, solo and in groups, using traditional instruments – *kannel*, bagpipe, herder's horn, reed pipe and willow whistle – with some archive recordings from as early as 1912.

Estonian Traditional Music 2001 (Viljandi Folk Music Festival, Estonia). Recordings of many of the young Estonian groups playing at the country's biggest folk festival in 2001.

The Folk Music of Estonia (Melodiya, USSR). Compiled by leading ethnomusicologist Ingrid Rüütel (wife of Estonian president Arnold Rüütel), these 44 tracks are mostly runo-songs – lyric, narrative and wedding – from regions of Estonia including Setumaa, plus some instrumentals on horn, wooden trumpet, *hiiu kannel*, bagpipe, fiddle and accordion.

Setu Songs (Mipu, Finland). Setu women's singing groups from the villages of Helbi, Kosselka, Obinitsa, Uusvada and Meremäe, plus the Leiko group from Värska, recorded in situ and in Helsinki.

Estonia artists

Kirile Loo *Saatus* (Fate) (Erdenklang, Germany; Alula, US). Runo-song-based material in sparse, atmospheric settings arranged by Peeter Vähi with traditional instruments – *kannel*s (played by Tuule Kann), bagpipe, straw whistle, Jew's harp – plus keyboards and guitar. Her second album, *Lullabies for Husbands* (Erdenklang, Germany, 1999) moves to a hefty world-beat sound, in which all the instruments – violin, flutes, guitar, *hiiu kannel*, synths and samples – are played by Tiit Kikas.

Veljo Tormis *Forgotten Peoples* (ECM, Germany). Critically acclaimed double CD of six compositions by Veljo Tormis, an influential composer celebrated for his choral works, here based on the music of Livonian, Votic, Izhorian and Karelian Finno-Ugric peoples and sung by the Estonian Philharmonic Chamber Choir.

Latvia compilations

Beyond the River: Seasonal Songs of Latvia (EMI Hemisphere, UK). Released back in 1998, but still a useful introduction to the pioneering work of four bands playing and singing traditional music with traditional instruments: Iļģi, Rasa, Auri and Grodi.

Ligo (UPE, Latvia) Six singers, including Zane Smite and Ainars Mielavs, focus on the songs associated with the main Latvian calendar celebration, Ligo (midsummer night). The minimalist instrumentation isn't specifically Latvian traditional, but the result – veiled, breathy and grainy, with a prevailing sense of wistfulness – is very distinctively Latvian.

Music from Latvia (Cooking Vinyl, UK; UPE, Latvia). A 2001 compilation from the catalogue of UPE, the label that has initiated and released most of the recent CDs of Latvian roots music. Tracks by Iļģi, Ugis Praulins, Biruta Ozoliņa, Laiksne, Vilki, Ainars Mielavs and more.

CONTEXTS

Auļi Sendzirdēju (Lauska, Latvia). Material from the small surviving Latvian bagpipe repertoire by this young band of nine bagpipers and percussionists, plus dance and song tunes, played in skirling harmony on Latvian bagpipes and big drums. That might suggest that it sounds like a Scottish pipe band, but it doesn't.

Marija Golubova Stāsti Un Dziesmas (UPE, Latvia). A recording, made in 2003, of Marija Golubova (born 1907) singing folksongs and telling of her life in the language of the Latvian region of Latgale and also in Russian. Even for a non-speaker of these languages, her spirit is so strong and the cadences of her voice so clear that somehow the meaning comes across.

Iļģi Kaza Kāpa Debesīs (A Goat Climbed Up Into the Sky) (UPE, Latvia). Formed in 1981 by singer and fiddler Ilga Reiznice, Iļģi has continued to develop and inspire throughout all Latvia's changes. The most recent line-up consists of Reiznice, Valdis Muktupāvels on *kokles*, Latvian bagpipe, whistle, Jew's harp and vocals, Gatis Gaujenieks on bass and gīgas, guitarist Egons Kronbergs and drummer Vilnis Strods.

Valdis Muktupāvels *Kokles* (UPE, Latvia) A double CD, one of traditional tunes, the other of Muktupāvels' own compositions for *kokles*. A prime mover in maintaining and reviving Latvian traditional music during the difficult Soviet days and carrying it through to the new Latvia, Muktupāvels is a player of *kokles* and bagpipes, a singer and an ethnomusicologist.

Biruta Ozoliņa *Balta Eimu* (UPE, Latvia) This singer from the eastern Latvian region of Latgale has an unaffected, clear voice, and is an able *kokles* player – the sparse, elegant performances of traditional material here are mainly just Ozoliņa with her *kokles*.

Ugis Praulins *Paganu Gadagramata* (UPE, Latvia) Programmer, producer and singer, and keyboard, *kokles* and flute player, Praulins combines traditional music with current studio technology. Material on this album is from the folk-song collections of Emilis Melngailis, featuring Jauns Mēness guitarist Gints Sola and the voices and traditional instruments of Ilga Reizniece and Māris Muktupāvels.

Skandinieki *Skandinieki* (UPE, Latvia) Folk vocal group Skandinieki sings thirty songs of rural life, nature, seasons, gods and symbolism in which Saule, the sun, is prominent. With natural female and male vocals, occasionally accompanied on fiddle, accordion or Jew's harp, they have a warm, unaffected, hypnotic folk-chorale sound with a quiet dignity that's very Latvian/Livonian.

Lithuanian Folk Dreams (Kuku, Lithuania). A sampler of roots-progressive bands such as Atalyja.

Lithuanian Folk Music (33 Records, Lithuania). Forty-six recordings, from the 1930s to the 1980s, of work, ritual, wedding, nature, children's, historical and war songs, plus instrumental music – with extensive English notes.

Lituanie: le pays des chansons (Ocora, France). Excellent, varied collection of 35 traditional songs and instrumentals, including horn, *kanklés* and *sutartinės*, recorded for Lithuanian Radio between 1958 and 1990. Notes in French and English.

Songs and Music from Suvalkija (Institute of Lithuanian Literature and Folklore, Lithuania). Recordings made in 1935–39 in southwest Lithuania, including reaping, wedding, family and love songs, waltzes, marches, schottisches, krakowiaks and mazurpolkas on fiddle or whistle, and *kanklés* playing by the founder of the Skriaudžiai Kanklés Ensemble.

Songs, Sutartinės and Instrumental Music from Aukštaitija (Institute of Lithuanian Literature and Folklore, Lithuania). Recordings made in 1935–41 in northeastern

Lithuania. Polyphonic vocal *sutartinės* and some played on *kanklės*, plus shepherds' songs and wedding songs, polkas and waltzes.

Atalyja *Atalyja* (Sutaras/Kuku, Lithuania). Powerful and fresh 2001 debut by this large band with five singers, plus instruments including *kanklės*, bagpipes, fiddle, viola, flute, *skudučiai*, guitar and tabla.

Veronika Povilionienė *Vai Ant Kalno* (Sutaras/Kuku, Lithuania). Compilation of recordings by a singer long highly regarded in Lithuania for her serene, rich-toned voice. The songs were recorded between 1986 and 2000, some unaccompanied except for the sounds of the forest where they were recorded, others involving unexpected and wonderfully eccentric collisions with rock, jazz and avant-garde.

Rinkinys *Sutartinės* (Studija, Lithuania). A group with several albums of traditional song and instrumentals, performed straight without added arrangement, here performing *sutartinės* in strong male voices, or played on *kanklės* or wind instruments.

Sutaras *Call of the Ancestors* (Lituanus, Lithuania). This five-strong group specializes in reviving ancient instruments and repertoire. The 38 tracks on this CD include vocal and instrumental *sutartinės*, the playing of *kanklės*, horns, whistles and *pūslinė*, and polkas and other dance tunes on fiddle, accordion, harmonica and *basetlė*.

---

century many women, who were predominantly the creators and carriers of songs, had repertoires of a hundred or more songs.

Singing can be solo or in a group, in unison or in parallel chords of thirds, fourths or fifths. Aukštaitija, Lithuania's northeastern region, has a distinctive and well-known tradition of polyphonic songs, **sutartinės**, whose melody and form are also transferred to instrumental music. They are duophonic – two voices, or groups of voices in harmony. In the case of **dvejinės** (by twos) and **keturinės** (by fours), two harmonizing lines are sung together, then they stop and are replaced by a second group of singers and two different harmonizations, while in **trejinės** three parts overlap, two at a time, as in a canon. The word stresses create a syncopating internal rhythm.

Instruments

There is a relatively large range of Lithuanian traditional instruments. The basic form of the Lithuanian version of the Baltic zither, the **kanklės**, differs regionally in playing style and in the number of strings, which can be anywhere between five and twelve. The repertoire of the traditional *kanklės* consisted of old-style material such as *sutartinės* and more modern dance tunes such as polkas, waltzes and quadrilles. A "concert series" of large, many-stringed box *kanklės* was devised for the Soviet-style ensembles.

Whereas the old round dances (*rateliai*) were traditionally accompanied by singing only, during the nineteenth and twentieth centuries instrumental ensembles commonly played the newer dance forms. Instrumental groups playing *kanklės* and *lamzdeliai* (wooden or bark whistles) existed as far back as the sixteenth century. Later the fiddle and three-stringed bass *basetlė* joined them, followed in the nineteenth and early twentieth centuries by accordions, bandoneons, concertinas, Petersburg accordions and harmonicas, mandolins, balalaikas, guitars, modern clarinets and cornets. During the Soviet era, dressed-up ensembles emerged using box *kanklės* and *birbynės* (folk clarinets – they used the developed form which is a mellow-sounding thick tube with a cowhorn bell). These groups actually made quite a pleasant sound, not so different from a disciplined village band, but they were often used, to the annoyance of those searching out the "real thing", in classically influenced arrangements to accompany choral singing of harmonized and denatured so-called *sutartinės* with all their dissonances smoothed out.

In the northeast, tunes of the *sutartinė* type were played on *skudučiai* – rather like dismantled pan-pipes, played by a group of men. The same type of tune was played by five-piece sets of birchbark-bound wooden trumpets (*ragai*), or alternatively, by pairs of the straighter, longer *daudytės*; each of the latter could produce up to five natural harmonics, so only two *daudytės* were needed for a set.

Other wind instruments include *švilpas* (overtone whistle), goat-horns and *sekminių ragelis* (a single-drone bagpipe). Percussion instruments include *tabalas* (a flat piece of wood hung and hit like a gong) and drums. A curious instrument, rarely seen today, is the *pūslinė* – a musical bow with an inflated pig's bladder resonator containing a rattling handful of dried peas.

Ensembles to bands

As the social structure changed, and Sovietization altered Lithuanian society from the outside, the old ways of music lost much of their role. Tradition moved to post-traditional, or "secondary folklore", with material collected from those who remembered the old ways converted to a form considered suitable for performance to an audience.

The first Lithuanian folklore ensembles were formed around the beginning of the twentieth century. One was the **Skriaudžiai Kanklės Ensemble** – formed by maker and player Pranas Puskunigis in 1906 – which is now based at the folk museum in Skriaudžiai, near Kaunas. Subsequently, ethnographic plays such as *The Kupiskenai Wedding* were staged. While these tried to reflect genuine village life, concert ensembles worked on the premise that the rough old folk songs needed sprucing up.

A strong choral movement developed, resulting in the huge song festival, **Dainų Šventė** ("The Feast of Songs"), which takes place every five years. The state folk song and dance ensemble **Lietuva**, founded in 1940, appeared at such events. "Modernized" folk instruments were created, and traditional dress was formalized into national costume.

While this was the form of national expression acceptable to the Soviet regime, considerably more suspicious was the back-to-the-villages folklore movement that began in the 1960s and was spurred on later that decade by the Prague Spring events in Czechoslovakia. Rasa (the summer solstice) and other Baltic pagan events were publicly celebrated despite persecution by the KGB. **Folklore ensembles** sprang up in towns and cities, and the village musicians from whom they collected formed performing units themselves, usually known as "ethnographic ensembles". The annual **Skamba Skamba Kankliai** festival in Vilnius' old town began in 1975, while the first **Baltica** International Folklore Festival, which moves between the Baltic States each year, took place in 1987 in Vilnius.

The current undisputed doyenne of Lithuanian folk singing is **Veronika Povilionienė**, a native of the Dzūkija region who has been the nation's outstanding performer of unaccompanied female narrative songs ever since her student days in the late 1960s. Her repertoire consists of traditional material from all over the country, although she has also made several excursions into crossover territory – the 1993 album *Povilionienė/Vyšniauskas* (recorded with jazz saxophonist Petras Vyšniauskas) is one of the most startling exercises in fusion to come out of the Baltics, and can still be picked up from Vilnius record shops.

The next generation of tradition-rooted progressive bands, such as folk-rock band **Atalyja**, combine *kanklės*, bagpipes and other traditional instruments with those of rock for an emphatic, wild expression of *sutartinės* and other traditional material. Beyond folk-rock stretches a spectrum of post-Soviet, pan-Baltic, neo-pagan bands, from "ritual folk" such as that of **Kulgrinda**, through "martial-folklore", "folk-metal", "dark-metal" and "dark-ambient", to the sort of black-metal bands whose CDs come with a lighter inscribed "Visit your local church at night".

Written and researched by Andrew Cronshaw

Books

Plenty of books were written about the Baltic States during the collapse of the Soviet Union and its aftermath, and if a brief grounding in the region's history and politics is what you're after, there's a good deal to choose from. Other aspects of Baltic culture are much less visible in the bookshops and many of the most perceptive accounts of travel in the area were produced by nineteenth- and early twentieth-century writers whose works are nowadays hard to find. A number of non-Baltic writers have used the Baltic States as a background for their fiction, but – curiously, and rather depressingly – the rich traditions of Lithuanian, Latvian and Estonian literature are almost invisible in English-speaking countries, with Estonia's grand old man of letters Jaan Kross the only novelist who regularly gets translated. Titles marked with the ⚑ symbol are particularly recommended. The abbreviation "o/p" means "out of print".

General Baltics

History and politics

Eric Christiansen *The Northern Crusades*. Definitive account of the thirteenth-century conquest of Estonia and Latvia by German-speaking knights and priests. The mixture of missionary zeal and near-genocidal savagery that characterized the times comes in for thought-provoking scrutiny.

John Hiden and Patrick Salmon *The Baltic States and Europe*. Excellent introduction to the main themes of Baltic history, concentrating on the twentieth century.

⚑ David Kirby *The Baltic World. Vol. I 1492–1772; vol II 1772–1993*. General, wide-screen history examining long-term German, Swedish and Russian interests in the region, as well as the fates of the Baltic peoples themselves.

⚑ Anatol Lieven *Baltic Revolution*. Witty, erudite and endlessly stimulating book which successfully

mixes history, reportage and where-do-the-Baltics-go-from-here analysis, written by the journalist descendant of a long line of Latvian aristocrats.

R.J. Misiunas & R. Taagepera *The Baltic States: Years of Dependence, 1940–1980*. Baltic society and politics under Soviet occupation, Nazi occupation and Soviet occupation again, examined by a pair of leading scholars.

Georg von Rauch *The Baltic States: Years of Independence, 1917–1940* (o/p). The definitive work on the inter-war period, covering the intrigues of internal politics, as well as the growing threats posed to the three Baltic States by outside powers, notably the Soviet Union.

Clare Thomson *The Singing Revolution*. The main events of the late 1980s and early 1990s, presented with involving immediacy by a journalist who was there at the time.

Memoirs and travel

Walter Duranty *I Write as I Please* (o/p). Rollicking war-correspondent memoirs

from an eyewitness to the Latvian and Estonian wars of independence. If you

49

want to know what conflict-scarred cities like Tallinn and Rīga were like in 1919, this is a good start.

J.G. Kohl *Russia* (o/p). Indefatigable German guide-book writer who ventured all over Europe in the 1830s and 1840s and wrote lengthy tomes about his travels. This one covers much of the Tsarist Empire, including an account of a journey through Latvia and Estonia that documents the semi-feudal, manorial culture that prevailed in the countryside at the time.

E. Alexander Powell *Undiscovered Europe* (o/p). An American journalist who visited Lithuania, Latvia and Estonia in the 1930s, Powell is a sympathetic and well-informed observer who offers the occasional insightful nugget.

Owen Rutter *The New Baltic States and their Future* (o/p). Travelling through the Baltic in the early 1920s, Rutter never quite got to grips with the region and comes across as a bit of a bumbler. The resulting text is pooterish in the extreme, but remains a wonderful source of local colour.

Literature about the Baltic States

Johannes Bobrowski *Shadow Lands*. One of Germany's greatest twentieth-century poets, Bobrowski grew up in an East Prussian town shaped by German, Lithuanian, Polish and Jewish influences, only to see this cosmopolitan world destroyed during World War II. Feelings of cultural loss (and German guilt) fill his poems.

Ed Carey. *Alva & Irva*. Fantasmagorical modern fable focusing on the adventures of two girls in the mythical city of Entralla, loosely based on the Lithuanian capital Vilnius. Dark, quirky, mesmeric stuff.

Stephan Collishaw *The Last Girl*. Eminently readable offering in which an elderly Lithuanian poet stalks the streets of post-Soviet Vilnius, haunted by memories of wartime betrayal. The atmosphere of Lithuania in the 1990s is authentically rendered.

Jonathan Franzen *The Corrections*. Award-winning novel about contemporary America and its discontents, centring on a Midwestern couple and their far-flung offspring – one of whom ends up in the Lithuanian capital in the early 1990s. The Vilnius portrayed by Franzen – a post-communist wild east characterized by organized crime and pollution – is rather different from the one that exists today.

Tadeusz Konwicki *Bohin Manor*. Elegaic novel set among the Polish-Lithuanian gentry in the wake of the 1863 anti-Tsarist uprising, written by one of Poland's leading twentieth-century novelists – himself a native of the Vilnius region. Capturing wonderfully the tone of manor-house life in the Lithuanian backwoods, this is an attempt to update *Pan Tadeusz* (see below) for a modern audience.

Henning Mankell *The Dogs of Rīga*. World-weary Swedish cop Kurt Wallender heads for Rīga looking for help in solving a murder case. Set in 1990, with Latvia in an uneasy limbo between communism and independence, this book paints a convincing picture of the paranoia and uncertainty of the times.

Adam Mickiewicz *Pan Tadeusz*. Poland's national epic, a poem of Homeric proportions describing the ructions and reconciliations of a Polish-Lithuanian gentry family on the eve of Napoleon's invasion of the Tsarist Empire.

Czesław Miłosz *The Issa Valley*. Wonderfully lyrical, semi-autobiographical account of a post-World War I boyhood spent in the Lithuanian countryside by Nobel Prize-winning Miłosz. The Issa of the title is based on the real-life River Nevėžis, north of Kaunas.

Denise Neuhaus *The Christening*. Spellbinding novel about the fates of three Estonian women split between Stockholm and Tallinn in the 1970s and 80s. Combining elements of family saga and political thriller, its depiction of life in the last decades of Soviet Estonia is totally believable.

William Palmer *The Good Republic*. Well-written, intelligent and thought-provoking novel about a London-based émigré returning to the unnamed Baltic state of his birth (an artistic amalgam of Estonia and Latvia), to be confronted by the ghosts of his politically ambiguous past.

Anthony Powell *Venusberg* (o/p). An inter-war novel involving a junior English diplomat who is posted to an East European capital – clearly based on a mixture of Tallinn and Rīga – where he falls in with a bunch of tedious ex-pats and ridiculously Ruritanian locals. A whimsically intriguing period piece, but hardly Powell's best.

Marguerite Yourcenar *Coup de Grace* (o/p). Sombre meditation on fate and responsibility set during the Latvian War of Independence, with a Baltic German officer discovering that the object of his desire is fighting on the opposite side.

Estonia

History, politics and culture

E. Nodel *Estonia: Nation on the Anvil* (o/p). A handy introduction to Estonian politics and culture, from the earliest times to the Soviet occupation.

Madli Puhvel *Symbol of Dawn*. A well-researched biography of Estonia's leading nineteenth-century poetess, Lydia Koidula, written in accessible style by an American-Estonian academic, and providing background on the formation of nineteenth-century society and culture. Available in big bookshops in Tallinn and Tartu.

Toivo U. Raun *Estonia and the Estonians*. Best of the general histories, covering the main themes of Estonian society and politics from the earliest times up to 1991, in readable style.

Rein Taagepera *Estonia: Return to Independence*. A useful addition to the above titles, this provides plenty of detailed analysis on the fall of the Soviet Union and the political landscape of the 1990s.

Travel and memoirs

Tania Alexander *A Little of All of These* (o/p). Memories of a childhood spent on an Estonian country estate during the inter-war years, among a cosmopolitan bunch of Russo-German aristocrats.

Arthur Ransome *Racundra's First Cruise* (o/p). The author of children's classic *Swallows and Amazons* spent the summer of 1922 sailing from Rīga to Tallinn, stopping off at sundry Estonian ports

and islands on the way. If you know your sextant from your spinnaker, this is an absorbing read.

Elizabeth Rigby *Letters from the Shores of the Baltic* (o/p). Account of a sojourn on a baronial estate in Estonia in the 1840s, a best-seller in its day, written by a formidable woman of letters who noted elsewhere that "well-read, solid-thinking, early-rising, sketch-loving, light-footed, trim-waisted, straw-hatted" Englishwomen always made the best travel writers.

Ronald Seth *Baltic Corner: Travels in Estonia* (o/p). Engaging, if low-key, memoirs of an English teacher in inter-war Estonia. Some good stuff on

daily life in the Tallinn of the 1930s, and lively descriptions of trips to Narva and Petseri monastery – the latter a Setu shrine which was then part of Estonia, but subsequently awarded to Russia by post-World War II border changes.

Literature

  ELM (Estonian Literary Magazine). Quarterly magazine published by the Estonian Institute and available from Tallinn bookstores, featuring contemporary poetry and prose in English translation, and a round-up of literary news. Find out more on ⓦwww.einst.ee/literary.

  Jaan Kaplinski *The Same Sea in us All* and *The Wandering Border*. Two collections from Estonia's leading contemporary poet, whose verse is imbued with an almost spiritual appreciation of nature. You can read more of his poems on ⓦhttp://jaan .kaplinski.com.

  Jaan Kross *The Czar's Madman*. First published in Estonia in 1978, the best-known work from the country's greatest living prose writer functions both as a rich historical

novel and subtle allegory of life in Brezhnev's USSR – which makes it all the more remarkable that it ever got past the censor. The kernel of the story involves a nineteenth-century Baltic German aristocrat who is locked up in the madhouse for daring to criticize the Tsar, with the stoical, self-denying lives of rural Estonians providing the intricate background weave. Kross's most recent work to be translated into English, *Treading Air*, is a richly textured guide to twentieth-century Estonia in the form of a civil servant's life story, and comes with an invaluable introduction to Kross's life and times by translator Eric Dickens. *Professor Martens' Departure*, in which a nineteenth-century Estonian adviser to the Tsar looks back on his life, is an altogether less penetrable meditation on the Estonian-Russian relationship.

Latvia

History, travel and memoirs

Lucy Addison *Letters from Latvia* (o/p). Addison was an Anglo-Latvian who chose to stay in Latvia throughout World War II and the Soviet occupation, recording the madness of war and political repression from the sanctuary of a wooden cottage in Jūrmala. These letters are both gripping historical narrative and a touching read.

Peggie Benton *Baltic Countdown* (o/p). Recollections of Rīga in the late 1930s, written by the wife of

a British diplomat. From beach holidays in Jūrmala to the arrival of Soviet tanks in 1940, this is an enjoyable slice of Englishwoman-abroad writing.

  Modris Eksteins *Walking Since Daybreak*. Mixing family memoir with a general history of Latvia's tragic twentieth century, this is beautifully written, totally engrossing stuff. If you only ever buy one book about Latvia, choose this one.

Silvija Grosa *Art Nouveau in Rīga*. With a good balance of glossy photos and informative texts, this is the best of many books about the Latvian capital's dominant architectural style. Published by Jumava and available from most big bookshops in Rīga.

George Popoff *City of the Red Plague* (o/p). Memoirs of life in Bolshevik-ruled Rīga during the first months of 1919. A winter of disease, starvation and political terror is recounted in wide-eyed style by a scandalized Popoff – an impressionable Red-hating misogynist who believed that the commies had recruited street prostitutes to command their firing squads.

Ernst von Salomon *The Outlaws* (o/p). Combat reminiscences of a young volunteer who headed for Latvia to join up with General von der Goltz's Baltic-German army in 1919. Characterized by nationalist euphoria, love of comradeship and bloodlust, it's a disturbing document.

Stephen Tallents *Man and Boy* (o/p). Lively, self-deprecating autobiography of the man who led the British mission to Latvia in 1919–20, serving (albeit briefly) as governor of Rīga. For a full account of what went on during those war-torn years, there is no better starting point.

Literature

Alberts Bels *The Cage* (o/p). Beginning like a hard-boiled detective story and ending as a disturbingly surreal fable, this is an outstanding piece of contemporary fiction – and subtle critique of the Soviet system (it first appeared in 1971). It's also one of the few morsels of Latvian literature that's available in English.

Various *All Birds Know This*. Well-translated and representative anthology of contemporary Latvian poets, including formidable national literary figures like Vesma Belševica and Imants Ziedonis. Available from the bigger Rīga bookshops.

Lithuania

History, politics and travel

E. J. Harrison *Lithuania Past and Present* (o/p). Harrison was British vice-consul in Vilnius in the wake of World War I, left it just as the Poles took over and returned as a newspaper correspondent. Eye-witness accounts of a turbulent period are mixed with satisfying chunks of history, cultural commentary and travelogue.

Czesław Miłosz *Native Realm* (o/p). Born in Lithuania to Polish parents, Miłosz's meditative autobiography is especially illuminating on the Polish–Lithuanian relationship in particular, and East European culture

in general. The same author's *Beginning with my Streets* (o/p) is a collection of essays, including some invigorating pieces about Vilnius.

S.C. Rowell *Lithuania Ascending*. Few sources reveal the exact processes by which Lithuania rose from being a tribal statelet to a huge empire stretching from the Baltic to the Black Sea, but Rowell has done a remarkable job in sifting the evidence; this ground-breaking analysis of thirteenth-century power politics is the result. One for the medievalist rather than the general reader.

Alfred Eric Senn *Lithuania Awakening* (o/p). Account of the rise of Sąjūdis and the push towards freedom, written with eyewitness freshness by an American academic who was there for most of the events described.

V. Stanley Vardys and Judith B. Sedaitis *Lithuania the Rebel Nation*. Good overview of twentieth-century history and a blow-by-blow account of the drive to independence. Eager to nail Western darling Gorbachev for his part in the anti-democratic crackdown of January 1991.

Various authors *Lithuania: past, culture, present*. Published in Lithuania by Baltos Lankos and sold in most bookshops in central Vilnius, this coffeetable book contains intelligent, readable essays on key aspects of Lithuanian identity, accompanied by a wonderful selection of photographs.

Literature

Sigitas Geda *Biopsy of Winter*. Arrow-sharp shards of verse from one of the country's leading literati, deftly translated by American poet Kerry Shawn Keys. Published by Vaga and available from their bookshop in Vilnius (see p.341).

Jonas Mekas *There is no Ithaca*. Collection of poems by the Lithuanian-born, New-York-based writer and avant-garde film-maker. Contains *Idylls of Semeniskiai*, a lyrical evocation of Lithuanian village life. Parallel English/Lithuanian texts.

Kornelijus Platelis *Snare for the Wind*. Varied, career-spanning selection from one of Lithuania's most respected contemporary poets. Available from Vaga and other big bookshops in Vilnius.

Balys Sruoga *Forest of the Gods*. Powerful, concentration-camp memoirs from a poet and playwright who was imprisoned in Stutthof towards the end of World War II. Available in Vilnius bookshops.

Lithuanian-Jewish history and memoirs

Lucy S. Dawidowicz *From That Place and Time* (o/p). American academic Dawidowicz went to study at Vilnius's YIVO (Yiddish Institute) as a young graduate in 1938 and wrote this memoir as a nostalgic tribute to the city. The same author's *The War Against the European Jews* is one of the best overall histories of the Holocaust.

Waldemar Ginsburg *And Kovno Wept*. Gripping, unforgettable account of ghetto life in Kaunas (Kovno to its Jewish inhabitants), written by a survivor.

Dan Jacobson *Heshel's Kingdom*. Involving account of a voyage through Lithuania inspired by memories of Jacobson's grandfather Heshel, who was a rabbi in the western Lithuanian town of Varniai. This is a wistful, elegiac book with insights into contemporary Lithuania's ambiguous relationship with its multicultural past.

Howard Jacobson *Roots Schmoots*. Both humorous travelogue and identity-seeking enquiry, this book ends up in the southern Lithuanian town of Lazdijai – home town of Jacobson's great-grandparents. Lithuania sounds pretty grim the way Jacobson describes it, but then he was travelling in the post-Soviet early 1990s.

Dovid Katz *Lithuanian Jewish Culture*. Excellent introduction to the all-but-vanished world of the Litvaks. Handsomely illustrated, and written with enthusiasm and verve, this is one that will satisfy both the specialist and the general reader. Published by Baltos Lankos and available from Vilnius bookshops.

Herman Kruk *The Last Days of the Jerusalem of Lithuania*. Chronicle of Vilnius's wartime ghetto, scribbled down nightly by Kruk, who dedicated himself to documenting a culture he knew was being snuffed out. Enormously valuable as a social document, this also makes for gut-wrenching reading.

Hillel Levine *In Search of Sugihara*. Well-researched and engagingly written biography of the diplomat frequently dubbed the "Japanese Schindler". Levine clearly likes his subject, and yet his determination to portray him as a complex, often flawed human being has earned the enmity of the Sugihara family.

William W. Mishell *Kaddish for Kovno*. The story of Kaunas's Jewish community, with a sensitive overview of Lithuanian–Jewish relations over the centuries, and an unflinching narrative of the Nazi occupation.

Avraham Tory *Surviving the Holocaust: Kovno Ghetto Diary*. Harrowing tale of survival in World War II Kaunas, written by the deputy secretary of the ghetto council. Retained as a personal memoir by Tory, the manuscript was dusted off in 1982, when the author was called to testify against Kazys Palciauskas, the city's wartime mayor.

Lithuanian-Jewish literature

Chaim Grade *My Mother's Sabbath Days* (o/p). Outstanding prose from one of Vilnius's best Yiddish-language writers. The first half of this book consists of quirky short-story snapshots of life in Jewish Vilnius on the eve of World War II; the second is harrowing autobiography, with Grade escaping the Nazi invasion while his wife chooses to stay in the Vilnius ghetto.

Menke Katz *Burning Village*. Powerful cycle of poems set on the eve of World War II in the author's native Michalishek, a Jewish village in the Lithuanian–Belorussian borderlands.

Avram Sutzkever *Selected Poetry and Prose*. Leading light of the Yung Vilne movement, who escaped from the Vilnius ghetto and lived as a partisan in the forest before emigrating to Israel after the war. Electrifying verse and experimental prose poems about Vilnius and the war, highly charged with imagery and nostalgia.

Language

Language

Estonian 465

Latvian 469

Lithuanian 473

Estonian

stonian belongs to the Finno-Ugric family of languages; it's closely related to Finnish and somewhat more distantly to Hungarian. Despite the importance of Germans, Swedes and Slavs in Estonia's history, the language itself has remained remarkably free of foreign-influenced words, and its relative purity is regarded by the locals as a powerful symbol of their own ability to survive hundreds of years of foreign domination with their culture unscathed. Bearing little relation to any Indo-European language, Estonian is a difficult language for outsiders to master. Although it has no masculine or feminine gender, the situation is complicated by the existence of fourteen noun cases, which take the form of a fiendishly difficult-to-learn set of suffixes. "Tallinna" ("Tallinn's"), "Tallinas" ("in Tallinn"), "Tallinast" ("from Tallinn") are just three examples of the way the system works.

If you wish to investigate further, *Colloquial Estonian* (Routledge) makes an admirable attempt to render this notoriously impenetrable language both fun and accessible.

Pronunciation

In Estonian, words are pronounced exactly as they're written, with the stress almost always falling on the first syllable. Estonian consonants are pronounced pretty much as they are in English, and it's only really the vowels, listed below that require particular attention. If you're leafing through an Estonian dictionary, bear in mind that the vowels õ, ä, ö and ü usually come at the end of the alphabet, just after z.

a "a" as in attitude
aa "a" as in cart
ä midway between the "a" in hat and "e" in met
e "e" as in met
ee "é" as in café
j "y" as in yellow
o "o" as in dog
oo "o" as in port
ö the same as German ö; a combination of o and e that sounds like the "u" in fur
õ no equivalent in English; midway between the "ur" in fur and the "i" in sit
š "sh" as in shiny
u "oo" as in fool
ü the same as German "ü"; a combination of u and e that sounds like the French "u" in "sur"

Estonian words and phrases

Basics

Kas te räägite inglise keelt?	Do you speak English?
Jah	Yes
Ei	No
Ma ei saa aru	I don't understand
Palun	Please
Tänan/aitäh	Thank you
Vabandage	Excuse me
Tere	Hello
Tere hommikust	Good morning
Head õhtust	Good evening
Head ööd	Goodnight
Nägemiseni/ nägemist	Goodbye
Hüvasti!	Bye!
Kuidas sa elad?	How are you?
Tänan, hästi	Fine thanks
Kuidas sinu nimi on?	What is your name?
Minu nimi on...	My name is...
Eile	Yesterday
Täna	Today
Homme	Tomorrow
Hommikul	In the morning
Pärastlõunat	In the afternoon
Õhtul	In the evening

Some signs

Sissepääs	Entrance
Väljapääs	Exit
Saabumine	Arrival
Väljumine	Departure
Avatud	Open
Suletud	Closed
Tualett	Toilet
Mitte suitsetada!	No smoking!

Questions and directions

Kus on..?	Where is..?
Millal?	When?
Mis?	What?
Miks?	Why?
Rong/buss/laev/ jalgratas	Train/bus/ferry/bicycle
Kui palju?	How much?
Kui palju see maksab?	How much does this cost?
Ma soovin...	I'd like...
Odav	Cheap
Kulukas	Expensive

Hea	Good
Halb/paha	Bad
Siin	Here
Seal	There
Vasak	Left
Parem	Right
Otse	Straight on
Pilet/piletikassa	Ticket/ticket office
Jaam, vaksal	Train station
Bussijaam/peatus	Bus station/bus stop

Days and months

Esmaspäev	Monday
Teisipäev	Tuesday
Kolmapäev	Wednesday
Neljapäev	Thursday
Reede	Friday
Laupäev	Saturday
Pühapäev	Sunday
Jaanuar	January
Veebruar	February
Märts	March
Aprill	April
Mai	May
Juuni	June
Juuli	July
August	August
September	September
Oktoober	October
November	November
Detsember	December

Numbers

üks	1
kaks	2
kolm	3
neli	4
viis	5
kuus	6
seitse	7
kaheksa	8
üheksa	9
kümme	10
üksteist	11
kaksteist	12
kolmteist	13
neliteist	14
viisteist	15
kuusteist	16
seitseteist	17

kaheksateist	18
üheksateist	19
kakskümmend	20
kolmkümmend	30
nelikümmend	40
viiskümmend	50
kuuskümmend	60
seitsekümmend	70
kaheksakümmend	80
üheksakümmend	90
sada	100
kaksada	200
tuhat	1000

Some countries

Eesti	Estonia
Läti	Latvia
Leedu	Lithuania
Poola	Poland
Rootsi	Sweden
Saksamaa	Germany
Soome	Finland
Valgevene	Belarus
Venemaa	Russia

Food and drink

Basic words and phrases

Menüü/toidukaart	Menu
Hommikueine	Breakfast
Lõuna	Lunch
Head isu!	Bon appetit!
Terviseks!	Cheers!
Arve	Bill

Essentials

Eelroad	Starters
Juust	Cheese
...kastmes	In ... sauce
Kaste	Sauce
Leib	(Brown) bread
Päevapraad	Dish of the day
Pipar	Pepper
Roog	Dish, course
Sai	(White) bread
Sool	Salt
Suhkur	Sugar
Või	Butter
Vorm	Stew

Snacks and starters

Kartulisalat	Potato salad
Pannkook	Pancake
Pelmeenid	Pelmeny
Pirukas	Dough parcel stuffed with cabbage and bacon
Salat	Salad
Sült	Cold meat in jelly
Supp	Soup

Meat (liha)

Kana	Chicken
Kanapraad	Roast chicken
Karbonaad	Pork chop in batter
Lammas	Lamb
Peekon	Bacon
Šašlõkk	Shish kebab
Sealiha	Pork
Seapraad	Roast pork
Sink	Ham
Šnitsel	Schnitzel (usually veal, but can be pork or chicken)
Verivorst	Blood sausage, black pudding

Fish (kala) and seafood (mereannid)

Haug	Pike
Krevet	Shrimp
Makra	Crab
Räim	Baltic herring
Sprott	Sprat
Tuunikala	Tuna

Vegetables (köögivili)

Ahjukartulid	Roast potatoes
Hapukapsas	Sauerkraut
Hapukurk	Pickled gherkin
Hernes	Pea
Kartulid	Potatoes
Küüslauk	Garlic
Mädarõigas	Horseradish

Porgand	Carrot	Õun	Apple
Sibul	Onion	Pirn	Pear
Tomat	Tomato	Ploom	Plum
		Vaarikas	Raspberry

Desserts (desserdid)

		### Drinks (joogid)	
Jäätis	Ice cream		
Juustukook	Cheesecake	Hõõgvein	Mulled wine
Kook	Cake	Kohv	Coffee
Piparkook	Gingerbread	Mahl	Juice
Saiake	Bun	Õlu	Beer
Šokolaadikook	Chocolate cake	Piim	Milk
		Vesi	Water

Fruit (puuvili)

		Vein	Wine
Apelsin	Orange	Viin	Vodka

Glossary

Aed	Garden	Pank	Bank
Apteek	Pharmacy	Pood	Shop
Järv	Lake	Postkontor	Post office
Jõgi	River	Raba	Bog
Kauplus	Shop	Saar	Island
Kesklinn	Town centre	Saatkond	Embassy
Kirik	Church	Sild	Bridge
Laht	Gulf	Soo	Bog
Linn	Town	Supelrand	Beach
Linnus	Castle	Tänav	Street
Loss	Castle	Toidupood	Food shop
Maantee	Road	Toomkirik	Cathedral
Mägi	Hill	Turg	Market
Mõis	Manor house	Tuulik	Windmill
Muuseum	Museum	Väljak	Square
Pakihõid	Left-luggage office		

Latvian

A long with Lithuanian, Latvian is a member of the Baltic family of languages and in terms of grammar and basic vocabulary is very close to its southerly neighbour. There, however, the similarity ends: unlike the staccato, almost Mediterranean-sounding delivery of Lithuanian, Latvian has a melodic, rolling quality that sounds closer to Scandinavia than the European mainland. The stress always falls on the first syllable of the word (the only exception to this rule being "paldies", meaning "thank you"); accented vowels are pronounced in a long, drawled-out way; and unaccented vowels are clipped back in everyday speech to the extent that you can't always hear that they're there at all. *Colloquial Latvian* (Routledge) is a good place to start if you're learning, although it's less fun than the excellent *Palīgā!* series of textbooks published by Latvian television (and available from the Zvaigzne bookshop; see p.219) – although they're intended for Russian-speakers and don't have any instructions in English.

Pronunciation

Aside from a few tricky consonants not found in English, Latvian pronunciation is pretty straightforward, providing you pay attention to the vowel sounds below.

a "a" as in clap
ā "a" as in hard
c "ts" as in cats
č "ch" as in church
e usually pronounced like "e" as in bet, but in some words resembles the "aa" in aah
ē like French "é" in café, but in some words resembles the "aa" in aah
ģ somewhere between the "d" in endure and the "j" in jeep
i "i" as in hit
ī "ee" as in green
j "y" as in yesterday
ķ "t" as in future
ļ rolled combination of "l" and "y"; like the final "l" and initial "y" of "cool yule" pronounced together
ņ "n" as in new
o "wo" as in water
š "sh" as in shut
u "u" as in put
ū "oo" as in fool
ž "s" as in pleasure

Latvian words and phrases

Basics

Vai Jūs runājat angliski?	Do you speak English?
Jā	Yes
Nē	No
Es nesaprotu	I don't understand
Lūdzu	Please
Paldies	Thank you
Labi	OK
Atvainojiet/Piedodiet	Excuse me/Sorry
Sveiks! (sing); sveiki! (pl); čau!	Hi!
Labdien	Hello/Good day
Esiet sveicināti	Welcome
Labrīt	Good morning
Labvakar	Good evening
Ar labu nakti	Good night
Uz redzēšanos	Goodbye
Atā!	Bye!
Kā Jūs sauc? (formal); kā tevi sauc? (informal)	What is your name?
Mani sauc...	My name is...
Šodien	Today
Vakar	Yesterday
Rīt	Tomorrow
Rītā	In the morning
Pēcpusdienā	In the afternoon
Vakarā	In the evening

Some signs

Ieeja	Entrance
Izeja	Exit
Pienākšana, pienāk	Arrival
Atiešana, atiet	Departure
Atvērts	Open
Slēgts	Closed
Tualete	Toilet
Smēķēt aizliegts!	No smoking!

Questions and directions

Kur?	Where?
Kur atrodas...?	Where is...?
Kad?	When?
Kas?	What?
Kāpēc?	Why?
Kur ir dzelceļa stacija?	Where is the railway station?

Vilciens/autobuss/velosipēds	Train/bus/bicycle
Cik?	How much?
Cik tas maksā?	How much does it cost?
...Es vēlos...	I'd like
Lēts	Cheap
Dārgs	Expensive
Labs	Good
Slikts	Bad
Karsts	Hot
Auksts	Cold
Šeit	Here
Tur	There
Pa kreisi	Left
Pa labi	Right
Taisni	Straight on
Tuvu/tālu	Near/far
Biļete/biļešu kase	Ticket/ticket office
Stacija/autoosta/pietura	Train/bus station/bus stop
Uz Rīgu	To Rīga
Uz Ventspili	To Ventspils
Tagad	Now
Agri, agrāk	Early, earlier
Vēlu, vēlāk	Late, later
Cik ir pulkstenis?	What time is it?

Countries

Baltakrievija	Belarus
Igaunija	Estonia
Somija	Finland
Vācija	Germany
Latvija	Latvia
Lietuva	Lithuania
Polija	Poland
Krievija	Russia
Zviedrija	Sweden

Numbers

viens (m); viena (f)	1
divi (m); divas (f)	2
trīs	3
četri	4
pieci	5
seši	6
septiņi	7
astoņi	8
deviņi	9

desmit	10
vienpadsmit	11
divpadsmit	12
trīspadsmit	13
četrpadsmit	14
piecpadsmit	15
sešpadsmit	16
septiņpadsmit	17
astoņpadsmit	18
deviņpadsmit	19
divdesmit	20
trīsdesmit	30
četrdesmit	40
piecdesmit	50
sešdesmit	60
septiņdesmit	70
astoņdesmit	80
deviņdesmit	90
simts	100
divi simti	200
tūkstotis	1000

Days and months

Pirmdiena	Monday
Otrdiena	Tuesday
Trešdiena	Wednesday
Ceturtdiena	Thursday
Piektdiena	Friday
Sestdiena	Saturday
Svētdiena	Sunday
Janvāris	January
Februāris	February
Marts	March
Aprīlis	April
Maijs	May
Jūnijs	June
Jūlijs	July
Augusts	August
Septembris	September
Oktobris	October
Novembris	November
Decembris	December

Food and drink terms

Essentials

Cukurs	Sugar
Krējums	Sour cream
Maize	Bread
Merce	Sauce
Olas	Eggs
Pipari	Pepper
Rupjmaize	Rye bread
Sāls	Salt
Siers	Cheese
Soļanka	Meat-and-vegetable broth
Sviests	Butter
Zupa	Soup

Latvian staples

Cūkas galerts	Pork in aspic
Pelēkie zirņi	Peas with bacon
Pelmeņi	Dough parcels with meat stuffing
Pīrāgs/pīrādziņš	Doughy pasty stuffed with bacon and/or cabbage
Rasols	Salad consisting of chopped meat and vegetables dressed in sour cream

Zirņu pikas	Mashed peas with bacon

Meat (gaļa)

Cāļīšu gaļa	Chicken
Cūkas gaļa	Pork
Desa	Sausage
Karbonāde	Pork chop
Liellopu gaļa	Beef
Teļu gaļa	Veal
Žāvēta desa	Smoked sausage

Fish (zivs)

Forele	Trout
Lasis	Salmon
Siļķe	Herring
Šprotes	Sprats
Tuncis	Tuna
Zandarts	Pike-perch
Zutis	Eel

Vegetables (dārzeņi)

Burkāni	Carrots
Gurķi	Cucumbers
Kartupeļi	Potatoes
Kāposti	Cabbage
Ķiploks	Garlic
Loki	Spring onions

Salāti	Lettuce
Sēnes	Mushrooms
Sīpoli	Onions
Skābie kāposti	Sauerkraut
Skābie gurķi	Pickled gherkins
Tomāti	Tomatoes

Desserts and fruit

Ābols	Apple
Apelsīns	Orange
Biezpiens	Curd cheese
Kūka	Cake
Ķīselis	Sweet porridge with fruit
Pankūkas	Pancake
Pudiņš	Pudding
Rieksti	Nuts

| Saldējums | Ice cream |
| Torte | Gateau |

Drinks (dzerieni)

Alus	Beer
Balzāms	Balsam – gloppy black liqueur
Degvīns	Vodka
Kafija	Coffee
Karstvīns	Mulled wine
Piens	Milk
Sula	Juice
Šņabis	Vodka
Tēja	Tea
Ūdens	Water
Vīns	Wine

Glossary

Aptieka	Pharmacy
Banka	Bank
Baznīca	Church
Darzs	Garden
Dome	Cathedral
Ezers	Lake
Iela	Street
Laukums	Square
Mežs	Forest
Muiža	Manor house
Muzejs	Museum

Parks	Park
Pasts	Post office
Pils	Castle
Pilskalns	(Iron Age) castle mound
Purvs	Bog
Sala	Island
Slimnīca	Hospital
Tilts	Bridge
Tirgus	Market
Upe	River

Lithuanian

L ithuanian is an Indo-European language belonging to the Baltic family, of which Latvian is the only other surviving member – other Baltic peoples such as the Prussians and the Yotvingians having died out in the Middle Ages. It's thought that the vocabulary and grammar of Lithuanian have changed little over the centuries, leading some linguists to argue that it is closer to ancient Sanskrit than any other living language. Few Lithuanian words bear much resemblance to those you may have encountered elsewhere in Europe, lending the language an exotic aura – and although it's a difficult language to pick up at first, it soon becomes addictive. If you are interested in learning, then *Colloquial Lithuanian* published by Routledge is the best of the available self-study courses. Once you get to Vilnius, a range of Lithuanian-produced textbooks aimed at foreign students is available from bigger bookshops.

There are two **genders** in Lithuanian – masculine and feminine. Masculine nouns almost always end with –s, feminine nouns usually with –a or –ė. Even foreign names are made to fit in with Lithuanian rules, as you will see from local newspaper references to figures as diverse as Georgeas Bushas and Saddamas Husseinas. Plurals are formed by adding –ai or –iai to masculine nouns; –s to feminine ones. It's also worth bearing in mind that there are six noun **cases** in Lithuanian, ensuring that each noun changes its ending according to which part of the sentence it occupies: thus "į Vilnių" means "to Vilnius", "iš Vilniaus" "from Vilnius", and "Vilniuje" "in Vilnius".

Pronunciation

Pronunciation is not as difficult as it first appears. Every word is spoken exactly as it's written, and each letter represents an individual sound. Most letters are pronounced as they are in English, with the following exceptions:

a "a" as in clap
ą originally a nasal vowel; nowadays pronounced in much the same way as "a"
c "ts" as in cats
č "ch" as in church
e usually pronounced like "e" as in bet, but in some words resembles the "ai" in fair
ė like French "é" in café
ę "e" as in bet
i "i" as in hit
į "i" as in hit
j "y" as in yesterday
š "sh" as in shut
u "u" as in put
ū "oo" as in fool
ų "u" as in put
y "i" as in hit
ž "s" as in pleasure

Lithuanian words and phrases

Basics

Ar Jūs kalbate angliškai?	Do you speak English?
Nesuprantu	I don't understand
Taip	Yes
Ne	No
Prašau, prašom	Please
Ačiū	Thank you
Gerai	OK
Atsiprašau	Excuse me/sorry
Labas!, Sveikas (m)/sveika (f)!	Hi!
Laba diena	Hello/Good day
Labas rytas	Good morning
Labas vakaras	Good evening
Labanakt	Goodnight
Viso gero	Goodbye
Ate!	Bye!
Iki!	See you!
Kaip gyveni?/Kaip sekasi?	How are you?
Ačiū, gerai	Fine, thanks
Koks tavo vardas?/ Kuo tu vardu?	What is your name?
Mano vardas...	My name is...
Šiandien	Today
Vakar	Yesterday
Rytoj	Tomorrow
Rytą	In the morning
Popiet	In the afternoon
Vakare	In the evening

Some signs

Įejimas	Entrance
Įšejimas	Exit
Atvykimas	Arrival
Išvykimas	Departure
Atidaryta	Open
Uždaryta	Closed
Turgus	Market
Ligoninė	Hospital
Vaistinė	Pharmacy
Tualetas	Toilet
Nerūkyti/Nerūkoma!	No smoking!

Questions and directions

Kur yra...?	Where is...?
Kada?	When?
Kas?	What?
Dabar	Now

Anksti, ankščiau	Early, earlier
Vėlu, vėliau	Late, later
Kiek valandų/Kelinta valanda?	What time is it?
Didelis/mažas	Big/small
Pigus/brangus	Cheap/expensive
Karštas/šaltas	Hot/cold
Arti/toli	Near/far
Geras/blogas	Good/bad
Daugiau/mažiau	More/less
Kairė/dešinė	Left/right
Tiesiai	Straight on
Traukinys/autobusas /laivas/keltas/ dviratis	Train/bus/boat/ ferry/ bicycle
Bilietas/bilietų kasa	Ticket/ticket office
Prašom, vieną bilietą į...	A ticket to... please
Į vieną pusę	Single
Pirmyn ir atgal	Return/round-trip
Norėčiau	I'd like...
Vienutė	Single room
Kambarys dviems	Double room
Kiek kainuoja?	How much is it?
Ar tūrite ką nors pigiau?	Do you have anything cheaper?

Numbers

vienas (m), viena (f)	1
du (m), dvi (f)	2
trys	3
keturi (m), keturios (f)	4
penki (m), penkios (f)	5
šeši (m), šešios (f)	6
septyni (m), septynios (f)	7
aštuoni (m), aštuonios (f)	8
devyni (m), devynios (f)	9
dešimt	10
vienuolika	11
dvylika	12
trylika	13
keturiolika	14
penkiolika	15
šešiolika	16
septyniolika	17
aštuoniolika	18
devyniolika	19
dvidešimt	20
trisdešimt	30
keturiasdešimt	40

penkiasdešimt	50	Balandis	April
šešiasdešimt	60	Gegužė	May
septyniasdešimt	70	Birželis	June
aštuoniasdešimt	80	Liepa	July
devyniasdešimt	90	Rugpjūtis	August
šimtas	100	Rugsėjis	September
du šimtai	200	Spalis	October
tūkstantis	1000	Lapkritis	November
		Gruodis	December

Days and months

Pirmadienis	Monday
Antradienis	Tuesday
Trečiadienis	Wednesday
Ketvirtadienis	Thursday
Penktadienis	Friday
Šeštadienis	Saturday
Sekmadienis	Sunday
Sausis	January
Vasaris	February
Kovas	March

Countries

Baltarusija	Belarus
Estija	Estonia
Suomija	Finland
Vokietija	Germany
Latvija	Latvia
Lietuva	Lithuania
Lenkija	Poland
Rusija	Russia
Švedija	Sweden

Food and drink terms

Basic words and phrases

Prašom, meniu	The menu, please
Prašom, kavos	A coffee, please
Prašom, du alaus	Two beers please
Aš vegetaras (m), vegetarė (f)	I am a vegetarian
Ar yra kas nors be mėsos?	Do you have anything without meat?
Į sveikatą!	Cheers!
Skanaus!	Bon appetit!
Prašom, sąskaitą	The bill, please

Essentials

Cukrus	Sugar
Druska	Salt
Duona	Bread
Grietinė	Sour cream
Kiaušiniai	Eggs
Medus	Honey
Padažas	Sauce
Pienas	Milk
Pipirai	Pepper
Sriuba	Soup
Sūris	Cheese
Sviestas	Butter

Lithuanian staples

Blynai	Pancakes
Bulvių blynai	Potato pancakes
Bulvių plokštainis	Baked slab of potato
Cepelinai	Zeppelin-shaped potato parcels stuffed with meat
Didžkukuliai	see "cepelinai"
Kibinas	Meat pasty
Koldūnai	Ravioli-like parcels with meat stuffing
Kugelis	see "bulvių plokštainis"
Šaltibarščiai	Cold beetroot soup
Vedarai	Pig intestine stuffed with potato

Meat (mėsa)

Dešra	Thick, salami-like sausage
Dešrelė	Frankfurter-like sausage
Jautiena	Beef
Kalakutiena	Turkey
Karbonadas	Pork chop
Kepsnys	Fried or roast cut of meat
Kumpis	Ham
Kiauliena	Pork
Vištiena	Chicken

Fish (žuvis)

Lašiša	Salmon
Menkė	Cod
Rukyta žuvis	Smoked fish
Unguris	Eel
Upėtakis	Trout

Vegetables (daržovės)

Agurkas	Cucumber
Bulvės	Potato
Česnakas	Garlic
Grybai	Mushrooms
Kopūstas	Cabbage
Moliūgas	Pumpkin
Morkos	Carrots
Pomidoras	Tomato
Pupelės	Beans
Svogūnas	Onion
Žirniai	Peas

Fruit (vaisiai)

Apelsinas	Orange
Avietės	Raspberries

Braškės	Strawberries
Citrina	Lemon
Kriaušė	Pear
Obuolys	Apple
Slyva	Plum
Vyšnia	Cherry

Desserts (desertai)

Ledai	Ice cream
Pyragaitis	Small cake
Pyragas	Cake or pudding
Riešutai	Nuts
Tortas	Cake
Uogienė	Jam

Drinks (gerimai)

Alus	Beer
Arbata	Tea
Degtinė	Vodka
Kava	Coffee
Sultys	Juice
Vanduo	Water
Vynas	Wine

Glossary

Aikštė	Square
Autobusų stotelė	Bus stop
Autobusų stotis	Bus station
Bankas	Bank
Bažnyčia	Church
Dviračių takas	Cycle path
Ežeras	Lake
Gatvė	Street
Giria	Forest
Kaimas	Village
Kalnas	Hill
Katedra	Cathedral
Kopa	Dune
Ligoninė	Hospital
Miestas	Town
Miškas	Forest
Muziejus	Museum

Naujamiestis	New Town
Parkas	Park
Paštas	Post office
Piliakalnis	(Iron Age) castle mound
Pilis	Castle
Rotušė	Town hall
Sodas	Garden
Senamiestis	Old Town
Stotis	Station
Takas	Path
Tiltas	Bridge
Turgus	Market
Upė	River
Vaistinė	Pharmacy
Vienuolynas	Abbey

Travel store

UK & Ireland
Britain
Devon & Cornwall
Dublin **D**
Edinburgh **D**
England
Ireland
The Lake District
London
London **D**
London Mini Guide
Scotland
Scottish Highlands
& Islands
Wales

Europe
Algarve **D**
Amsterdam
Amsterdam **D**
Andalucía
Athens **D**
Austria
Baltic States
Barcelona
Barcelona **D**
Belgium &
Luxembourg
Berlin
Brittany & Normandy
Bruges **D**
Brussels
Budapest
Bulgaria
Copenhagen
Corfu
Corsica
Costa Brava **D**
Crete
Croatia
Cyprus
Czech & Slovak
Republics
Denmark
Dodecanese & East
Aegean Islands
Dordogne & The Lot
Europe
Florence & Siena
Florence **D**
France
Germany
Gran Canaria **D**
Greece
Greek Islands

Hungary
Ibiza & Formentera **D**
Iceland
Ionian Islands
Italy
The Italian Lakes
Languedoc &
Roussillon
Lanzarote &
Fuerteventura **D**
Lisbon **D**
The Loire Valley
Madeira **D**
Madrid **D**
Mallorca **D**
Mallorca & Menorca
Malta & Gozo **D**
Menorca
Moscow
The Netherlands
Norway
Paris
Paris **D**
Paris Mini Guide
Poland
Portugal
Prague
Prague **D**
Provence
& the Côte D'Azur
Pyrenees
Romania
Rome
Rome **D**
Sardinia
Scandinavia
Sicily
Slovenia
Spain
St Petersburg
Sweden
Switzerland
Tenerife &
La Gomera **D**
Turkey
Tuscany & Umbria
Venice & The Veneto
Venice **D**
Vienna

Asia
Bali & Lombok
Bangkok
Beijing

Cambodia
China
Goa
Hong Kong & Macau
Hong Kong
& Macau **D**
India
Indonesia
Japan
Kerala
Laos
Malaysia, Singapore
& Brunei
Nepal
The Philippines
Rajasthan, Dehli
& Agra
Singapore
Singapore **D**
South India
Southeast Asia
Sri Lanka
Taiwan
Thailand
Thailand's Beaches
& Islands
Tokyo
Vietnam

Australasia
Australia
Melbourne
New Zealand
Sydney

North America
Alaska
Baja California
Boston
California
Canada
Chicago
Colorado
Florida
The Grand Canyon
Hawaii
Honolulu **D**
Las Vegas **D**
Los Angeles
Maui **D**
Miami & South Florida
Montréal
New England
New Orleans **D**
New York City

New York City **D**
New York City Mini
Guide
Orlando & Walt
Disney World® **D**
Pacific Northwest
San Francisco
San Francisco **D**
Seattle
Southwest USA
Toronto
USA
Vancouver
Washington DC
Washington DC **D**
Yellowstone & The
Grand Tetons
Yosemite

Caribbean
& Latin America
Antigua & Barbuda
Argentina
Bahamas
Barbados **D**
Belize
Bolivia
Brazil
Cancùn & Cozumel
Caribbean
Central America
Chile
Costa Rica
Cuba
Dominican Republic
Dominican Republic
Ecuador
Guatemala
Jamaica
Mexico
Peru
St Lucia **D**
South America
Trinidad & Tobago
Yúcatan

Africa & Middle East
Cape Town & the
Garden Route
Dubai **D**
Egypt
Gambia
Jordan

D: Rough Guide
DIRECTIONS for
short breaks

enya
arrakesh **D**
orocco
outh Africa, Lesotho
  & Swaziland
yria
anzania
unisia
est Africa
anzibar

ravel Specials
irst-Time Africa
irst-Time Around
  the World
irst-Time Asia
irst-Time Europe
irst-Time Latin
  America
ravel Health
ravel Online
ravel Survival
Valks in London
  & SE England
Vomen Travel
Vorld Party

Maps
Algarve
Amsterdam
Andalucia
  & Costa del Sol
Argentina
Athens
Australia
Barcelona
Berlin
Boston & Cambridge
Brittany
Brussels
California
Chicago
Chile
Corsica
Costa Rica
  & Panama
Crete
Croatia
Cuba
Cyprus
Czech Republic
Dominican Republic
Dubai & UAE
Dublin
Egypt

Florence & Siena
Florida
France
Frankfurt
Germany
Greece
Guatemala & Belize
Iceland
India
Ireland
Italy
Kenya & Northern
  Tanzania
Lisbon
London
Los Angeles
Madrid
Malaysia
Mallorca
Marrakesh
Mexico
Miami & Key West
Morocco
New England
New York City
New Zealand
Northern Spain
Paris
Peru
Portugal
Prague
Pyrenees & Andorra
Rome
San Francisco
Sicily
South Africa
South India
Spain & Portugal
Sri Lanka
Tenerife
Thailand
Toronto
Trinidad & Tobago
Tunisia
Turkey
Tuscany
Venice
Vietnam, Laos
  & Cambodia
Washington DC
Yucatán Peninsula

**Dictionary
Phrasebooks**
Croatian
Czech
Dutch
Egyptian Arabic
French
German
Greek
Hindi & Urdu
Italian
Japanese
Latin American
  Spanish
Mandarin Chinese
Mexican Spanish
Polish
Portuguese
Russian
Spanish
Swahili
Thai
Turkish
Vietnamese

Computers
Blogging
eBay
iPhone
iPods, iTunes
  & music online
The Internet
Macs & OS X
MySpace
PCs and Windows
PlayStation Portable
Website Directory

Film & TV
American
  Independent Film
British Cult Comedy
Chick Flicks
Comedy Movies
Cult Movies
Film
Film Musicals
Film Noir
Gangster Movies
Horror Movies
Kids' Movies
Sci-Fi Movies
Westerns

Lifestyle
Babies
Ethical Living
Pregnancy & Birth
Running

Music Guides
The Beatles
Blues
Bob Dylan
Book of Playlists
Classical Music
Elvis
Frank Sinatra
Heavy Metal
Hip-Hop
Jazz
Led Zeppelin
Opera
Pink Floyd
Punk
Reggae
Rock
The Rolling Stones
Soul and R&B
Velvet Underground
World Music
  (2 vols)

Popular Culture
Books for Teenagers
Children's Books,
  5-11
Conspiracy Theories
Crime Fiction
Cult Fiction
The Da Vinci Code
His Dark Materials
Lord of the Rings
Shakespeare
Superheroes
The Templars
Unexplained
  Phenomena

Science
The Brain
Climate Change
The Earth
Genes & Cloning
The Universe
Weather

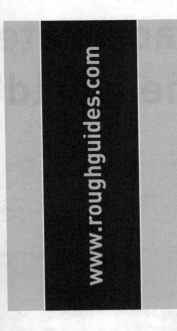

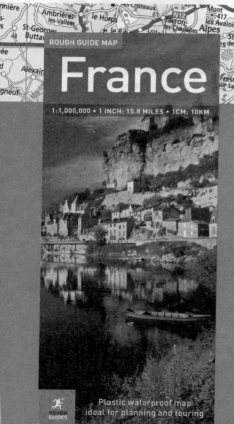

NOTES

Small print and Index

A Rough Guide to Rough Guides

Published in 1982, the first Rough Guide – to Greece – was a student scheme that became a publishing phenomenon. Mark Ellingham, a recent graduate in English from Bristol University, had been travelling in Greece the previous summer and couldn't find the right guidebook. With a small group of friends he wrote his own guide, combining a highly contemporary, journalistic style with a thoroughly practical approach to travellers' needs.

The immediate success of the book spawned a series that rapidly covered dozens of destinations. And, in addition to impecunious backpackers, Rough Guides soon acquired a much broader and older readership that relished the guides' wit and inquisitiveness as much as their enthusiastic, critical approach and value-for-money ethos.

These days, Rough Guides include recommendations from shoestring to luxury and cover more than 200 destinations around the globe, including almost every country in the Americas and Europe, more than half of Africa and most of Asia and Australasia. Our ever-growing team of authors and photographers is spread all over the world, particularly in Europe, the USA and Australia.

In the early 1990s, Rough Guides branched out of travel, with the publication of Rough Guides to World Music, Classical Music and the Internet. All three have become benchmark titles in their fields, spearheading the publication of a wide range of books under the Rough Guide name.

Including the travel series, Rough Guides now number more than 350 titles, covering: phrasebooks, waterproof maps, music guides from Opera to Heavy Metal, reference works as diverse as Conspiracy Theories and Shakespeare, and popular culture books from iPods to Poker. Rough Guides also produce a series of more than 120 World Music CDs in partnership with World Music Network.

Visit www.roughguides.com to see our latest publications.

Rough Guide travel images are available for commercial licensing at www.roughguidespictures.com

Rough Guide credits

Text editor: Natasha Foges
Layout: Ajay Verma
Cartography: Amod Singh
Picture editor: Mark Thomas
Production: Rebecca Short
Proofreader: Jennifer Speake
Cover design: Chloë Roberts
Photographer: Kerry Dean
Editorial: **London** Kate Berens, Claire
Saunders, Ruth Blackmore, Alison Murchie,
Karoline Densley, Andy Turner, Keith Drew,
Edward Aves, Nikki Birrell, Alice Park, Sarah
Eno, Lucy White, Jo Kirby, James Smart, Roísín
Cameron, James Rice, Emma Traynor, Emma
Gibbs, Kathryn Lane, Joe Staines, Duncan
Clark, Peter Buckley, Matthew Milton, Tracy
Hopkins, Ruth Tidball; **New York** Andrew
Rosenberg, Steven Horak, AnneLise Sorensen,
Amy Hegarty, April Isaacs, Ella Steim, Anna
Owens, Joseph Petta, Sean Mahoney; **Delhi**
Madhavi Singh, Karen D'Souza
Design & Pictures: **London** Scott Stickland,
Dan May, Diana Jarvis, Chloë Roberts, Nicole
Newman, Sarah Cummins; **Delhi** Umesh

Aggarwal, Jessica Subramanian, Ankur Guha,
Pradeep Thapliyal, Sachin Tanwar, Anita Singh
Production: Vicky Baldwin
Cartography: **London** Maxine Repath, Ed
Wright, Katie Lloyd-Jones; **Delhi** Jai Prakash
Mishra, Rajesh Chhibber, Ashutosh Bharti, Rajesh
Mishra, Animesh Pathak, Jasbir Sandhu, Karobi
Gogoi, Alakananda Bhattacharya, Swati Handoo
Online: Narender Kumar, Rakesh Kumar,
Amit Verma, Rahul Kumar, Ganesh Sharma,
Debojit Borah
Marketing & Publicity: **London** Liz Statham,
Niki Hanmer, Louise Maher, Jess Carter, Vanessa
Godden, Vivienne Watton, Anna Paynton, Rachel
Sprackett; **New York** Geoff Colquitt, Megan
Kennedy, Katy Ball
Manager India: Punita Singh
Series Editor: Mark Ellingham
Reference Director: Andrew Lockett
Publishing Coordinator: Helen Phillips
Publishing Director: Martin Dunford
Commercial Manager: Gino Magnotta
Managing Director: John Duhigg

Publishing information

This second edition published January 2008 by
Rough Guides Ltd,
80 Strand, London WC2R 0RL
345 Hudson St, 4th Floor,
New York, NY 10014, USA
14 Local Shopping Centre, Panchsheel Park,
New Delhi 110017, India
Distributed by the Penguin Group
Penguin Books Ltd,
80 Strand, London WC2R 0RL
Penguin Group (USA)
375 Hudson Street, NY 10014, USA
Penguin Group (Australia)
250 Camberwell Road, Camberwell,
Victoria 3124, Australia
Penguin Books Canada Ltd,
10 Alcorn Avenue, Toronto, Ontario,
Canada M4V 1E4
Penguin Group (NZ)
67 Apollo Drive, Mairangi Bay, Auckland 1310,
New Zealand

Cover concept by Peter Dyer.

Typeset in Bembo and Helvetica to an original
design by Henry Iles.

Printed and bound in China

© Jonathan Bousfield

504pp includes index

A catalogue record for this book is available from
the British Library

ISBN: 978-1-84353-922-3

1   3   5   7   9   8   6   4   2

Help us update

We've gone to a lot of effort to ensure that
the second edition of **The Rough Guide
to The Baltic States** is accurate and up to
date. However, things change – places get
"discovered", opening hours are notoriously
fickle, restaurants and rooms raise prices or lower
standards. If you feel we've got it wrong or left
something out, we'd like to know, and if you can
remember the address, the price, the hours, the
phone number, so much the better.

Please send your comments with the subject
line "**Rough Guide The Baltic States Update**"
to ⓔmail@roughguides.com. We'll credit all
contributions and send a copy of the next edition
(or any other Rough Guide if you prefer) for the
very best emails.

Have your questions answered and tell others
about your trip at
ⓦcommunity.roughguides.com

Acknowledgements

Jonathan Bousfield would like to thank Kerry and Sonata, Indrė Trakimaitė, Nijolė Beliukevičienė, Gabija Thomson, Martiņš Zaprauskis, Steve Roman, Baiba Plume, Inga Vonoga, Ieva Pigozne, Jurgita and Henrieta in Birštonas, Edita Mongirdaitė, Ingrida Nasvytė, Inga Pazereckaitė, Jurgita Neniskienė, Romena Savickienė, Jurgita Eglinskienė, Howard Jarvis, Andrew Quested, Neil Taylor and Renate at Skanu mezs. Thanks also go to Natasha Foges

for unflagging enthusiasm and encouragement, Jennifer Speake for proofreading, Mark Thomas for picture research, Ajay Verma for his patience and layout skills and Amod Singh for preparing the maps.

Shafik Meghji would like to thank Darryl Andrade and Keef Llewellyn-Burke for their insight into Tallinn's nightlife, Kate Berens, Ruth Blackmore, Jon Bousfield, Natasha Foges, Jean, Nizar and Nina Meghji, Steve Roman and Kadri Suni.

SMALL PRINT

Readers' letters

Thanks to all the readers who have taken the time to write in with comments and suggestions (and apologies if we've inadvertently omitted or misspelt anyone's name):

Patricia Abt; Bill Burnham; Geir Johne Carlsen; Henrik Clausen; Winn Faria; Ton Geldens; Nicole Gmuer; Helena Granlund; Victoria Herriott; Chris Keeling; Brendan Kirwan; Karen Koyanagi and Fraser Shaw; Richard Mackey; Nick Nicolaides;

JCE Rhodius; Arnon Rosenthal; Bob and Rose Sandham; Marius Sekse; Daniele, Pia and Jörg Sendele; John Stainsby; Claire Stansfield; Sander Van den Oord; Rudi Wesselius; Gillian White; Stephen Wilson.

Photo credits

All photos © Rough Guides except the following:

SMALL PRINT

Index

Map entries are in colour.

A

accommodation
Estonia 54
Latvia............................... 171
Lithuania.......................... 286
Āraiši (LAT)...............22, 268
Abava valley
(LAT).....................237–242
Aglona (LAT) ... 23, 276–278
Aizkraukle (LAT) 272
Alatskivi (EST)............... 163
Altja (EST) 137
Amata valley (LAT)........ 265
amber 416
Angla (EST) 114
Anykščiai
(LITH) 353–355
August, Sigismund
.............................298, 308
Aukštaitija National Park
(LITH) 350–353
Aukštaitija National
Park............................351

B

B&Bs...............................37
banks
Estonia 62
Latvia............................... 179
Lithuania.......................... 295
Barclay de Tolly,
Mikhail 148, 203
Barons, Krišjānis........... 434
Basanavičius, Jonas..... 441
Bathory, Stefan....182, 298,
313
Bauska (LAT)................. 225
Beržoras (LITH)............. 421
birdwatching....................39,
The great outdoors colour
insert
Birštonas 378
Biržai (LITH) 355
Bižai (LITH) 383
bogs ..... 15, 139, *The great
outdoors* colour insert
books.................... 455–461
borscht.........*Baltic food &
drink* colour insert

Bulduri (LAT) 222
buses
to the Baltic States 31
in Estonia 53
in Latvia............................. 169
in Lithuania........................ 285
between the Baltic
States........................... 36

C

Čaks, Aleksandrs 207
camping...........................37
Estonia 56
Latvia............................... 173
Lithuania.......................... 288
canoeing...........................39
canoeing, Dzūkija National
Park 380
canoeing,
Gauja Valley 257
carbon offset
schemes 29
Čepkelių bog (LITH)...... 383
Čiurlionis, Mikalojus
Konstantinis......317, 332,
366, 381
Cēsis (LAT) 265–268
Cēsis 267
cinema
Estonia 60
Latvia............................... 177
Lithuania.......................... 294
changing money
Estonia 62
Latvia............................... 179
Lithuania.......................... 295
classical music
Estonia 60
Latvia............................... 176
Lithuania.......................... 293
climate..................... 11–13
climate change............... 29
clubbing
Estonia 60
Latvia............................... 177
Lithuania.......................... 290
consulates 41
costs
Estonia 61
Latvia............................... 179
Lithuania.......................... 295
Courland, Duchy of 224,
226

credit cards
Estonia 62
Latvia............................... 180
Lithuania.......................... 295
crime................................40
Curonian Spit
(LITH) 405–412,
The great outdoors colour
insert
Curonian Spit................ 406
currency............................43
cycling 39

D

Darius, Steponas.......... 365
Daugava valley
(LAT)................... 269–273
Daugavpils (LAT)... 274–276
Daugavpils 275
dialling codes 44
disabled travellers 40
drinks
Estonia 57
Latvia............................... 174
Lithuania.......................... 290
driving
to the Baltic States 31
in Estonia 53
in Latvia............................. 171
in Lithuania........................ 285
Druskininkai
(LITH) 384–389
Druskininkai 384
Duke Jakob of
Courland ...226, 229, 238,
239, 241, 272
Dzerzhinsky, Felix.........311
Dzintari (LAT) 222
Dzūkija National Park
(LITH) 380–384
Dzūkija National Park ... 381

E

Eastern and Central
Lithuania 349
Eastern Estonia 129
Eastern Latvia 256
Eisenstein, Sergei
Mikhailevich............... 204

INDEX

electricity 41
embassies 41
entertainment
Estonia 60
Latvia 176
Lithuania.......................... 293
Erratic boulders 14, 132
Estonia 52

F

ferries
to the Baltic States 31
in Estonia 53
festivals
Estonia 56
Latvia 175
Lithuania 290
Fish *Baltic food & drink*
colour insert
flights
to the Baltic States from
Britain and Ireland 27
to the Baltic States from the
US and Canada 28
to the Baltic States from
Australia and New
Zealand 28
folk music 445–454
food ...... *Baltic food & drink*
colour insert
Estonia 56
Latvia 173
Lithuania 288

G

Gary, Romain 328
Gauja National
Park 21, 258
Gauja National Park 258
Gauja Valley (LAT)
.... 257–269
Gaujasmala (LAT) 264
gay travellers 41
Gediminas ... 297, 308, 342,
439
getting there
from Britain and
Ireland 27
from the US and
Canada 28
from Australia and New
Zealand 28
from Poland 31
from Finland 32
from Sweden 32
Ginuičiai (LITH) 352

Girėnas, Stasys 365
global warming 29
Godeliai (LITH) 421
Grūtas park
(LITH) 23, 389

H

Haanja (EST) 162
Haapsalu
(EST) 98–103
Haapsalu 99
Hanseatic
League 66, 182
Harilaid peninsula
(EST) .... 116, *The great
outdoors* colour insert
health 42
Hiiumaa (EST) 103,
The great outdoors colour
insert
Hiiumaa 103
hiking 38
Hill of Crosses (LITH) 15,
393
history
Estonia 427–432
Latvia 433–438
Lithuania 438–444
hostels 37
Estonia 56
Latvia 172
Lithuania 288
hotels 37
Estonia 54
Latvia 172
Lithuania 286

I

Ignalina (LITH) 351
Iia (EST) 124
information 44
insurance 42

J

Jakobson,
Karl Robert 121, 126
Jannsen, Johann
Voldemar 126, 429
Jēkabpils (LAT) 272
Jelgava (LAT) 229–231
Jõesuu (EST) 124

Jogaila 306, 439
Jūrmala (LAT) 220–222
Juodkrantė (LITH) 407

K

Kaali (EST) 114
Kallaste (EST) 164
Kaarma (EST) 114
Käina (EST) 105
Kalevipoeg 85, 121, 160,
161, 429, 445
Kapiniškės (LITH) 383
Karaim 344
Kärdla (EST) 104
Karja (EST) 115
Karosta (LAT) 17, 251
Kasepää (EST) 163
Käsmu (EST) 135
Kassari (EST) 105
Kaunas (LITH) 356–375
Kaunaš 358–359
Kaunas Old Town 361
accommodation 357
airlines 375
arrival 357
bars 374
Botanical Garden 369
car rental 375
clubs 374
Devil Museum 367
drinking 372
eating 372
entertainment 373
festivals 374
history 356
information 357
Internet cafés 375
Jewish Kaunas 370
Laisvės alėja 362
left luggage 375
M.K. Čiurlionis Art
Museum 366
Military Museum 365
Mykolas Žilinskas
Art Gallery 368
Ninth Fort 370
Old Town 362–364
Pažaislis monastery 372
pharmacy 375
Rumšiškės 375
shopping 374
Sugihara House 369
taxis 375
Town Hall 362
travel agents 375
Kėdainiai (LITH) ... 376–378
Ķemeri (LAT) 236,
The great outdoors colour
insert
Kernavė (LITH) 346

Kihelkonna (EST) 115
Kihnu (EST)..................... 123
Klaipėda (LITH) 398–405
Klaipėda 399
Koguva (EST)................... 107
Koidula, Lydia...... 121, 154, 161, 457
Koknese (LAT)............... 272
Kõljala (EST) 114
Kolka (LAT) 232
Kolkja (EST) 163
Koosa (EST) 162
Kõpu (Hiiumaa, EST) ... 105, *The great outdoors* colour insert
Kõpu (near Viljandi, EST)..... 124
Košrags (LAT) 234
Kretinga (LITH)............... 418
Kreuzwald, Friedrich Reinhold 85, 161, 429
Krimulda (LAT) 263
Kuldīga (LAT) 239–242
Kuldīga 240
Kuressaare (EST) 107–114
Kuressaare 110
Kurzeme (LAT) 231–235

L

Lāčplēsis...... 193, 270, 271, 272
Lahemaa National Park (EST) 130–138
Lahemaa National Park 131
landscapes, Baltic .... 38–40 *The great outdoors* colour insert
language
  Estonian 465–468
  Latvian 469–471
  Lithuanian.................. 473–476
Latgale (LAT) 273–280
Latvia................................ 170
Latvian Riflemen... 195, 199
left luggage
  Estonia 62
  Latvia 179
  Lithuania............................. 295
lesbian travellers............. 41
Lielvārde (LAT) 270
Liepāja (LAT) .. 17, 246–253
Liepāja 248–249
Līgatne (LAT)................. 264
Līgatne Nature Trail (LAT)..........264, *The great outdoors* colour insert

Lihula (EST) 103
Liiva (EST)...................... 107
Linakūla (EST)............... 123
Lipchitz, Jacques 322, 324
Liškiava (LITH) 390
Lithuania 284
Livs 226, 233, 433
Ludza (LAT)................... 279

M

mail................................... 43
Majori (LAT)................... 221
Mann, Thomas 410
maps................................. 43
Marcinkonys (LITH)....... 382
Margionys (LITH).......... 383
Matsalu Nature Reserve (EST) ....103, *The great outdoors* colour insert
Mazirbe (LAT)................ 234
media............................... 38
  Estonia 58
  Latvia 174
  Lithuania............................. 290
Mērsrags (LAT) 232
Merkinė (LITH) 381
Mežotne Palace (LAT)... 228
Mickiewicz, Adam 309, 312, 314
Midsummer's Eve.............. 9
Miłosz, Czesław... 297, 314, 319, 377, 459
Mindaugas... 297, 306, 346, 396, 439
mobile phones
  Lithuania............................. 296
  Estonia 63
  Latvia 180
money............................... 43
  Estonia 62
  Latvia 179
  Lithuania............................. 295
Muhu (EST)..................... 107
Museum of the Centre of Europe (LITH).............. 347
Musteika (LITH) 383

N

Narva (EST).......... 138–141
Narva................................ 139
Narva-Jõesuu (EST) 141
newspapers and magazines
  Estonia 58

Latvia................................ 174
Lithuania........................... 290
Nida (LITH) .... 408–412, *The great outdoors* colour insert
Nida-Preila-Pervalka cycling route............. 411, *The great outdoors* colour insert
Niūronys (LITH)............. 354

O

Oandu (EST) .... 137, *The great outdoors* colour insert
Obinitsa (EST)............... 165
Old Believers 163
opening hours
  Estonia 62
  Latvia................................. 180
  Lithuania............................. 296
Orvydas Garden (LITH) 423
Otepää (EST)........ 157–159
outdoor activities............ 38

P

Palanga (LITH) 413–418
Palanga 414
Palmse (EST) 134
Palūšė (LITH) 352
Panevėžys (LITH).......... 355
Pape (LAT) 22, 254
Pape, Lake (LAT) 253–255
Pärispea (EST) 136
Pärnu (EST).... 23, 116–123
Pärnu................................ 117
Pedvāle (LAT)................ 239
Peipsi, Lake (EST) 162–164
Pervalka (LITH) 408
Peter the Great.......... 7, 43, 65, 84, 86, 141, 143, 163, 182, 192, 203, 225, 250, 354, 428, 434
phones............................. 43
  Estonia 63
  Latvia................................. 180
  Lithuania............................. 296
Piirisaar (EST) 164
Piłsudski, Józef 331
Piusa sand caves (EST) 17, 166

Plateliai (LITH).............. 420
Plokštinė rocket base
  (LITH) 422
Plungė (LITH)................. 420
police............................ 40
pop music
  Estonia 60
  Latvia.............................. 177
  Lithuania......................... 293
pork...........*Baltic food &
  drink colour insert*
post offices
  Estonia 62
  Latvia.............................. 179
  Lithuania......................... 295
potatoes.........*Baltic food
  & drink colour insert*
potato pancakes ...17, 289,
  *Baltic food & drink colour
  insert*
Preiļi (LAT)..................... 277
Preila (LITH) 411
private rooms
  Estonia 56
  Latvia.............................. 172
  Lithuania......................... 286
public holidays
  Estonia 62
  Latvia.............................. 180
  Lithuania......................... 296
Pühajärv, Lake (EST) ...159,
  *The great outdoors colour
  insert*
Pumpurs, Andrējs .. 193, 271

R

Radvila family 323, 355,
  376, 398
rail passes 30
Rainis, Jānis 204
Rakvere (EST).............. 138
Rēzekne (LAT).............. 278
Rīga (LAT)....... 16, 181–220
Rīga and around 181
Rīgā 184–185
Rīga Old Town 191
  accommodation 187
  airlines............................ 220
  airport............................. 220
  Arcadia Park.................... 209
  arrival............................. 183
  Biķernieku forest............. 210
  Botanical Gardens 209
  Braļu kapi 209
  cathedral 190
  Central Market 200
  cinema 217
  City Park 201
  classical music................ 217
  clubs 217
  consulates....................... 220
  drinking 216
  eating 213
  embassies....................... 220
  entertainment 217
  Esplanāde 202
  exchange......................... 220
  Foreign Art Museum 194
  Freedom Monument 201
  Grebenshchikov
    Church 208
  history 182
  History and Navigation
    Museum 192
  Holocaust Memorial... 22, 210
  hospital........................... 220
  hostels 187
  hotels 188
  House of the
    Blackheads 197
  information 186
  Internet cafés 220
  Jānis Rozentāls and Rudolfs
    Blaumanis Museum 205
  Krišjanis Barons Memorial
    Museum 206
  Latvian Architecture
    Museum 194
  Latvian History
    Museum 194
  Latvian Open-air Ethnographic
    Museum 19, 212
  Latvian Railway
    Museum 208
  Latvian Riflemen's
    Square 198
  Latvian Theatre
    Museum 208
  Latvian War Museum 195
  laundry 220
  left luggage 220
  libraries........................... 220
  Menzendorff House 199
  Mežaparks....................... 210
  Motor Museum 210
  Museum of Decorative and
    Applied Arts.................. 196
  Museum of Latvia's
    Jews 205
  Museum of Medical
    History 201
  Museum of the
    Barricades 193
  Museum of Writing, Theatre
    and History 194
  National Theatre.............. 201
  Occupation Museum 198
  Old Town 190–200
  opera 217
  Parliament 194
  Photography Museum....... 199
  Pils laukums 194
  public transport............... 187
  Rātslaukums 196
  Rumbula.......................... 212
  St Gertrude's Church 206
  St John's Church 196
  St Peter's Church............. 196
  Salaspils.......................... 213
  shopping 219
  sport............................... 218
  Sports Museum 200
  State Art Museum............ 202
  taxis................................ 220
  Town Hall 197
  travel agents 220
Rīgas melnais
  balzams ....15, 174, *Baltic
  food & drink colour insert*
Riisa (EST) 124
Ristna (EST)................... 106,
  *The great outdoors colour
  insert*
Roja (LAT) 232
Rõuge (EST) 162
Rozentāls, Jānis
  ....202, 205, 260
Rundāle Palace (LAT) 21,
  226
Rupsi (EST)..................... 163
rural homestays
  Latvia.............................. 172
  Lithuania......................... 286

S

Saaremaa (EST).............20,
  106–116, *The great out-
  doors colour insert*
Saaremaa............. 108–109
Sabile (LAT)................... 238
Sagadi (EST)................. 137
St Casimir...................... 307
saunas 44
Setumaa (EST)
  164–166
Šiauliai (LITH)....... 390–393
Šiauliai............................ 391
Sigulda (LAT) 259
Sigulda 262
Sillamäe (EST) 142
Skamba skamba
  kankliai................19, 291
skiing 40
Skrīveri (LAT)................. 271
Slītere National Park
  (LAT)............................ 233
Smiltynė (LITH) 407
Song festivals................... 7
Soomaa National Park
  (EST) 123
sport
  Estonia 56
  Latvia.............................. 178
  Lithuania......................... 292

Stone Plantation
  (EST) ....135, *The great
  outdoors* colour insert
Storks 10
Stripeikai (LITH) 353
studying in the Baltic
  States 45
Sugihara, Chiune ... 369, 461
Suur Munamägi (EST) ...161
Suuremõisa (EST) 105

T

Tahkuna Penisula 106
Tallinn (EST) 18, 64–166
Tallinn and around 64
Tallinn 68–69
Tallinn Old Town 74–75
  accommodation 69–72
  Adamson-Eric Museum 79
  Aegna 88
  airlines 95
  Applied Art and Design
    Museum 77
  arrival 66
  ballet 93
  Botanical Gardens 88
  car rental 95
  cathedral 81
  Church of the Holy
    Ghost 73
  cinema 94
  city walls 77
  consulates 95
  Dominican Monastery 78
  drinking 91
  eating 89
  embassies 95
  entertainment 92
  Estonian Drama Theatre 82
  Estonian History
    Museum 73, 87
  Estonian Maritime
    Museum 76
  Estonian Open-Air
    Museum 88
  Estonian Theatre and
    Concert Hall 82
  gay and lesbian info 95
  Hirvepark 82
  history 65
  hostels 70
  hotels 70
  House of the Blackheads ... 76
  House of the Great Guild... 73
  information 66
  Internet cafés 95
  Kadriorg Art Museum 85
  Kadriorg Palace.................. 85
  Kadriorg Park 84
  Kiek-in-de-Kök 81
  Kumu Art Museum 19, 86

left luggage 95
libraries............................... 95
literary museum 84
Mikkel Museum................... 85
Museum of Occupation and of
  the Fight for Freedom..... 82
Museum of Theatre and
  Music 80
music.................................. 93
Naissar 88
Old Town 72–80
Peter the Great House
  Museum......................... 86
pharmacies 95
phones 96
Pirita 87
police.................................. 96
post office 96
public transport................... 67
Raekoja plats 72
Riigikogu 81
Ruasalka Memorial 87
St Bridget's Convent
  Ruins 87
St Nicholas's Church 78
St Olaf's Church................. 76
Salt Storage Warehouse 83
shopping 94
Song Bowl.......................... 86
Tallinn Art Hall 82
Tallinn City Museum........... 77
Tallinn Science and
  Technology Centre........ 83
taxes.................................. 96
telephones 96
Television Tower................. 88
theatre 93
Toompark 77
Toompea 80–82
Toompea Castle 81
Town Hall 72
travel agents 96
Vabaduse väljak 82
Zoo.................................... 88
Talsi (LAT)....................... 235
Tammsaare, Anton
  Hansen 84
Tartu (EST) 22, 142–157
Tartu 144–145
Central Tartu 146
  accommodation 147
  arrival 147
  Art Museum 150
  bike rental 157
  Botanical Garden 151
  car rental 157
  cathedral 151
  cinema 156
  clubs 156
  drinking 155
  eating 154
  entertainment.................... 156
  Estonian National
    Museum 152
  ferry trips.......................... 157
  history 143

information 147
Internet cafés 157
Karlova 153
KGB Cells Museum........... 153
Museum of the Nineteenth-
  Century Citizen 150
Oskar Luts Museum.......... 153
pharmacy 157
public transport................. 147
Raekoja plats 148
St John's Church 150
Song Festival Grounds 154
Supilinn 154
swimming 157
Tartu City Museum............ 154
Tartu University 150
theatre 156
Toomemägi........................ 151
Town Hall 148
travel agents 157
University 150
University History
  Museum 151
telephones........................ 43
  Estonia 63
  Latvia................................ 180
  Lithuania........................... 296
television
  Estonia 58
  Latvia................................ 174
  Lithuania........................... 290
temperature 13
Tērvete (LAT) 230
time.................................. 44
tipping 61, 178
Tõramaa (EST) 124
tourist boards 45
tourist information 44
trains
  to the Baltic States 30
  in Estonia 53
  in Latvia 171
  in Lithuania....................... 285
Trakai (LITH).................. 20,
  342–346, *The great out-
  doors* colour insert
Tukums (LAT) 236
Turaida (LAT) 260

U

Ūla valley (LITH)............ 383
Ulmanis, Karlis.....200, 246,
  435

V

Vaide (LAT)..................... 234
Vaišniūnai (LITH)........... 353

Varnja (EST) 162
Värska (EST) 165
Ventspils (LAT) 242–246
Ventspils........................ 243
Viinistu (EST)................ 136
Viitna (EST) 134
Viki (EST) 115
Vilde, Eduard 150
Viljandi (EST)........ 124–128
Viljandi.......................... 125
Vilnius
  (LITH) 17, 297–348
Vilnius and around....... 298
Vilniuš................. 302–303
Vilnius Old Town 310
  accommodation 301–305
  airport............................... 341
  Antakalnis cemetery......... 329
  Applied Art Museum 309
  arrival............................... 299
  Artillery Bastion............... 319
  ballet 338
  Bernardine Church........... 309
  car rental 341
  cathedral 306
  Church of SS Peter and
    Paul.............................. 329
  Church of the Holy
    Spirit 318
  Church of the Holy
    Trinity 318
  classical music................. 338
  clubs 337
  consulates........................ 341
  Contemporary Arts
    Centre 317
  Dominican Church 321
  drinking 335
  eating 333
  embassies........................ 341
  entertainment................... 337
  exchange.......................... 341
  Gate of Dawn............. 17, 318
  Gedimino prospektas....... 323
  Hill of Three Crosses........ 329
  history 297
  hospitals........................... 341
  hostels.............................. 305
  hotels 301
  House of Signatories 312
  information 300
  Internet cafés 341
  Jewish Museum 312

laundry 341
left luggage 341
libraries............................. 341
Lithuanian Genocide
  Museum........................ 326
Lithuanian National
  Museum........................ 309
Lower Castle..................... 308
Naujamiestis..................... 327
opera................................. 338
Paneriai 332
Parliament Building........... 326
pharmacies 341
phones 342
Picture Gallery.................. 316
police................................ 342
post office 342
Presidential Palace 315
public transport................. 300
Pushkin Museum 331
Pyatnitskaya Church 315
Rasų cemetery 331
St Anne's Church 311
St Casimir's Church 317
St John's Church 314
St Michael's Church.......... 311
St Theresa's Church......... 318
shopping 340
taxis.................................. 342
Television Tower............... 332
theatre 339
travel agents 342
University 313
Upper Castle.................... 308
Užupis 327
Vilsandi National Park
  (EST) 16, 115,
  The great outdoors colour
  insert
Viru Bog (EST) 133,
  The great outdoors colour
  insert
visas 41
volunteer work................. 45
von Biron, Ernst
  Johann......................... 226
von Buxhoeveden, Albert
  ....182, 192, 270, 433
von der Goltz,
  Rudiger 435
von Herder, Johann
  Gottfried 193

Vormsi (EST) 102
Võru (EST)..................... 159
Võsu (EST) 134
Vytautas.......319, 342, 344,
  364, 370, 439–440

W

weather...................... 11–13
Western Estonia 97
Western Latvia............. 224
Western Lithuania 397
wildlife...........................39,
  The great outdoors colour
  insert
working in the Baltic
  States 45

Y

youth hostels
  Estonia 56
  Latvia.................................. 172
  Lithuania............................ 288

Z

Zackagiris nature
  path ....382, *The great
  outdoors* colour insert
Žemaičių Kalvarija
  (LITH) 422
Žemaitija National Park
  (LITH) 418–424
Žemaitija National
  Park............................... 419
Žiūrai (LITH) 383
Zemgale (LAT)...... 225–231
Zervynos (LITH) 383

INDEX

Map symbols

maps are listed in the full index using coloured text

----	Chapter boundary	★	Bus stop
-----	International border	⚓	Boat
·-·-	Provincial boundary	⧫	Point of interest
	Motorway	@	Internet access
	Road	ⓘ	Information office
	Unpaved/gravel road	⊠	Post office
··········	Track	⊞	Hospital
	Pedestrianized street	⛣	Public gardens
⊞⊞⊞⊞⊞	Steps	⚠	Campsite
	Railway	◉	Swimming pool
··············	Funicular railway	◉	Accommodation
-----	Footpath	♜	Castle
	Waterway	⚲	Museum
— —	Ferry route	🏛	Monument
●---●	Cable car and station	⊙	Statue/memorial
▄▄▄	Wall	⚰	Concentration camp
⊠	Gate	🕌	Mosque
⤬	Bridge/tunnel	✡	Synagogue
▲	Mountain peak	⚜	Christian cemetery
ᚕᚕᚕᚕ	Rocks	⚜	Church (regional maps)
⌓	Cave	+─	Church/cathedral
⚶	Viewpoint		Building
☀	Crater	▢	Market
⛰	Cliff	⬭	Stadium
/I\	Hill	◡◡	Jewish cemetery
⟨	Dune	+⊤	Christian cemetery
⚶	Spring	▓	Park/national park
⚶	Waterfall	◰	Forest
⚲	Lighthouse	◰	Marshland/bog
✚	Border post	⫶	Beach
✗	Airport